Cambridge English

Complete IELTS

Bands 6.5–7.5

Student's Book *without Answers*

Guy Brook-Hart and Vanessa Jakeman

CAMBRIDGE
UNIVERSITY PRESS

University Printing House, Cambridge CB2 8BS, United Kingdom

One Liberty Plaza, 20th Floor, New York, NY 10006, USA

477 Williamstown Road, Port Melbourne, VIC 3207, Australia

314–321, 3rd Floor, Plot 3, Splendor Forum, Jasola District Centre,
New Delhi – 110025, India

103 Penang Road, #05-06/07, Visioncrest Commercial, Singapore 238467

Cambridge University Press is part of the University of Cambridge.

It furthers the University's mission by disseminating knowledge in the pursuit of
education, learning and research at the highest international levels of excellence.

www.cambridge.org
Information on this title: www.cambridge.org/9781107657601

© Cambridge University Press 2013

First published 2013

21 20 19 18

Printed in Malaysia by Vivar Printing

A catalogue record for this publication is available from the British Library

ISBN 978-1-107-62508-2 Student's Book with Answers with CD-ROM
ISBN 978-1-107-65760-1 Student's Book without Answers with CD-ROM
ISBN 978-1-107-64281-2 Class Audio CDs (2)
ISBN 978-1-107-60964-8 Teacher's Book
ISBN 978-1-107-63438-1 Workbook with Answers with Audio CD
ISBN 978-1-107-66444-9 Workbook without Answers with Audio CD
ISBN 978-1-107-68863-6 Student's Pack (Student's Book with Answers with
CD-ROM and Class Audio CDs (2))

Contents

Unit title	Reading	Listening	Speaking
1 Getting higher qualifications	Reading Section 1: *The MIT factor: celebrating 150 years of maverick genius* • True / False / Not Given • Note completion • Short-answer questions	Listening Part 1: A graduate recruitment fair • Form completion	Speaking Part 1 • Answering questions about yourself • Using advanced vocabulary • Using *used to* and *would* to talk about the past
2 Colour my world	Reading Section 2: *Learning color words* • Matching headings • Summary completion • Pick from a list	Listening Part 2: A colour exhibition • Table completion • Pick from a list	Speaking Part 2 • Beginning and ending the talk • Introducing points within the talk • Maintaining fluency and coherence
Vocabulary and grammar review Units 1 and 2			
3 A healthy life	Reading Section 3: *Examining the placebo effect* • Yes / No / Not Given • Summary completion with a box • Multiple choice	Listening Part 3: Interview with a physiotherapist • Matching • Flow-chart completion	Speaking Part 2 • Addressing the task and making useful notes • Talking about ambitions and aspirations
4 Art and the artist	Reading Section 1: *The history of the poster* • Table completion • Flow-chart completion • True / False / Not Given	Listening Part 4: A lecture on Aboriginal art • Note completion	Speaking Parts 2 and 3 • Using advanced vocabulary • Addressing abstract topics • Generalising and distancing
Vocabulary and grammar review Units 3 and 4			
5 Stepping back in time	Reading Section 2: *Last man standing* • Matching information • Sentence completion • Matching features	Listening Part 3: A talk by a palaeontologist • Multiple choice • Labelling a diagram	Speaking Parts 2 and 3 • Fluency strategies: speaking for the full two minutes • Speculating and hypothesising • Giving reasons and examples
6 IT society	Reading Section 3: *The new way to be a fifth-grader* • Multiple choice • Yes / No / Not Given • Matching sentence endings	Listening Part 4: A lecture about animation technology in the film industry • Note completion	Speaking Parts 2 and 3 • Paraphrasing unknown or forgotten vocabulary • Discussing advantages and disadvantages
Vocabulary and grammar review Units 5 and 6			
7 Our relationship with nature	Reading Section 2: *Gold dusters* • Matching headings • Sentence completion • Pick from a list	Listening Part 3: Student discussion about a photography assignment • Labelling a plan • Sentence completion • Short-answer questions	Speaking Parts 2 and 3 • Structuring the talk • Using advanced vocabulary • Speculating and talking about the future
8 Across the universe	Reading Section 3: *The Earth and Space Foundation* • Yes / No / Not Given • Multiple choice • Summary completion with a box	Listening Part 4: A lecture on space observation • Note completion	Speaking Parts 2 and 3 • Understanding the question and giving an appropriate answer • Using a range of language functions
Vocabulary and grammar review Units 7 and 8			

Writing	Vocabulary	Pronunciation	Key grammar
Writing Task 1 • Writing an introduction to the task • Selecting and summarising main features • Grouping information in paragraphs • Advanced use of superlatives	Dependent prepositions	Sentence stress 1 • Stressing important words, including pronouns and contractions	Past simple, present perfect simple and past perfect simple
Writing Task 2 • Analysing the task and brainstorming ideas • Planning an answer • Using attitude adverbials	Phrasal verbs	Intonation 1 • Using intonation to show how you feel	Nouns and articles
Writing Task 1 • Summarising key features in more than one chart • Paragraphing and the overview • Using your own words • Expressing amount, extent or category	Verb + noun collocations	Linking and pausing	Expressing large and small differences
Writing Task 2 • Brainstorming main ideas • Maintaining a clear position • Using reasons and examples for support • Introducing arguments	Collocations and phrases with *make*, *take*, *do* and *have*	Speech rate and chunking • Pausing between word groups	Expressing purpose, cause and effect
Writing Task 1 • Summarising a diagram • Analysing the task and organising the answer • Linking information, signalling and comparing stages • Using participle clauses to express consequences	Word formation – negative affixes	Sentence stress 2 • Highlighting important aspects of an answer, e.g. a reference, contrast, etc.	Speaking hypothetically
Writing Task 2 • Describing advantages and disadvantages • Structuring an answer and linking paragraphs • Presenting a balanced view: discourse markers	Adjective + noun collocations	Intonation 2 • Showing you are engaged in discussion • Helping the conversation flow	Referencing
Writing Task 1 • Categorising data • Organising information • Proofing your work: punctuation	Idiomatic expressions	Word stress	Speculating and talking about the future
Writing Task 2 • Linking ideas and views across paragraphs • Writing a conclusion • Using advanced vocabulary	Verbs and dependent prepositions	Rhythm and chunking • Achieving natural-sounding rhythm	Emphasising

Introduction

Who this book is for

Complete IELTS Bands 6.5–7.5 is a short preparation course of 50–60 classroom hours for students who wish to take the Academic module of the International English Language Testing System (IELTS). It teaches you the reading, writing, listening and speaking skills that you need for the exam. It covers all the exam question types, as well as key grammar and vocabulary which, from research into the Cambridge Learner Corpus, are known to be useful to candidates needing to achieve a high band score in the test. If you are not planning to take the exam in the near future, the book teaches you the skills and language you need to reach an advanced level of English (Common European Framework (CEF) level C1).

What the book contains

In the **Student's Book** there are:

- **eight units for classroom study**, each containing:
  - one section on each of the four papers in the IELTS test, with relevant language input and skills practice.
  - a range of enjoyable and stimulating speaking activities, designed to enhance your fluency and your ability to speak at length and express complex ideas.
  - a coherent approach to IELTS Writing tasks.
  - key grammar exercises relevant to the exam, including exercises based on the Cambridge Learner Corpus ⊙ that highlight common problem areas for advanced students.
  - vocabulary exercises that aim to raise your knowledge of advanced vocabulary items and help demonstrate your ability to use these in Writing and Speaking tasks.
  - a unit review which revises the vocabulary and grammar that you have studied in each unit.
- **Speaking and Writing reference sections** which explain the tasks you will have to do in the Speaking and Writing papers. They give you examples, together with additional exercises and advice on how best to approach these two IELTS papers.
- a **Language reference section** which clearly explains all the areas of grammar and vocabulary covered in the book and which will help you prepare for the IELTS test.

- a complete **IELTS practice test**
- eight photocopiable **word lists** (one for each unit) containing topic-based vocabulary found in the units, accompanied by a definition supplied by a corpus-informed Cambridge dictionary, e.g. the *CALD*.
- complete **recording scripts** for all the listening material
- a **CD-ROM** which provides you with many interactive exercises, including further listening practice exclusive to the CD-ROM. All these extra exercises are linked to the topics in the Student's Book.

Also available are:

- two **audio CDs** containing listening material for the eight units of the Student's Book plus the Listening Test in the IELTS practice test. The listening material is indicated by different coloured icons in the Student's Book as follows: ⌒ CD1, ⌒ CD2.
- a **Teacher's Book** containing:
  - **step-by-step guidance** for handling all the activities in the Student's Book.
  - a large number of suggestions for **alternative treatments** of activities in the Student's Book and suggestions for **extension activities**.
  - information and advice on the test and task types for teachers to pass on to students.
  - **extra photocopiable materials** for each unit of the Student's Book, to practise and extend language.
  - **complete answer keys**, including sample answers to writing tasks.
  - four **photocopiable progress tests**, one for every two units of the book.
  - eight **photocopiable word lists** (one for each unit) taken from the International Corpus which extend the vocabulary taught in the units. Each item in the word list is accompanied by a definition supplied by a corpus-informed Cambridge dictionary, e.g. the *CALD*.
- a **Workbook** containing:
  - **eight units for homework and self-study**. Each unit contains **full exam practice** in one part of the IELTS Reading and Listening papers.
  - **further practice** in analysing the tasks from the Writing paper and writing answers.
  - further practice in the **grammar and vocabulary** taught in the Student's Book.
  - an **audio CD** containing all the listening material for the Workbook.

IELTS Academic Module: content and overview

part/timing	content	test focus
LISTENING approximately 30 minutes	• **four parts** • **40 questions** • **a range of question types** • **Part 1:** a conversation on a social topic, e.g. someone making a booking • **Part 2:** a monologue about a social topic, e.g. a radio report • **Part 3:** a conversation on a study-based topic, e.g. a discussion between students • **Part 4:** a monologue on a study-based topic, e.g. a lecture Students have ten minutes at the end of the test to transfer their answers onto an answer sheet. The recording is heard ONCE.	• Candidates are expected to listen for specific information, main ideas and opinions. • There is a range of task types which include completion, matching, labelling and multiple choice. • Each question scores 1 mark; candidates receive a band score from 1 to 9.
READING 1 hour	• **three sections** • **40 questions** • **a range of question types** • **Section 1:** a passage with 13 questions • **Section 2:** a passage usually divided into paragraphs with 13 questions • **Section 3:** a passage with 14 questions At least one passage contains arguments and/or views. This is usually Section 3. Candidates are advised to spend no more than 20 minutes on each section.	• Candidates are expected to read for / understand specific information, main ideas, gist and opinions. • Each section contains more than one task type. They include completion, matching, paragraph headings, True / False / Not Given and multiple choice. • Each question scores 1 mark; candidates receive a band score from 1 to 9.
WRITING 1 hour	• **two compulsory tasks** • **Task 1:** a 150-word summary of information presented in graphic or diagrammatic form • **Task 2:** a 250-word essay presenting an argument on a given topic Candidates are advised to spend 20 minutes on Task 1 and 40 minutes on Task 2, which is worth twice as many marks as Task 1.	• Candidates are expected to write a factual summary and a discursive essay. • Candidates are assessed on a nine-band scale for content, coherence, vocabulary and grammar.
SPEAKING 11–14 minutes	• **three parts** • **one examiner + one candidate** • **Part 1:** The examiner asks a number of questions about familiar topics such as the candidate's studies/work, hobbies, interests, etc. *4–5 minutes* • **Part 2:** After a minute's preparation, the candidate speaks for two minutes on a familiar topic provided by the examiner. *3–4 minutes* • **Part 3:** The examiner and the candidate discuss some general questions based on the theme of the Part 2 topic. *4–5 minutes*	• Candidates are expected to be able to respond to questions on familiar and unfamiliar topics and to speak at length. • Candidates are assessed on a nine-band scale for fluency, vocabulary, grammar and pronunciation.

All candidates who take the test receive an Overall Band Score between 1 and 9 that is an average of the four scores for each part of the test. For information on courses, required band scores and interpreting band scores, see www.ielts.org.

Unit 1 Getting higher qualifications

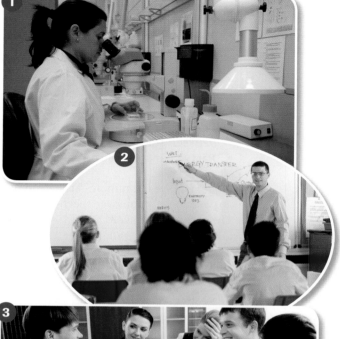

Starting off

1 Work in small groups. Explain what it means to have each of these personal qualities, using your own words. When you have finished, look at page 96 to check your answers.

> **a** *You do things like read documents very carefully and focus on all the small points, checking their accuracy.*

a   an eye for detail
b   creativity
c   an enquiring mind
d   the ability to work in a team
e   vision
f   an outgoing personality
g   good communication skills
h   management skills

2 Which of the qualities in Exercise 1 do you think each of the photos illustrates? Some could illustrate more than one quality.

3 Work in pairs.

- What type of work do you do or want to do? Why?
- Which of the qualities in Exercise 1 do you need? Why?
- What other qualities would be useful? Why?

Listening Part 1

1 Work in pairs. You are going to hear a conversation between a university student and a company representative at a graduate fair. Before you listen, look at this advertisement, then discuss the questions below.

Are you a high achiever?

Do you want a job as soon as you graduate?
The world's biggest companies in IT, marketing, finance, and telecoms want graduates!

Visit the fair and register with them now!

1 What do you think happens at a graduate fair? Why do you think they are useful?
2 Why do many jobs require you to have a university degree? When is vocational training more useful than a university degree?
3 What might improve a graduate's chances of getting the job they want?

2 Look at Questions 1–10 and quickly check what type of information you need to fill each gap.

Questions 1–10

Complete the form below.

Write **NO MORE THAN THREE WORDS AND/ OR A NUMBER** *for each answer.*

Graduate Fair Registration
TGS Global

Graduate details

Area of work:	Example: Marketing
Name:	Dominika 1 ....
Nationality:	2 ....
Email address:	3 ....@qmail.com
University:	London
Type of course:	4 .... BA
Date available:	5 ....

Personal information

Other activities:	organised a 6 .... for charity
Interests:	7 .... and ....
Previous job(s):	8 ....
Career plans:	wants to be a 9 ....
Heard about fair through:	10 ....

3 🎧 Now listen and answer Questions 1–10.

4 Work in pairs. Imagine you are talking to another student who you have met at the coffee bar at a graduate fair. Introduce yourselves and tell each other about your:

- studies and qualifications / current job
- career plans and reasons for them
- free-time interests and related qualifications.

Vocabulary

Dependent prepositions

❶ **Complete these extracts from the Listening section by writing a preposition in each gap. Sometimes more than one answer is possible.**

1 Obviously our interest is related .... the class of degree that you get.
2 I haven't actually had any experience .... business yet.
3 I want to concentrate .... getting my qualifications first.
4 So when would you be available .... an interview?
5 I'm quite good .... cooking.
6 Have you done any other work in the past that would be relevant .... a marketing career?

❷ **Choose the correct preposition in *italics* in each of these sentences.**

1 The money spent *on / in* research was more than expected.
2 Some bosses are not very sensitive *for / to* their employees' needs.
3 The company has a reputation *of / for* producing top-quality toys.
4 It is important to have confidence *in / at* your own abilities.
5 A lot of students participated *on / in* the job fair.
6 Working parents have little time to take care *of / for* their children.

❸ ⊙ **IELTS candidates often make mistakes with prepositions after adjectives and verbs. Find and correct the mistakes in these sentences by changing or adding a preposition.**

1 To be a leader, you have to compete‸your colleagues. *with/against*
2 Youngsters today are better prepared with working life.
3 It is sometimes hard to get involved into your studies.
4 Universities should provide students the facilities they need.
5 Managers have to be responsible to the staff below them.
6 The government should pay more attention on the education of women.
7 In my job, I have to deal many different types of people.

Reading Section 1

❶ **Work in pairs. You are going to read a passage about a prestigious university. Before you read, discuss these questions.**

1 What are the most prestigious universities in your country?
2 In general, what makes a university prestigious?
3 Why do many students want to go to a prestigious university?

❷ **Scanning and skimming are skills that will save you time when you do the IELTS Reading paper.**

1 Complete these definitions by writing *scanning* or *skimming* in each gap.
  a .... involves running your eyes down the passage quickly in order to find a particular word or phrase. Often these words or phrases will stand out because they are proper nouns, e.g. names.
  b .... means reading something quickly in order to understand the main points, without studying it in detail.
2 How will each skill save you time?

❸ **Skim the passage on pages 11–12. Which of these best describes the writer's purpose?**

a to review the courses at MIT
b to explain why MIT has been so successful
c to describe the history of MIT

❹ **Writers use referencing techniques to link their ideas and avoid repetition. Understanding referencing can help you do IELTS questions. Scan the passage to find these phrases, then <u>underline</u> the idea(s) that they refer back to.**

1 This unusual community MIT (as a whole)
2 that single unifying ambition
3 the list of innovations
4 This down-to-earth quality
5 That symbiosis of intellect and craftsmanship
6 As such
7 You can see that

The MIT factor: celebrating 150 years of maverick genius

by Ed Pilkington

The Massachusetts Institute of Technology has led the world into the future for 150 years with scientific innovations.

The musician Yo-Yo Ma's cello may not be the obvious starting point for a journey into one of the world's great universities. But, as you quickly realise when you step inside the Massachusetts Institute of Technology, there's precious little going on that you would normally see on a university campus. The cello, resting in a corner of MIT's celebrated media laboratory – a hub of creativity – looks like any other electric classical instrument. But it is much more. Machover, the composer, teacher and inventor responsible for its creation, calls it a 'hyperinstrument', a sort of thinking machine that allows Ma and his cello to interact with one another and make music together. 'The aim is to build an instrument worthy of a great musician like Yo-Yo Ma that can understand what he is trying to do and respond to it,' Machover says. The cello has numerous sensors across its body and by measuring the pressure, speed and angle of the virtuoso's performance it can interpret his mood and engage with it, producing extraordinary new sounds. The virtuoso cellist frequently performs on the instrument as he tours around the world.

Machover's passion for pushing at the boundaries of the existing world to extend and unleash human potential is not a bad description of MIT as a whole. This unusual community brings highly gifted, highly motivated individuals together from a vast range of disciplines, united by a common desire: to leap into the dark and reach for the unknown.

MIT students at a physics class take measurements in 1957

The result of that single unifying ambition is visible all around. For the past 150 years, MIT has been leading the world into the future. The discoveries of its teachers and students have become the common everyday objects that we now all take for granted. The telephone, electromagnets, radars, high-speed photography, office photocopiers, cancer treatments, pocket calculators, computers, the Internet, the decoding of the human genome, lasers, space travel … the list of innovations that involved essential contributions from MIT and its faculty goes on and on.

From the moment MIT was founded by William Barton Rogers in 1861, it was clear what it was not. While Harvard stuck to the English model of a classical education, with its emphasis on Latin and Greek, MIT looked to the German system of learning based on research and hands-on experimentation. Knowledge was at a premium, but it had to be useful.

This down-to-earth quality is enshrined in the school motto, *Mens et manus* – Mind and hand – as well as its logo, which shows a gowned scholar standing beside an ironmonger bearing a hammer and anvil. That symbiosis of intellect and craftsmanship still suffuses the institute's classrooms, where students are not so much taught as engaged and inspired.

Take Christopher Merrill, 21, a third-year undergraduate in computer science. He is spending most of his time on a competition set in his robotics class. The contest is to see which student can most effectively program a robot to build a house out of blocks in under ten minutes. Merrill says he could have gone for the easiest route – designing a simple robot that would build the house quickly. But he wanted to try to master an area of robotics that remains unconquered – adaptability, the ability of the robot to rethink its plans as the environment around it changes, as would a human. 'I like to take on things that have never been done before rather than to work in an iterative way just making small steps forward,' he explains.

Merrill is already planning the start-up he wants to set up when he graduates in a year's time. He has an idea for an original version of a contact lens that would augment reality by allowing consumers to see additional visual information. He is fearful that he might be just too late in taking his concept to market, as he has heard that a Silicon Valley firm is already developing something similar. As such, he might become one of many MIT graduates who go on to form companies that fail. Alternatively, he might become one of those who go on to succeed in spectacular fashion. And there are many of them. A survey of living MIT alumni* found that they have formed 25,800 companies, employing more than three million people, including about a quarter of the workforce of Silicon Valley.

What MIT delights in is taking brilliant minds from around the world in vastly diverse disciplines and putting them together. You can see that in its sparkling new David Koch Institute for Integrative Cancer Research, which brings scientists, engineers and clinicians under one roof. Or in its Energy Initiative, which acts as a bridge for MIT's combined work across all its five schools, channelling huge resources into the search for a solution to global warming. It works to improve the efficiency of existing energy sources, including nuclear power. It is also forging ahead with alternative energies from solar to wind and geothermal, and has recently developed the use of viruses to synthesise batteries that could prove crucial in the advancement of electric cars.

In the words of Tim Berners-Lee, the Briton who invented the World Wide Web, 'It's not just another university. Even though I spend my time with my head buried in the details of web technology, the nice thing is that when I do walk the corridors, I bump into people who are working in other fields with their students that are fascinating, and that keeps me intellectually alive.'

adapted from the Guardian

people who have left a university or college after completing their studies there

---

❺ Work in pairs.

1 Look at Question 1 in the task below and the underlined words. Scan the passage to find the same or similar words.
2 Underline words or phrases in Questions 2–5 that might also occur in the passage.
3 Scan the passage and underline the same or similar words to those in the question.

Questions 1–5

Do the following statements agree with the information in the reading passage?

Write

TRUE   *if the statement agrees with the information*

FALSE   *if the statement contradicts the information*

NOT GIVEN *if there is no information on this*

1 The activities going on at the MIT campus are like those at any other university.
2 Harvard and MIT shared a similar approach to education when they were founded.
3 The school motto was suggested by a former MIT student.
4 MIT's logo reflects the belief that intellect and craftsmanship go together.
5 Silicon Valley companies pay higher salaries to graduates from MIT.

---

❻ Read Questions 1–5 carefully, then read around the words you have underlined in the passage and decide whether each question is True, False or Not Given.

Exam advice   True / False / Not Given

- Underline words or phrases in the question that will help you quickly scan for the right place in the passage.
- Read each statement carefully and decide on the main idea. Compare this with what is stated in the passage.
- Write 'TRUE' if the ideas are the same. If the passage says the opposite of the information in the question, write 'FALSE'; if the passage does not include the information expressed in the question, write 'NOT GIVEN'.

7 Read Questions 6–9 and quickly check what information you need for each gap. Then, using the title to find the right part of the passage, answer the questions.

Questions 6–9

Complete the notes below.

*Choose **NO MORE THAN TWO WORDS** from the passage for each answer.*

Christopher Merrill – student at MIT

Degree subject: **6** ....

Competition: to **7** .... the automated construction of a house

Special focus on: the **8** .... of robots

Future plans: to develop new type of **9** ....

Exam advice   Note completion

- Use the title to find the right place in the passage.
- Read the notes and decide what type of information you need for each gap.
- The information in the notes may be in a different order from the information in the passage.
- Be careful to copy words from the passage in exactly the same form.

8 Work in pairs.

1 Read Questions 10–13 and quickly check what information you need.

2 Underline words in the questions which will help you to find the right place in the passage.

3 Answer Questions 10–13.

Questions 10–13

Answer the questions below.

*Choose **NO MORE THAN TWO WORDS** from the passage for each answer.*

10 What proportion of workers at Silicon Valley are employed in companies set up by MIT graduates?

11 What problem does MIT's Energy Initiative aim to solve?

12 Which 'green' innovation might MIT's work with viruses help improve?

13 In which part of the university does Tim Berners-Lee enjoy stimulating conversations with other MIT staff?

Exam advice   *Short-answer questions*

- Underline words in each question which help to find the right place in the passage. The questions follow the order of information in the passage.
- Read that part carefully and underline the answer.
- Copy the answer exactly, without including any unnecessary words.

9 Check your answers. You can lose marks with:

- answers that are hard to spell.
  Did you copy your answers for Questions 6, 8 and 9 correctly?
- answers that consist of a phrase, rather than a word.
  Did you write both words for Questions 6, 9, 11 and 12?
- questions that can easily be misinterpreted.
  Is your answer to Question 10 a proportion and not a number?
  Is your answer to Question 12 an innovation?

10 Work in small groups.

1 What personal qualities do you think inventors require?

2 Which areas of technology do you think governments should spend money on at the moment? Why?

3 What sort of things do you think will be invented in the future?

4 If you could invent something, what would it be?

Speaking Part 1

1 (2) – (5) **Listen to four students answering some Part 1 questions. As you listen, decide on the focus of each student's answer, then complete the examiner's question by writing one word in each gap. In some cases, more than one answer is possible.**

Student	Examiner's question
	Why are you taking your current 1 ..course.. of study?
	Have you ever owned a 2 .... ?
	When did you last make something by 3 .... ?
	How much 4 .... do you do now compared with the past?

2 (2) – (5) **In order to achieve a vocabulary score of Band 6 or more, you need to use some advanced vocabulary. Listen again and complete each of these extracts with a word/phrase.**

1 A couple of years ago, I decided that I wanted to work in the ....
2 I'm looking forward to graduating and getting into ....
3 We used to have a .... black and white cat.
4 She would make these .... when we came home after school.
5 He's two, he's a .... now.
6 My sister and her husband were ....
7 Now I'm older, I'm .... my health.
8 I joined a gym last year and I've been making use of its ....

3 **The speakers use *used to* and *would* to talk about past habits or states or to mean 'accustomed to'. Choose the correct verb form in *italics* in these extracts.**

1 I used to *have / having* a casual part-time job as a waiter when I was 16.
2 She would *sit / sitting* on our laps at night ...
3 We used to *think / thinking* she was a real person.
4 They were used to *see / seeing* me as someone who couldn't play or make things ...
5 I didn't use to *do / doing* very much exercise ...
6 I just got used to *be / being* lazy!
7 I think my fitness level's a bit better than it used to *be / being*!

▶ page 120 used to *and* would

4 **Work alone. Complete these sentences so that they are true for you. Then compare your ideas with a partner.**

1 When I was a child, I used to ...
2 When I started secondary school, I had to get used to ...
3 After school, my classmates would ...
4 I have never got used to ...
5 Compared to the past, I am .... than I used to be.
6 By the time I went to secondary school, I was used to ...

▶ Pronunciation: *Sentence stress 1*

5 **Work in pairs. Ask and answer these Part 1 questions using:**

- some advanced vocabulary
- the different forms of *used to* and *would*
- sentence stress to express yourself clearly.

Your school days

1 At what time did you used to get up to go to school?
2 How did you feel about getting up early as a child?
3 Which teacher did you like best at school? Why?
4 What did you particularly dislike about your school days?
5 What did you look forward to most at school?
6 What skills did you learn at school that might be useful in your work?

- You can expect to be asked questions on a range of familiar topics. Prepare yourself for this by thinking of a range of higher-level vocabulary you can use with these topics (see Speaking reference, page 97).
- Aim to answer questions using two to three sentences, giving reasons and extra details.
- Use stress to emphasise important information.

Pronunciation
Sentence stress 1

> Speakers often stress nouns, adjectives and verbs when they answer questions. However, other words (pronouns, contractions, etc.) can be stressed, if they are important to your message.

❶ (6) Read and listen to these Part 1 extracts.

1 Underline the words in the sentences that the speakers stress.
  1 A couple of <u>years</u> ago, I <u>decided</u> that I wanted to work in the <u>hotel</u> industry.
  2 So that's why I've been doing a hotel-management course for the past two years.
  3 I know that cats don't talk, but this one did!
  4 He's two – he's a toddler now.
  5 I think my fitness level's a bit better than it used to be!

2 In which of the above sentences is stress used to emphasise a pronoun because the speaker is:
  a using it to refer to something in a previous sentence?
  b making a contrast between two things?

❷ (7) Work in pairs. Look at the sentences below.

1 Underline the words in each sentence that you think should be stressed, and say why.
2 Listen and check your answers.

1 I really don't like having animals in the home.
2 I go running in the afternoon because I feel more energetic at that time of day.
3 I think everyone's too busy these days to make anything by hand!
4 I tried sewing at school, but I just couldn't do it.
5 My brother did badly at school, yet he earns more than I do!

❸ Take turns to read the answers in Exercise 2 to your partner.

Writing Task 1

Exam information

- You write a summary of information from one or more graphs, tables, charts or diagrams.
- You must also compare some of the information and write an overview.
- You write at least 150 words in about 20 minutes.

❶ Work in pairs. Look at the Writing task below and complete this introductory sentence, using the words in the box to help you.

The graph gives information about how many …

| between | Canadian | graduated |
| male and female | students | |

> *The graph below shows the number of university graduates in Canada from 1992 to 2007.*
>
> *Summarise the information by selecting and reporting the main features and make comparisons where relevant.*
>
> **University graduates, Canada, 1992–2007**
>
>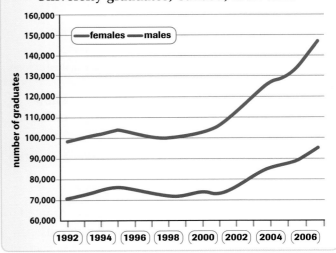

❷ Which FOUR of these statements (1–7) describe *main* features of the graph?

1 The number of graduates fell between 1996 and 1998.
2 The overall rise in numbers was not always steady.
3 Just under 75,000 male students graduated in 1992.
4 More women than men graduated between 1992 and 2007.

5 In 2007, there were nearly 150,000 female graduates.

6 The gap between the number of male and female graduates widened over the period.

7 The trends for male and female graduates were similar.

3 Work in pairs. Read this continuation of the sample answer from Exercise 1 and <u>underline</u> the sentences that describe the main features.

2 Graduate numbers rose during the 15 years and reached their highest levels in 2007, but there were always more female than male graduates. In 1992, the difference was less marked, with just over 70,000 males and about 100,000 females. However, by 2007 there had been more significant growth in female numbers. That year, they rose to 147,000, compared to just 95,000 males. Thus the gap between the number of male and female graduates had widened.

3 A more detailed look at the graph reveals that the overall growth in numbers was not always steady. Between 1992 and 1995, there was a slight increase. That was followed by a period of about five years, when numbers fell, then flattened out at just over 70,000 for men and 100,000 for women. After 2000, however, graduate numbers saw their strongest growth rate, and this was well above the increases that had been seen in the early 1990s.

4 Clearly, there were similar trends for male and female graduates over this period, but the number of women graduating increased at a higher rate than the number of men.

4 Draw two vertical lines on the graph to show how the student has grouped the information in paragraph 3 of the sample answer.

5 Work in pairs. Answer these questions about the sample answer.

1 What is the difference in focus between the second and third paragraphs?

2 What is the purpose of the last paragraph?

3 What phrases does the writer use in the second paragraph to mean ...
  a *not as great*?
  b *stronger*?

4 What verb is used to describe the changing size of the gap between men and women?

5 What phrase is used to introduce a close analysis of the graph?

6 What verb is used to mean *didn't change*?

7 What phrase is used with data to mean *a little more than*?

8 What adjective is used that means *small*?

6 IELTS candidates often make mistakes using superlative forms (e.g. *longest, most interesting*). <u>Underline</u> the superlative forms in the sample answer in Exercise 3.

▶ page 119 *Superlative forms*

7 ⊙ Choose the correct alternative in *italics* in these sentences, written by IELTS candidates.

1 The *steadiest / most steady* development can be seen in the USA.

2 The second *popular / most popular* university course is business studies.

3 In 2000, the *lowest / least* number of unemployed graduates was recorded.

4 *The most / Most* important change of school subjects occurred in the 1990s.

5 Regional colleges are where the *most / greatest* number of students choose to go.

6 Education is considered the *most important / most important area* in life.

7 Tuition fees are *the one / one* of the most important considerations for students.

8 Watching television is the *favourite / most favourite* activity for many 17-year-olds.

Exam advice   Writing Task 1

• Decide on the key features and the important details in the graph.

• Decide how to group the information into paragraphs, remembering that there are different ways this can be done.

• Write a short introductory paragraph saying what the graph shows. (This may be one sentence.)

• Support the key features with figures.

▶ Key grammar: *Past simple, present perfect simple and past perfect simple*

8 Work in pairs. Look at this Writing task, then answer the questions below.

> *The graph below shows the percentage change in the number of international students graduating from universities in different Canadian provinces between 2001 and 2006.*
>
> *Summarise the information by selecting and reporting the main features and make comparisons where relevant.*
>
> **International graduates, Canadian universities, 2001–2006**
>
>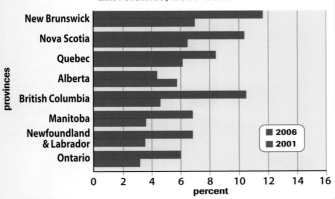

1 How would you introduce the task?
2 What are the key features in the information?
3 How would you highlight the key features?
4 How would you group the information?

9 Write your answer to the task in at least 150 words.

Key grammar
Past simple, present perfect simple and past perfect simple

1 Complete this table.

infinitive	past simple	past participle (*has/had* +)
reach	1 reached	2 reached
fall back	3	4
rise	5	6
widen	7	8
take place	9	10
experience	11	12

⊙ page 115 *Past simple, present perfect simple and past perfect simple*

2 ⊙ Choose the correct verb tense to complete these sentences written by IELTS candidates.

1 There was a ten-year period, during which figures *have gradually fallen / gradually fell*.
2 By 2008, the percentage of students choosing science subjects *decreased / had decreased* markedly.
3 Between 2000 and the present day, the numbers *remained / have remained* steady.
4 Over the past few decades, there *has been / was* a rapid development in educational technology.
5 After 2005, a more significant increase *took place / had taken place*.
6 Since the 1990s, graduates *have experienced / experienced* higher unemployment rates.
7 The situation *remained / had remained* unchanged for the next two years until more universities were opened.
8 In 2002, the university intake was stable, but prior to that, it *fluctuated / had fluctuated*.

3 Complete the summary of the graph by writing the correct form of the verbs in brackets.

Male graduates, science faculty, Callum University

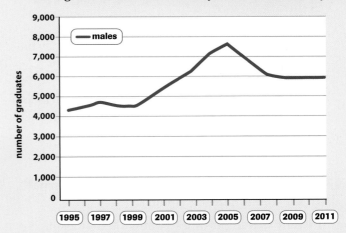

The number of men obtaining degrees in science from Callum University **1** .has risen. (*rise*) since 1995, but the trend **2** .... (*not always be*) steady. Between 1995 and 1997, the university **3** .... (*experience*) a slight increase from just over 4,000 science graduates to just under 5,000. This was followed by a period during which numbers **4** .... (*drop*) a little and then **5** .... (*remain*) stable. However, between 2000 and 2005, the faculty **6** .... (*see*) a dramatic increase in male graduates, and by 2005, their numbers **7** .... (*reach*) a peak of about 7,800, after which they **8** .... (*fall back*) to their current figure of 6,000.

Unit 2 Colour my world

Starting off

❶ Work in small groups. Each of these pictures illustrates the interior of a building.

1 How do the colours and designs make you feel? (Think about patterns, layout, etc.)
2 How appropriate do you think they are for the function of each place?

❷ Describe the colours and decoration that you have in a room in your home.

Reading Section 2

Exam information

- Reading passage 2 is usually divided into paragraphs or sections – A, B, C, etc. It may be descriptive, discursive or a combination of the two.
- There will usually be three tasks, often including either a 'matching headings' task (which comes before the passage) or a 'matching information' task.

❶ Work in pairs. You are going to read a journal article about naming colours.

1 Why is it important to know the names of colours? Did you have difficulty learning the names of any colours in English? Which ones?
2 Read the title and the subheading on page 19, then discuss what you expect to read about in the rest of the article.

❷ Skim the article on pages 19–20. Name two groups of people who you think would be interested in reading it, and explain why.

❸ Read the article and note down what you think is the main theme of each section. Then compare your notes with headings i–vii on page 19.

❹ Answer Questions 1–4.

Questions 1–4

The Reading Passage has four sections, **A–D**.

Choose the correct heading for each section from the list of headings below.

List of Headings

  i A possible explanation

  ii Why names of objects are unhelpful

  iii Checking out the theory

  iv A curious state of affairs

  v The need to look at how words are formed

  vi How age impacts on learning colours

  vii Some unsurprising data

1 Section A ....

2 Section B ....

3 Section C ....

4 Section D ....

Exam advice   *Matching headings*

• Read each paragraph / section of the passage carefully to identify the main idea or theme.

• Choose the correct heading for each paragraph/ section. Be careful to match the heading to the *main idea*, not just similar *words*.

Learning color words

Young children struggle with color concepts, and the reason for this may have something to do with how we use the words that describe them.

A In the course of the first few years of their lives, children who are brought up in English-speaking homes successfully master the use of hundreds of words. Words for objects, actions, emotions, and many other aspects of the physical world quickly become part of their infant repertoire. For some reason, however, when it comes to learning color words, the same children perform very badly. At the age of four months, babies can distinguish between basic color categories. Yet it turns out they do this in much the same way as blind children. "Blue" and "yellow" appear in older children's expressive language in answer to questions such as "What color is this?", but their mapping of objects to individual colors is haphazard and interchangeable. If shown a blue cup and asked about its color, typical two-year-olds seem as likely to come up with "red" as "blue." Even after hundreds of training trials, children as old as four may still end up being unable to accurately sort objects by color.

B In an effort to work out why this is, cognitive scientists at Stanford University in California hypothesized that children's incompetence at color-word learning may be directly linked to the way these words are used in English. While word order for color adjectives varies, they are used overwhelmingly in pre-nominal position (e.g. "blue cup"); in other words, the adjective comes before the noun it is describing. This is in contrast to post-nominal position (e.g. "The cup is blue") where the adjective comes after the noun. It seems that the difficulty children have may not be caused by any unique property of color, or indeed, of the world. Rather, it may simply come down to the challenge of having to make predictions *from* color words to the objects they refer to, instead of being able to make predictions *from* the world of objects to the color words.

To illustrate, the word "chair" has a meaning that applies to the somewhat varied set of entities in the world that people use for sitting on. Chairs have features, such as arms and legs and backs, that are combined to some degree in a systematic way; they turn up in a range of chairs of different shapes, sizes, and ages. It could be said that children learn to narrow down the set of cues that make up a chair and in this way they learn the concept associated with that word. On the other hand, color words tend to be unique and not bound to other specific co-occurring features; there is nothing systematic about color words to help cue their meaning. In the speech that adults direct at children, color adjectives occur pre-nominally ("blue cup") around 70 percent of the time. This suggests that most of what children hear from adults will, in fact, be unhelpful in learning what color words refer to.

C To explore this idea further, the research team recruited 41 English children aged between 23 and 29 months and carried out a three-phase experiment. It consisted of a pre-test, followed by training in the use of color words, and finally a post-test that was identical to the pre-test. The pre- and post-test materials comprised six objects that were novel to the children. There were three examples of each object in each of three colors—red, yellow, and blue. The objects were presented on trays, and in both tests, the children were asked to pick out objects in response to requests in which the color word was either a prenominal ("Which is the red one?") or a post-nominal ("Which one is red?").

In the training, the children were introduced to a "magic bucket" containing five sets of items familiar to 26-month-olds (balls, cups, crayons, glasses, and toy bears) in each of the three colors. The training was set up so that half the children were presented with the items one by one and heard them labelled with color words used pre-nominally ("This is a red crayon"), while the other half were introduced to the same items described with a post-nominal color word ("This crayon is red"). After the training, the children repeated the selection task on the unknown items in the post-test. To assess the quality of children's understanding of the color words, and the effect of each type of training, correct choices on items that were consistent across the pre- and post-tests were used to measure children's color knowledge.

D Individual analysis of pre- and post-test data, which confirmed parental vocabulary reports, showed the children had at least some knowledge of the three colour words: they averaged two out of three correct choices in response to both pre- and post-nominal question types, which, it has been pointed out, is better than chance. When children's responses to the question types were assessed independently, performance was at its most consistent when children were both trained and tested on post-nominal adjectives, and worst when trained on pre-nominal adjectives and tested on post-nominal adjectives. Only children who had been trained with post-nominal color-word presentation and then tested with post-nominal question types were significantly more accurate than chance. Comparing the pre- and post-test scores across each condition revealed a significant decline in performance when children were both pre- and post-tested with questions that placed the color words pre-nominally.

As predicted, when children are exposed to color adjectives in post-nominal position, they learn them rapidly (after just five training trials per color); when they are presented with them pre-nominally, as English overwhelmingly tends to do, children show no signs of learning.

❺ Read Questions 5–9 and the title of the gapped summary.

1 Quickly scan for the section of the passage that deals with this.
2 Read the words around the question to decide what information you need for each gap.
3 Answer Questions 5–9.

Questions 5–9

Complete the summary below.

*Choose **NO MORE THAN TWO WORDS** from the passage for each answer.*

The Hypothesis

Children learn many words quite quickly, but their ability to learn colour words takes longer than expected. In fact, despite **5** .... , many four-year-olds still struggle to arrange objects into colour categories. Scientists have hypothesised that this is due to the **6** Pre ...... of the adjectives in a phrase or sentence and the challenges this presents.

While objects consist of a number of **7** Cues that can be used to recognise other similar objects, the **8** ...... of a colour cannot be developed using the same approach. As a consequence, the way colour words tend to be used in English may be **9** .... to children.

Exam advice **Summary completion**

- Read the summary carefully first and decide what type of information is missing.
- Use the title to find the correct section of the passage, then read it carefully.
- Copy words exactly from the passage.
- Check your summary when you have finished to ensure that it makes sense grammatically and reflects the meaning of the passage.

❻ Look at Questions 10–13.

1 <u>Underline</u> the words in Questions 10–13 (not the options) that will help you find the answers in the passage.
2 Scan the passage until you find the right places.
3 Answer Questions 10–13 by matching what the writer says to the correct options.

Questions 10–13

*Choose **TWO** letters, **A–E**.*

Questions 10–11

*Which **TWO** of the following statements about the experiment are true?*

A The children were unfamiliar with the objects used in the pre- and post-test.

B The children had to place the pre- and post-test objects onto coloured trays.

C The training was conducted by dividing the children into two groups.

D Pre-nominal questions were used less frequently than post-nominal questions in the training.

E The researchers were looking for inconsistencies in children's knowledge of word order.

Questions 12–13

*Which **TWO** of the following outcomes are reported in the passage?*

A Average results contradicted parental assessment of children's knowledge.

B Children who were post-tested using post-nominal adjectives performed well, regardless of the type of training.

C Greatest levels of improvement were achieved by children who were trained and post-tested using post-nominal adjectives.

D Some children performed less well in the post-test than in the pre-test.

E Some children were unable to accurately name any of the colours in the pre- and post-tests.

Exam advice **Pick from a list**

- Use words in the question to help you find the right place(s) in the passage.
- <u>Underline</u> the answers in the passage and choose the correct options.
- The answers may come from one part or different parts of the passage.

7 Work in pairs.

1 What things did you find difficult to learn as a child?

2 How important is it for children to learn things (e.g. numbers, words, activities, skills) as quickly as possible?

3 What can parents do to encourage children to reach their maximum potential?

Vocabulary
Phrasal verbs

1 Using phrasal verbs correctly will help you raise your band score in the exam. Scan the passage on pages 19–20 for these phrasal verbs. Then match them with their definition a–h from the *Cambridge International Dictionary of Phrasal Verbs*.

1	comes to	5	turn up
2	turns out	6	narrow down
3	come up with	7	carried out
4	work out	8	pointed out

a to appear or be found

b to do/complete something, especially something important

c to happen in a particular way or to have a particular result

d to make something smaller and clearer by removing the things that are less important

e to find the answer by thinking about it

f to tell someone a fact that they did not already know

g to reach a particular state or situation

h to think of or suggest a plan, idea, solution or answer to a question

▶ page 115 *Phrasal verbs*

2 Complete these sentences by writing a phrasal verb from Exercise 1 in the correct form in each gap.

1 I have never succeeded in .... which colours suit me best.

2 The designer .... that the pattern on the fabric was unique.

3 Unfortunately, I couldn't .... any useful suggestions.

4 James has managed to .... his choice of subjects .... to three.

5 We chose the furniture, but when it .... the colours, we were undecided.

6 I'm going to .... a small study as part of my course work.

7 It .... that many workers preferred the coloured chairs.

8 The meeting had to be cancelled because too few people ....

3 Work in pairs. Find five more phrasal verbs in the reading passage and decide what each of them means.

4 Which phrasal verbs in Exercises 1–3 are examples of:

1 verb + adverb particle?

2 verb + preposition?

3 verb + adverb particle + preposition?

5 Complete these sentences in any way you wish using phrasal verbs from Exercises 1 and 3.

1 When it comes …

2 No one could come …

3 If you work too hard, you will end …

4 Their grandparents brought …

5 The judges had to narrow …

6 The instructor pointed …

7 One individual cannot carry …

8 The show turned …

9 It's important to turn …

Listening Part 2

Exam information
- You hear one speaker talking about a social or general topic.
- This part of the test is slightly harder than Part 1.

❶ Work in pairs. You are going to hear a radio programme about a colour exhibition.

1 What sort of exhibitions have you been to or heard about?
2 Do you prefer to look at museum exhibits or use hands-on, interactive displays? Why?
3 Think of one thing that you might see or do at a colour exhibition.

❷ Read Questions 1–6. <u>Underline</u> the key ideas around each gap and use these to help you decide what information you need to listen for.

Questions 1–6

Complete the table below.

Write **ONE** word for each answer.

Eye for Colour Exhibition

Section	Aim	Examples of activities
'Seeing colour'		view the gallery through a huge **1** ....
'Colour in culture'	to connect colour and **2**	• go to the colour café • learn how a **3** .... affects sight
'Colour in nature'	to look at the natural world	• put on a camouflage suit and pick a suitable **4** .... • see through the eyes of a dog or fish
'The **5** .... room'	to show how colours make us feel	listen to music as the colours and **6** .... change

❸ 🎧 8 Now listen and answer Questions 1–6.

Exam advice   Table completion
- Check how many words you are allowed to use.
- Read around the gaps and make sure the word(s) you choose make sense.
- Spell your answers correctly.

❹ 🎧 9 Read Questions 7–10 and <u>underline</u> the key ideas in the questions. Then listen and answer the questions.

Questions 7–10

*Choose **TWO** letters, A–E.*

Questions 7–8

*Which **TWO** colours were most popular among visitors?*

A blue   **D** purple

B deep pink   **E** red

C lime green

Questions 9–10

*Which **TWO** reasons did the children give for selecting their favourite colour?*

A They like wearing it.

B They notice it more than other colours.

C It makes them feel relaxed.

D It has a connection with a sport.

E Someone they admire wears it.

Exam advice   Pick from a list
- <u>Underline</u> the key ideas in the question.
- Read through the options and remember that only two of them are correct.
- As you listen, tick the options you hear. The correct answers may not come in the same order in the recording as they do in the question.
- You may hear a paraphrase of a correct option.

❺ Work in pairs.

1 How do children benefit from going to exhibitions?
2 Why are some exhibitions more popular among children than others?
3 Who should encourage children to enjoy exhibitions?

Speaking Part 2

1 Work in pairs. Read this Speaking task and briefly discuss what you could say for each point. Make some notes as you talk.

> Describe something colourful that you bought in the past.
>
> You should say:
>
> > why you bought the item
> >
> > what it looks/looked like
> >
> > what other people think/thought of it
>
> and explain how you feel/felt about this item.

2 🔊 Listen to Zandra doing the task in Exercise 1 and use the table to note down how she begins and ends her talk, and how she introduces the points on the card. Then tell your partner what you can remember about each point.

beginning of talk	One of the most **1** _colourful things_ that I've ever bought is …
why she bought the item	I **2** .... this doll because …
what it looked like	Actually, my doll **3** .... , even though …
what people thought of it	**4** .... think … and others …
how she felt about it (ending)	For me, well, **5** .... , I feel …

3 🔊 Zandra uses a number of strategies to help her talk flow. Listen again and complete this table.

when she has forgotten something	**1** _I'm afraid I can't remember_
to avoid hesitation	**2** ....
to clarify _made in this era_	**3** ....
to refer back to something she said earlier	**4** ....
	5 ....
to paraphrase _wooden rods_	**6** ....

4 Change partners.

1 Take a minute to review the notes you made in Exercise 1 and think how you can use phrases from Exercises 2 and 3 in your talk.
2 Take turns to give your talks.
3 While you listen, think of a brief question about your partner's talk you can ask at the end.

▶ Pronunciation: _Intonation 1_

5 Read this Part 2 task and take one minute to make some notes. Then take turns to do the task with a partner.

> Describe a colourful event that you particularly enjoyed.
>
> You should say:
>
> > why you were there
> >
> > who you were with
> >
> > what you saw around you
>
> and explain why you enjoyed the event so much.

Pronunciation
Intonation 1

Speakers use intonation to show how they feel. A rise helps your listener understand that something is exciting or shocking, while a fall can suggest a negative feeling, such as disappointment.

1 (11) **Work in pairs. Look at this extract from Zandra's talk and decide where you think her voice might rise or fall to show how she feels. If the word has more than one syllable, mark the syllable(s) that rise or fall. Then listen to check your answers.**

I mean, I've seen some terrible puppet shows in the past, but these dolls were expressive – they came alive.

2 (12) **Work in pairs. Decide where Zandra's voice will rise or fall in these sentences. Then listen to check your answers.**

1 I decided to buy this doll because we'd been to a puppet theatre and seen a performance, and it was just fantastic.
2 The story included a certain amount of fighting, which was probably quite frightening for children, but it was also magical – and the good guy won, which I like.
3 Actually, my doll looks pretty old, even though it was made – you know – made in this era.
4 It's only wooden, but dressed in really bright, attractive materials, like batik.
5 Some of my friends think she's very scary, and others, like me, are really drawn to her.
6 I feel that she protects me from bad things and brings me good luck.

3 **Work in pairs. Take turns to read the extracts in Exercises 1 and 2 to each other using the same intonation.**

Writing Task 2

1 **Work in pairs. Read this Writing task, then brainstorm some ideas that support the statement by discussing the questions below.**

Write about the following topic.

Psychologists have known for many years that colour can affect how people feel. For this reason, attention should be given to colour schemes when decorating places such as offices and hospitals.

How true is this statement?
How far does colour influence people's health and capacity for work?

Give reasons for your answer and include any relevant examples from your own knowledge or experience.

1 What activities take place in offices?
2 How would colour affect staff in these places?
3 Who else goes to offices? How might they feel?
4 How might colour affect patients in a hospital?
5 What about medical staff?

2 **When you write a discursive essay, you are expected to express your opinions on the topic and give reasons for them. Read the sample answer on page 26, then complete this plan.**

Essay plan
Introduction – my view – statement is very true
2nd and 3rd paragraphs – reasons why colour is important in offices
• can't concentrate with bright colours
•
•
4th and 5th paragraphs – reasons why colour is important in hospitals
•
•
•

Conclusion

Colour is <u>arguably</u> one of the earliest things that we learn about. As we grow up, we develop preferences for colour, and these are shown in the decoration of our homes, the products we buy and the clothes we wear. As colour plays such a huge role in our domestic lives, <u>it is inevitable that</u> it will also affect how we feel outside of the home, particularly in places such as hospitals and offices.

<u>As a matter of fact</u>, businesses have been aware of the impact of colour on employees for some time. <u>The general view has been that</u> if you work in an office that has too many colours and patterns on the walls, you will end up finding it hard to concentrate. Visitors may also be too taken up with the colours around them to focus on what they are doing.

<u>Interestingly</u>, however, there are some office areas that suit bright colours. For example, creative people often say they can carry out their work better if a room is painted in bold colours. In my university in Thailand, the creative room was painted entirely in yellow to inspire its users to come up with exciting and novel ideas. Students commented that they felt more energised in this type of environment.

While work is about output, hospitals are about the health of patients. <u>Clearly</u>, bright colours would be less welcome on a hospital ward, where patients are trying to recover from operations and illnesses. Here, relaxing shades are needed, such as pastels.

Having said that, some hospital areas are the opposite. Unlike adults, children need some form of entertainment, and walls painted in bright reds and oranges with pictures and posters can achieve that. Similarly, doctors and nurses might welcome brighter surroundings when they are taking a break from work.

<u>As far as I am concerned</u>, there is a direct link between colour and mood. This means that designers should think about who will occupy a building, and decorate its rooms in such a way that the occupants are able to get the best out of their surroundings.

❸ **In the sample answer, the writer uses words and phrases to express his attitude to what he is about to say. Which of the <u>underlined</u> words/phrases does he use to say he thinks something is:**

1 possibly true?
2 obvious?
3 his opinion (as opposed to anyone else's)?
4 the opinion of most people?
5 certain?
6 a curious or unexpected point?
7 important to emphasise?

▶ page 112 *Attitude adverbials*

❹ ⊙ **Work in pairs. IELTS candidates often make mistakes using attitude adverbials. Find and correct the mistakes at the start of these sentences.**

1 ~~Most important~~, people should be consulted about their views. *Most importantly*
2 In their opinion, some people totally disagree with this statement for the following reasons.
3 In my point of view, people who can still work should be encouraged to work regardless of their age.
4 Arguable, the media can play a significant role in conveying this message.
5 As the matter of fact, no matter what country you are in, you can always see rivalry between teams.
6 As far as I concerned, societies benefit from cultural differences.

Exam advice   *Writing Task 2*
• Analyse the task carefully first. You will lose marks if you misread the question or fail to deal with all parts of the task.
• Brainstorm ideas, make a quick plan and write following your plan.
• Use comment adverbials to indicate your views.

▶ Key grammar: *Nouns and articles*

❺ **Work in small groups.**

1 Brainstorm ideas you could put into an essay which expresses the idea that the statement in the task in Exercise 1 is not very true.
2 Complete this plan for the answer.

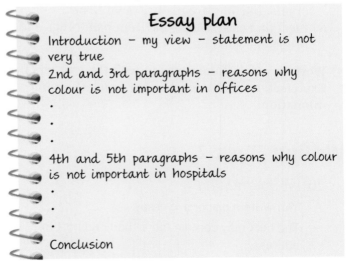

Essay plan
Introduction – my view – statement is not very true
2nd and 3rd paragraphs – reasons why colour is not important in offices
•
•
•
4th and 5th paragraphs – reasons why colour is not important in hospitals
•
•
•
Conclusion

❻ **Write your answer in 35 minutes. Write at least 250 words and leave a few minutes to check what you have written.**

Key grammar
Nouns and articles

❶ Read these sentences from the sample answer on page 26.

1 <u>Colour</u> is arguably <u>one of the earliest **things**</u> that we learn about.
2 … these are shown in <u>the **decoration** of our homes</u>, <u>the **products** we buy</u> and <u>the **clothes** we wear</u>.
3 … creative **people** often say they can carry out their work better if <u>a **room**</u> is painted in bold colours.
4 In my university in **Thailand**, <u>the creative room</u> was painted entirely in yellow to inspire its **users** to come up with exciting and novel ideas.
5 While **work** is about **output**, hospitals are about <u>the **health** of **patients**</u>.

Put the words in bold into one of these categories. Some can go in more than one category.

1 countable   *things, …*
2 uncountable
3 only found in the plural
4 a proper noun (i.e. a name)

❷ Which <u>underlined</u> words/phrases in Exercise 1 illustrate these rules of article use?

Use the definite article 'the'

a with particular or known places, e.g. *the supermarket*
b when you are talking about a particular example of a thing, e.g. *the education of young children*
c with superlative adjectives

Use the indefinite article 'a' or 'an'

d with a singular countable noun

Do not use an article

e before the names of most places
f when talking in general

▶ page 120 *Use and non-use of articles*

❸ Circle the correct option in *italics* in these sentences.

1 *The / A* lighting in many restaurants is too bright.
2 White clothes can quickly end up looking grey if you wash them with *the / –* other colours.
3 Only *a / –* small percentage of people can read in bright sunshine.
4 If you are colour blind, some colours like green and blue look *the / –* same.
5 In sport, colour is often used to identify *a / the* team of players.
6 We saw some very interesting displays at *the / –* Colour Exhibition.
7 Colour can have a positive effect on *a / –* mood.
8 *The / –* children's toyshops are usually very attractive to look at.

❹ ⊙ IELTS candidates often make mistakes using articles. Find and correct the mistakes in these sentences. One sentence is correct.

1 The government has encouraged ~~the people~~ to enjoy life. *people*
2 It is hard to find job in design after graduation.
3 In the capital of Czech Republic, there is a famous street that contains some old but very colourful shops.
4 We are living in the world where people have more choice.
5 Elderly have different views from young people.
6 Children should look forward to the bright future.
7 It can lead to a lack of communication between people.
8 In my opinion, it would be a wrong approach to the problem.

Vocabulary and grammar review **Unit 1**

Vocabulary

❶ Complete these sentences by writing the correct preposition in each gap. Sometimes more than one answer is possible.

1 Finding a course that is suitable ......*for*...... me hasn't been easy.
2 Some people are more capable than others .... studying late at night.
3 The interviewers were very impressed .... the candidate's qualifications.
4 Human beings should never underestimate their capacity .... knowledge.
5 I've realised that I'm not as suited as I thought I was .... working in an office.
6 After such dishonesty, all the belief that I had .... him has gone.
7 Blaming others .... your mistakes is never a good idea.
8 Most people regard me .... a shy person, but I'm really quite outgoing.

Grammar

❷ Complete these sentences by writing the past simple, present perfect simple or past perfect simple form of the verb in brackets in each gap.

1 Prior to 2010, South Korea ......*was*...... (*be*) the third leading source of international students in the US.
2 The research that .... (*conduct*) on the subject so far is minimal.
3 In 2009, there were 300 admissions, but by 2012, this figure .... (*treble*).
4 The presentation .... (*already begin*) when the fire alarm went off.
5 The bottles were washed, sterilised, inspected and finally .... (*fill*) with fluid.
6 Between 2009 and 2011, the percentage of school leavers .... (*not alter*).
7 Although I .... (*not have*) any experience as an analyst, I am very keen to learn.
8 When I asked for the bill, I was told it .... (*just pay*).

❸ Complete the gaps in the summary below of this graph using a comparative or superlative form of the words in brackets.

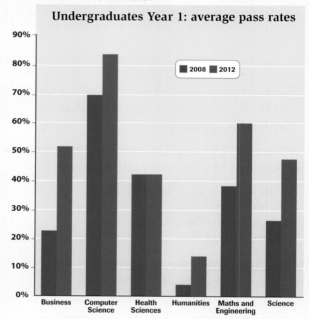

Undergraduates Year 1: average pass rates

The chart compares how well students from a range of disciplines did in their Year 1 assessments in 2008 and 2012.

At just over 80% in 2012 and 70% in 2008, average pass rates among Computer Science students were by far **1** *the highest* (*high*), while **2** .... (*high*) scores in 2012 were in Maths and Engineering. On the other hand, students studying Humanities had **3** .... (*low*) pass rates in both years.

Looking more closely at the percentage change between the two years, this was clearly **4** .... (*marked*) for those studying Business. 2008 pass rates in Business, Science, and Maths and Engineering were considerably **5** .... (*low*) in 2008 than in 2012, which means that **6** .... (*great*) level of improvement took place in these disciplines. Meanwhile, the Health Sciences experienced **7** .... (*stable*) pass rates.

Overall, students in 2008 did consistently **8** .... (*good*) than their counterparts in 2012, although there were significant differences among the subject areas in both years.

Vocabulary and grammar review **Unit 2**

Vocabulary

❶ Complete these sentences by writing a phrasal verb in the correct form in each gap. Add any necessary pronouns. The first letter of each word has been given.

1 Unfortunately, the shirt I thought was red _turned_ _out_ to be orange in daylight.

2 It is unwise to present an argument in your essay unless you can b............... i............... u............... with examples or evidence.

3 During the sales meeting, staff c............... u............... w............... some good ideas about how to improve the appearance of the showroom.

4 The assistant d............... w............... the customer's complaint by giving her a refund.

5 It was decided to s............... u............... the exhibition in the town square in order to attract as many passers-by as possible.

6 The assistant gave me a reference for the item, but unfortunately I forgot to n............... i............... d............... on my iPhone.

7 I cannot p............... u............... w............... these dark walls any longer – I'm going to paint them.

8 In this economic climate, it's hard to g............... b............... when you don't earn very much money.

❷ Find nine more words in the grid all connected with colour. You can find the words horizontally, vertically and diagonally and in any direction.

E	K	O	L	M	J	D	W	H	V	I	C
S	R	I	P	U	R	P	L	E	D	M	O
H	O	D	F	A	V	S	B	P	O	I	L
A	W	E	T	O	T	R	H	O	N	F	O
D	B	R	I	G	H	T	D	I	L	P	U
E	X	S	E	F	J	B	E	G	P	D	R
A	P	A	S	T	E	L	U	R	E	B	B
Q	J	P	E	N	C	R	O	V	N	I	L
T	U	R	Q	U	O	I	S	E	T	Y	I
I	D	I	S	N	K	C	U	O	L	E	N
C	A	M	O	U	F	L	A	G	E	W	D

Grammar

❸ Circle the most appropriate adverbial in *italics*.

1 Car colour is directly linked to safety; (*in fact*)/ *in my view*, surveys have shown that white cars have fewer accidents.

2 *Frankly / Apparently*, if you fill a black tin and a green tin with the same amount of paint, people will think that the black tin is heavier.

3 Everyone has some form of artistic talent, but some people are *understandably / arguably* more talented than others.

4 *Generally speaking / As far as I'm concerned*, I don't believe in making children do things they don't want to do.

5 You can ask children not to spill paints but, *inevitably / as a matter of fact*, they will.

❹ Complete this paragraph by writing *a, an, the* or – if you think no article is needed. In some cases, more than one answer is possible.

Making natural dyes

Natural dyes made from **1** .... plant material produce much softer colours than **2** .... commercial dyes and contain no chemicals. If you want to make **3** .... blue dye, for example, all you need to do is cut up **4** .... red cabbage and boil it in water for 30–40 minutes. Let **5** .... mixture stand overnight, then boil it again and remove **6** .... plant material.

Before you dye a garment, **7** .... important process known as fixing ensures that **8** .... colour will not run. **9** .... most common fixers are lemon juice and vinegar. They also need to be boiled with your garment as part of **10** .... dyeing process.

Once you have done this, you should put the garment into **11** .... stainless steel pot with **12** .... dye and simmer **13** .... two together for 30 to 40 minutes (until you get **14** .... right colour). **15** .... more you stir during this time, **16** .... better your dye will fix.

Unit 3 A healthy life

Starting off

1 Work in small groups. Complete the photo captions with these phrases (a–f).

a to inoculate her against disease.
b to relieve her headache.
c to treat an injured knee joint.
d to set a broken bone.
e to check his sight.
f to cure his migraine.

2 Which photo illustrates:

i an alternative form of medical treatment?
ii large-scale preventative medical treatment?
iii the use of medication to alleviate pain?
iv the treatment of a muscle injury?
v treatment following an accident in the playground?
vi a routine check-up?

3 Have you or someone you know ever experienced any of these treatments? When and where?

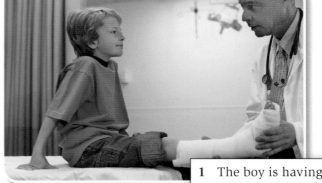

1 The boy is having a plaster cast put on his leg …

2 The young woman is taking a tablet …

3 The man is having acupuncture …

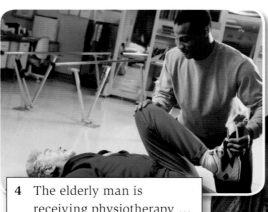

4 The elderly man is receiving physiotherapy …

5 The girl is being given an injection …

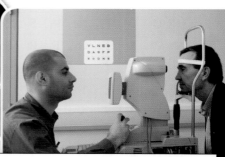

6 The man is having an eye test …

Listening Part 3

Exam information
- You hear a conversation between two or more speakers on a study-based topic.
- The questions may cover both factual information and opinions.

1 Work in pairs. You are going to hear two students talking to a physiotherapist. Discuss these questions before you listen.

1 What does a physiotherapist's work involve?
2 When might someone need a physiotherapist?

2 Look at Questions 1–5 below and the comments. Underline the key ideas in options A–F.

Questions 1–5

What comments do the speakers make about each treatment or service?

Choose FIVE answers from the box and write the correct letter, A–F, next to Questions 1–5.

Treatments and Services

1 Manual therapy   ....
2 Stability training   ....
3 Electrotherapy   ....
4 Video analysis   ....
5 Workstation analysis   ....

Comments
A It strengthens the whole body.
B It is the most popular.
C It requires special sportswear.
D It is the most effective.
E It is best done in the evening.
F It is rarely used.

---

3 (13) Now listen and answer Questions 1–5.

Exam advice   Matching
- Underline the key ideas in the questions and/or options.
- You will hear the questions in the same order as they are written on the question paper.
- Write your answers as you listen.

4 Look at Questions 6–10 below (ignoring the underlined words for now).

1 What does the flow chart describe?
2 What type of information is needed to complete each gap?

Questions 6–10

Complete the flow chart below.

*Write **NO MORE THAN TWO WORDS** for each answer.*

Example of patient route

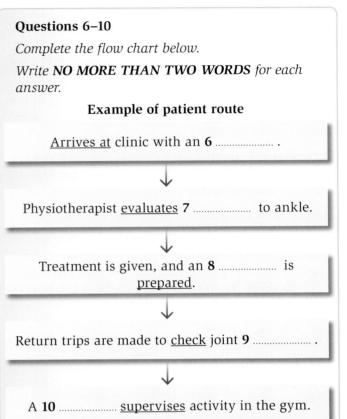

Arrives at clinic with an **6** ....

↓

Physiotherapist evaluates **7** .... to ankle.

↓

Treatment is given, and an **8** .... is prepared.

↓

Return trips are made to check joint **9** ....

↓

A **10** .... supervises activity in the gym.

---

5 (14) Now listen and answer Questions 6–10.

Exam advice   Flow-chart completion
- Use the title and the words around the gaps to decide what you need to listen for.
- Quickly read through the chart afterwards to check your answers make sense.

6 Look at the recording script on page 152.

1 For Questions 1–5, underline the words that gave you each answer.
2 For Questions 6–10, note down the words the speakers use that mean the same as the underlined verbs in Questions 6–10.

7 Work in pairs. Take turns to speak for a minute or two on this topic.

Describe a time when you or a friend experienced a minor injury. Say how it happened, what you did about it, and who helped you.

Reading Section 3

Exam information

- Reading Section 3 is generally more challenging than the other two sections.
- There are 14, rather than 13 questions.

1 Work in small groups. You are going to read an article about the 'placebo effect'. Before you read, discuss these questions.

1 Why do pharmaceutical companies have to test the drugs they are developing?

2 How do you think they do this?

2 Look at the illustration in the article and read the title and subheading. What does the 'placebo effect' refer to? What do you expect to read about?

3 Now skim the article and decide whether your answers to Exercise 2 were correct.

4 <u>Underline</u> words in Questions 1–5 below which will help you scan to find the relevant parts of the passage. Then read those parts of the passage and answer the questions.

Questions 1–5

Do the following statements agree with the claims of the writer?

Write

YES   *if the statement agrees with the claims of the writer*

NO   *if the statement contradicts the claims of the writer*

NOT GIVEN   *if it is impossible to say what the writer thinks about this*

1 Merck's experience with MK-869 was unique.

2 These days, a small number of unsuccessful test results can ruin a well-established drugs company.

3 Some medical conditions are more easily treated by a placebo than others.

4 It was to be expected that the third group in Kaptchuk's trial would do better than the other two groups.

5 Kaptchuk's research highlights the fact that combined drug and placebo treatments should be avoided.

Exam advice   *Yes / No / Not Given*

- You should use the same approach for *True / False / Not Given* and *Yes / No / Not Given* questions (see page 12). However, *True / False / Not Given* questions refer to information stated in the article, whereas these questions refer to the writer's opinions or claims.

- Remember that 'NO' statements say the opposite of what is stated in the passage, while the idea in 'NOT GIVEN' statements is not mentioned at all.

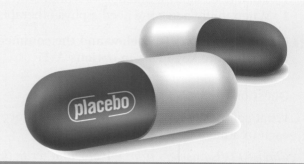

Examining the placebo effect

BY STEVE SILBERMAN

The fact that taking a fake drug can powerfully improve some people's health—the so-called placebo effect—was long considered an embarrassment to the serious practice of pharmacology, but now things have changed.

Several years ago, Merck, a global pharmaceutical company, was falling behind its rivals in sales. To make matters worse, patents on five blockbuster drugs were about to expire, which would allow cheaper generic products to flood the market. In interviews with the press, Edward Scolnick, Merck's Research Director, presented his plan to restore the firm to pre-eminence. Key to his strategy was expanding the company's reach into the anti-depressant market, where Merck had trailed behind, while competitors like Pfizer and GlaxoSmithKline had created some of the best-selling drugs in the world. "To remain dominant in the future," he told one media company, "we need to dominate the central nervous system."

His plan hinged on the success of an experimental anti-depressant codenamed MK-869. Still in clinical trials, it was a new kind of medication that exploited brain chemistry in innovative ways to promote feelings of well-being. The drug tested extremely well early on, with minimal side effects. Behind the scenes, however, MK-869 was starting to unravel. True, many test subjects treated with the medication felt their hopelessness and anxiety lift. But so did nearly the same number who took a placebo, a look-alike pill made of milk sugar or another inert substance given to groups of volunteers in subsequent clinical trials to gauge the effectiveness of the real drug by comparison. Ultimately, Merck's venture into the anti-depressant market failed. In the jargon of the industry, the trials crossed the "futility boundary".

MK-869 has not been the only much-awaited medical breakthrough to be undone in recent years by the placebo effect. And it's not only trials of new drugs that are crossing the futility boundary. Some products that have been on the market for decades are faltering in more recent follow-up tests. It's not that the old medications are getting weaker, drug developers say. It's as if the placebo effect is somehow getting stronger. The fact that an increasing number of medications are unable to beat sugar pills has thrown the industry into crisis. The stakes could hardly be higher. To win FDA* approval, a new medication must beat placebo in at least two authenticated trials. In today's economy, the fate of a well-established company can hang on the outcome of a handful of tests.

Why are fake pills suddenly overwhelming promising new drugs and established medicines alike? The reasons are only just beginning to be understood. A network of independent researchers is doggedly uncovering the inner workings and potential applications of the placebo effect.

A psychiatrist, William Potter, who knew that some patients really do seem to get healthier for reasons that have more to do with a doctor's empathy than with the contents of a pill, was baffled by the fact that drugs he had been prescribing for years seemed to be struggling to prove their effectiveness. Thinking that a crucial factor may have been overlooked, Potter combed through his company's database of published and unpublished trials—including those that had been kept secret because of high placebo response. His team aggregated the findings from decades of anti-depressant trials, looking for patterns and trying to see what was changing over time. What they found challenged some of the industry's basic assumptions about its drug-vetting process.

Assumption number one was that if a trial were managed correctly, a medication would perform as well or badly in a Phoenix hospital as in a Bangalore clinic. Potter discovered, however, that geographic location alone could determine the outcome. By the late 1990s, for example, the anti-anxiety drug Diazepam was still beating placebo in France and Belgium. But when the drug was tested in the U.S., it was likely to fail. Conversely, a similar drug, Prozac, performed better in America than it did in western Europe and South Africa. It was an unsettling prospect: FDA approval could hinge on where the company chose to conduct a trial.

Mistaken assumption number two was that the standard tests used to gauge volunteers' improvement in trials yielded consistent results. Potter and his colleagues discovered that ratings by trial observers varied significantly from one testing site to another. It was like finding out that the judges in a tight race each had a different idea about the placement of the finish line.

After some coercion by Potter and others, the National Institute of Health (NIH) focused on the issue in 2000, hosting a three-day conference in Washington, and this conference launched a new wave of placebo research in academic laboratories in the U.S. and Italy that would make significant progress toward solving the mystery of what was happening in clinical trials.

In one study last year, Harvard Medical School researcher Ted Kaptchuk devised a clever strategy for testing his volunteers' response to varying levels of therapeutic ritual. The study focused on a common but painful medical condition that costs more than $40 billion a year worldwide to treat. First, the volunteers were placed randomly in one of three groups. One group was simply put on a waiting list; researchers know that some patients get better just because they sign up for a trial. Another group received placebo treatment from a clinician who declined to engage in small talk. Volunteers in the third group got the same fake treatment from a clinician who asked them questions about symptoms, outlined the causes of the illness, and displayed optimism about their condition.

Not surprisingly, the health of those in the third group improved most. In fact, just by participating in the trial, volunteers in this high-interaction group got as much relief as did people taking the two leading prescription drugs for the condition. And the benefits of their "bogus" treatment persisted for weeks afterward, contrary to the belief—widespread in the pharmaceutical industry—that the placebo response is short-lived.

Studies like this open the door to hybrid treatment strategies that exploit the placebo effect to make real drugs safer and more effective. As Potter says, "To really do the best for your patients, you want the best placebo response plus the best drug response."

adapted from Wired Magazine

* *The Food and Drugs Administration (an agency in the United States responsible for protecting public health by assuring the safety of human drugs)*

line 80

⑤ Work in pairs.

1 Read the title of the summary below. Which paragraphs in the passage will you need to read carefully to do this task?

2 Read the summary and <u>underline</u> words around the gaps that express key ideas.

Questions 6–10

Complete the summary using the list of words, A–I, below.

Merck and MK-869

As a result of concerns about increasing **6** .... in the drugs industry, the pharmaceutical company Merck decided to increase its **7** .... in the anti-depressant market. The development of the drug MK-869 was seen as the way forward.

Initially, MK-869 had some **8** .... , but later trials revealed a different picture. Although key **9** .... could be treated with the drug, a sugar pill was proving equally effective. In the end, the **10** .... indicated that it was pointless continuing with the development of the drug.

A activity	**D** patients	**G** symptoms
B prices	**E** tests	**H** competition
C success	**F** diseases	**I** criticism

---

❻ Now read the paragraphs you identified in Exercise 5 and complete Questions 6–10 in the summary.

Exam advice   **Summary completion with a box**

• The answers may come from more than one part of the passage.

• Use the title and words in the summary to help you find the right parts.

• <u>Underline</u> the words in the passage that provide the missing information – you need to match these to the correct option in the box.

❼ <u>Underline</u> the key ideas in Questions 11–14 (not the options). Then scan the passage to find the relevant parts and read each part carefully to choose the correct options.

Questions 11–14

Choose the correct letter, A, B, C or D.

11 Which of the following is true of William Potter's research?

   A It was based on recently developed drugs that he had recommended.

   B It included trial results from a range of drugs companies.

   C Some of the trial results he investigated had not been made public.

   D Some of his findings were not accepted by the drugs industry.

12 What did William Potter's research reveal about the location of drugs trials?

   A The placebo effect was weakest in the US.

   B Results were not consistent around the world.

   C Results varied depending on the type of hospital.

   D The FDA preferred drugs to be tested in different countries.

13 What does the *tight race* refer to in line 80?

   A the standard tests

   B consistent results

   C ratings by trial observers

   D testing sites

14 What significant discovery was made by Ted Kaptchuk?

   A The effects of a placebo can last longer than previously thought.

   B Patients' health can improve while waiting to undergo a trial.

   C Patients respond better to a placebo if they are treated by the same clinician throughout the trial.

   D Those conducting a placebo trial need to know the subjects' disorder well.

Exam advice   **Multiple choice**

• Use names and other words to scan to find the right place in the passage.

• Read above and below that part of the passage and <u>underline</u> the words that answer the question.

Vocabulary
Verb + noun collocations

❶ Some verbs and nouns are often used together. Scan the passage on pages 32–33 for these verb + noun collocations (1–8). Then match each verb in bold with its meaning (a–h).

1 **promote** feelings
2 **gauge** the effectiveness (of something)
3 **overlook** a factor
4 **challenge** an assumption
5 **determine** an outcome
6 **yield** results
7 **devise** a strategy
8 **outline** the causes (of something)

a to invent – cleverly or imaginatively
b to supply or produce something positive, such as information
c to encourage the development or existence of something
d to give a general idea of the main items or parts of something
e not to notice, or to pretend not to notice
f to calculate or make a judgement about something
g to question or express doubt about the truth, legality or purpose of something
h to control or influence directly; to decide

❷ Choose the correct verb in *italics* to complete these sentences.

1 Seventy years ago, a nurse *devised / determined* a method of alleviating pain during operations without the use of an anaesthetic.
2 Using a placebo in trials allows scientists to *determine / yield* the true success of a drug.
3 Prior to the official use of placebos, researchers sometimes *gauged / overlooked* negative results.
4 Researchers have found that taking a sugar pill while believing it to be a medicine can *promote / outline* a sense of well-being.
5 In *gauging / devising* a patient's reaction to treatment, it is always important to look at side effects as well.
6 Some alternative medical treatments have *challenged / overlooked* conventional practice.
7 During a consultation, medical practitioners should *outline / promote* their treatment strategy.
8 A trial should be abandoned if the treatment is not *yielding / promoting* any real gains.

Speaking Part 2

❶ Work in pairs. Read this Speaking task and briefly discuss what you could say for each point. Make brief notes as you talk.

> Describe something you would like to do in the future that would be good for your health.
>
> You should say:
>
> what you would like to do
>
> what it would involve
>
> when you would like to do it
>
> and explain why it would be good for your health.

❷ 🔊(15) Listen to Faris doing the task in Exercise 1 and complete his notes.

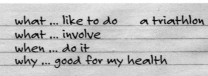

what ... like to do   a triathlon
what ... involve
when ... do it
why ... good for my health

❸ 🔊(15) Complete these sentences by putting the verb in brackets into the correct form. Then listen again to check your answers.

1 I've always dreamed of .... (*take part*) in a triathlon.
2 There's an Olympic distance, which I wish I .... (*can*) do.
3 I think I'm likely .... (*finish*) if I choose a shorter course.
4 I don't expect I'll be able .... (*tackle*) it until my academic year's ended.
5 I'm actually looking forward to .... (*do*) a triathlon.
6 I just hope I .... (*be*) successful at it.

▶ page 120 *Talking about ambitions and aspirations*

❹ Work in pairs. Take turns to complete these sentences about yourself.

1 When I have taken my IELTS test, I expect …
2 I have always dreamed of …
3 I hope one day I …
4 This year, I am looking forward to …
5 If I have a holiday next year, I am likely to …
6 I have always wished I …… , but I might find …… too difficult.

5 Work in small groups. Take a minute to review the notes you made in Exercise 1, then take turns to give your talk. As you listen, complete this checklist.

Did your partner …

- ☐ introduce the topic?
- ☐ talk about the points in the task?
- ☐ use the points to structure the talk?
- ☐ use vocabulary related to the task?
- ☐ end the talk appropriately?

▶ Pronunciation: *Linking and pausing*

6 Read this Speaking task and spend one minute preparing notes for each point. Then take turns to do the task with a partner. When your partner has finished, ask them for brief replies to the two questions below.

> **Describe your ideal healthy living environment.**
> **You should say:**
> > **where it would be**
> > **what features it would have**
> > **how easy it would be to live there**
> **and explain why this would be your ideal environment.**

1 Do you know many places like this?
2 Do you think you will live in this type of place in the future?

Pronunciation
Linking and pausing

Linking certain words together and then pausing between groups of words helps a speaker achieve the natural rhythm of English speech. The way words are linked depends on the letters that come at the end of one word and the beginning of the next.

1 🔈16 Listen to these extracts from Faris's talk. When is the *t* pronounced in the underlined words, and when is it silent? Why?

1 *Well, I'm <u>quite</u> fit …*
2 *… taking <u>part</u> in a triathlon.*

2 🔈17 Work in pairs. Decide whether the <u>underlined</u> consonants in these sentences should be pronounced or silent. Then listen and check your answers.

1 *… a triathlon<u>'s</u> a multi-spor<u>t</u> event, but rathe<u>r</u> a hard one.*
2 *As fo<u>r</u> when I'<u>d</u> take par<u>t</u> in it, I'm no<u>t</u> sure.*
3 *I'<u>m</u> actually looking forwar<u>d</u> to the triathlon.*

3 Take turns to read the sentences from Exercise 2 aloud.

4 🔈18 Work in pairs. Look at this longer extract and <u>underline</u> the words that you think Faris links together. Listen and check your answers. When you have finished, take turns to read the extract aloud.

That would be realistic because I'd need time to train and really get into shape. It's not something that I could do in a hurry! Um, obviously it would be a really healthy thing to do because it would force me to get even fitter than I am now. Plus I'd have to eat well during the training period and get plenty of sleep and that sort of thing.

Writing Task 1

❶ Work in pairs. Look at the task below.

1 How is the table linked to the chart?
2 Select the key features in the chart and table.
3 What general trends can you identify in the data as a whole?

> *The chart and table below give information about population figures in Japan.*
>
> *Summarise the information by selecting and reporting the main features and make comparisons where relevant.*

Japan's population: past, present and future trends

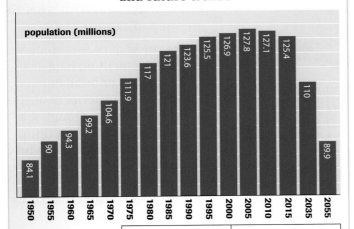

over-65s	population (millions)	percentage of total population
1950	4.1	4.9%
2005	25.7	20.0%
2035	37.2	34.0%
2055	36.5	41.0%

❷ Work in pairs. How would you organise the information and plan the paragraphs in your answer?

❸ Read the sample answer in the next column and complete this writer's plan. How does it compare with your plan?

> Paragraph 1 (Introduction): Topic and time period
>
> Paragraph 2:
>
> Paragraph 3:
>
> Paragraph 4 (Overview):

The table and chart provide information regarding population growth and the proportion of the population over 65 over a 100-year period in Japan.

According to the information, Japan's general population figures in 1950 were very different from those in 2005, and future predictions show even greater differences. In 1950, the number of people was just over 84 million, and only 4.9 percent (4.1 million) of these people were above the age of 65. By 2005, the percentage of older people had risen considerably to 20 percent, while the overall population had shown a parallel increase to nearly 128 million.

However, total population figures peaked in 2005, and it is expected that the number of people living in Japan will fall substantially over the next 50 years to a little below 90 million. In spite of this fall, the rise in the ageing population will continue, and at a faster rate, so that by 2055, 41 percent (36.5 million) of Japanese people will be over 65.

These statistics show two contrasting trends in Japan's demographics that will result in fewer citizens, but greater numbers of elderly people.

❹ Answer these questions about the sample answer.

1 What figures does the writer quote? Why?
2 What is the purpose of the first sentence in paragraph 2?
3 What similarities does the writer mention? What linker does she use to compare the points?
4 What differences does the writer mention? What linkers does she use to contrast the points?
5 What is the purpose of the overview at the end?

❺ Work in pairs. It is important to paraphrase words and phrases in the task and use precise language in your answer.

1 Find as many alternative expressions as you can in the sample answer for these phrases.
   a aged 65 and older
   b Japan's population
2 Find more precise words or phrases in the sample answer for these expressions.
   a more than
   b a lot (*two expressions*)
   c similar
   d under
   e more quickly
   f opposite
   g more

6 Work in pairs. Look at this Writing task and answer the questions below.

The charts below give information about the diet and general health of two groups of students.

Summarise the information by selecting and reporting the main features and make comparisons where relevant.

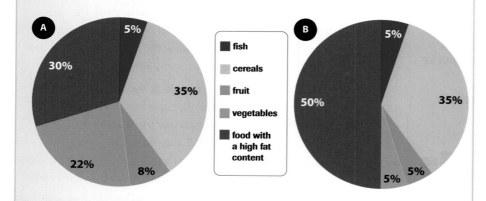

	Group A (%)	Group B (%)
overweight	10	20
illness in the past year	5	12
attendance at classes	90	75

1 What are the key features?
2 What comparisons could you make?
3 What should the overview contain?
4 Suggest two different ways you could organise the information.

7 Now read this sample answer, ignoring the gaps, and identify features 1–4 from Exercise 6: the key features, the comparisons, the overview and the organisation of the information.

The pie charts provide a breakdown of the 1 .... of food eaten by two groups of students, while the table highlights some 2 .... of their health. The data suggest that diet may have an impact on 3 .... of absenteeism and on student's ability to stay healthy.

The pie charts show that there are similarities and differences with regard to the two groups' diets. In both groups, about a third of the food students eat consists of cereals such as pasta, bread and rice. Similarly, they eat an equal 4 .... of fish (5 percent). However, the 5 .... of high-fat food eaten by Group B is considerably higher than in Group A, at 50 percent, while students in Group B eat far fewer vegetables than Group A and a slightly smaller 6 .... of fresh fruit.

The table indicates that there are twice as many overweight people in Group B (20 percent) as in Group A. What is more, Group B has experienced a much higher 7 .... of illness over the year, with over double the 8 .... of students being absent from classes. This has resulted in a 15 percent lower attendance 9 ....

8 When answering Task 1, you often need to use phrases that express amount, extent or categories. Complete the sample answer in Exercise 7 by writing one word from the box in each gap. In some cases, more than one answer may be possible, and you may need change the word to its plural form.

amount	aspect	incidence
level	number	proportion
quantity	rate	type

9 Match six of the words in the box in Exercise 8 with what they are used to express (1–6).

1 the speed at or frequency with which something happens
2 an amount or number of something material or abstract
3 the number or amount of a group or part of something when compared to the whole
4 one part of a situation, problem, etc.
5 the occurrence of something
6 the position of something abstract or concrete on a scale

10 Choose the correct option in *italics* in each of these sentences written by IELTS candidates.

1 It is important to control the *quantity / amount* of sunshine children are exposed to.
2 To discourage driving, certain *aspects / qualities* of the public transport system should be improved.
3 The *proportion / rate* of smokers to non-smokers is greater in some parts of the world than in others.
4 The *quantity / number* of workers doing shifts is very high.
5 The water *levels / percentages* were highest at midday.
6 This solution will reduce the unemployment *rate / number*.

- If there is more than one chart, decide how they relate to each other.
- Ensure key features are clearly expressed.
- Include an overview, summarising the main trends or features.
- Vary your vocabulary and use your own words as far as possible (e.g. do not lift long phrases from the task instructions).

▶ Key grammar: *Expressing large and small differences*

⑪ Write your answer to this task in at least 150 words.

The chart and table below give information about healthcare resources and life expectancy in different countries.

Summarise the information by selecting and reporting the main features and make comparisons where relevant.

Hospital beds per thousand of the population

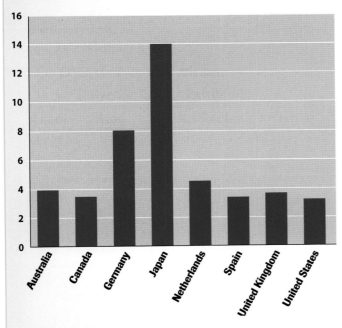

Government health spending

	Japan	Netherlands	US
health spending per person	$2,581	$3,481	$6,719
average life expectancy	83	80	78

Key grammar
Expressing large and small differences

❶ Answer these questions relating to comparisons in the two sample answers on pages 37 and 38.

1 Which adverb is used to emphasise *different* in the first sample answer?
2 What are the two opposites of *more*? Which is used with countable nouns?
3 Which adverbs are used to emphasise *higher* in the second sample answer?
4 Which two adverbs are used with *fewer* and *smaller* in the second sample answer? Which adverb expresses a big difference, and which one expresses a small difference?
5 What phrase does the writer use to compare the incidence of illness in the two groups?

▶ page 113 *Expressing large and small differences*

❷ Rewrite these sentences so that they have the same meaning, using the words in brackets. Emphasise the adjectives where necessary.

1 My brother eats less food than I do. (*quantity*)
My brother eats a smaller quantity of food than I do.
2 Some people's sleep patterns are not at all the same as mine. (*different*)
3 There are nowhere near as many injuries among pedestrians now. (*fewer*)
4 A much greater number of people are choosing alternative medical treatment in my country. (*popular*)
5 Now that I'm seeing a physiotherapist, I don't have nearly as much pain. (*less*)
6 Inoculations have resulted in fewer childhood illnesses. (*incidence*)

❸ IELTS candidates often make mistakes making comparisons. Choose the correct alternative in *italics* in each of these sentences.

1 Group A's statistics are *much more / very* different from the others.
2 The number of working women is much *less / lower* than it used to be.
3 Men need to consume twice as *many / greater* calories a day as women.
4 The gap between the different cultures is growing *less and less / smaller and smaller*.
5 Living for a long time is not nearly as important *as / than* staying healthy.

Unit 4 Art and the artist

Starting off

❶ Work in small groups. Look at the photos of different art forms.

1 Match the labels to the photos.
2 Where would you expect to see each art form?
3 Which of these works of art do you think is the most impressive? Why?

a antique jewellery
b modern sculpture
c modern painting
d antique vase
e modern graffiti

❷ Would you like to have any of these works of art in or near your home? Why? / Why not?

Reading Section 1

❶ Work in small groups. You are going to read an article about the history of poster art. Before you read, discuss these questions.

1 Where do you normally see posters?
2 What features are commonly seen in poster design?

❷ Now quickly read the title and the subheading of the passage on page 41. How do you think the passage will be structured?

❸ Skim the passage to find out what techniques for producing posters are mentioned.

The history of the poster

The appearance of the poster has changed continuously over the past two centuries.

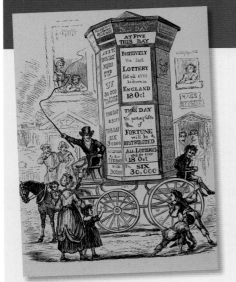

The first posters were known as 'broadsides' and were used for public and commercial announcements. Printed on one side only using metal type, they were quickly and crudely produced in large quantities. As they were meant to be read at a distance, they required large lettering.

There were a number of negative aspects of large metal type. It was expensive, required a large amount of storage space and was extremely heavy. If a printer did have a collection of large metal type, it was likely that there were not enough letters. So printers did their best by mixing and matching styles.

Commercial pressure for large type was answered with the invention of a system for wood type production. In 1827, Darius Wells invented a special wood drill – the lateral router – capable of cutting letters on wood blocks. The router was used in combination with William Leavenworth's pantograph (1834) to create decorative wooden letters of all shapes and sizes. The first posters began to appear, but they had little colour and design; often wooden type was mixed with metal type in a conglomeration of styles.

A major development in poster design was the application of lithography, invented by Alois Senefelder in 1796, which allowed artists to hand-draw letters, opening the field of type design to endless styles. The method involved drawing with a greasy crayon onto finely surfaced Bavarian limestone and offsetting that image onto paper. This direct process captured the artist's true intention; however, the final printed image was in reverse. The images and lettering needed to be drawn backwards, often reflected in a mirror or traced on transfer paper.

As a result of this technical difficulty, the invention of the lithographic process had little impact on posters until the 1860s, when Jules Cheret came up with

his 'three-stone lithographic process'. This gave artists the opportunity to experiment with a wide spectrum of colours. Although the process was difficult, the result was remarkable, with nuances of colour impossible in other media even to this day. The ability to mix words and images in such an attractive and economical format finally made the lithographic poster a powerful innovation.

Starting in the 1870s, posters became the main vehicle for advertising prior to the magazine era and the dominant means of mass communication in the rapidly growing cities of Europe and America. Yet in the streets of Paris, Milan and Berlin, these artistic prints were so popular that they were stolen off walls almost as soon as they were hung. Cheret, later known as 'the father of the modern poster', organised the first exhibition of posters in 1884 and two years later published the first book on poster art. He quickly took advantage of the public interest by arranging for artists to create posters, at a reduced size, that were suitable for in-home display.

Thanks to Cheret, the poster slowly took hold in other countries in the 1890s and came to celebrate each society's unique cultural institutions: the café in France, the opera and fashion in Italy, festivals in Spain, literature in Holland and trade fairs in Germany. The first poster shows were held in Great

Britain and Italy in 1894, Germany in 1896 and Russia in 1897. The most important poster show ever, to many observers, was held in Reims, France, in 1896 and featured an unbelievable 1,690 posters arranged by country.

In the early 20th century, the poster continued to play a large communication role and to go through a range of styles. By the 1950s, however, it had begun to share the spotlight with other media, mainly radio and print. By this time, most posters were printed using the mass production technique of photo offset, which resulted in the familiar dot pattern seen in newspapers and magazines. In addition, the use of photography in posters, begun in Russia in the twenties, started to become as common as illustration.

In the late fifties, a new graphic style that had strong reliance on typographic elements in black and white appeared. The new style came to be known as the International Typographic Style. It made use of a mathematical grid, strict graphic rules and black-and-white photography to provide a clear and logical structure. It became the predominant style in the world in the 1970s and continues to exert its influence today.

It was perfectly suited to the increasingly international post-war marketplace, where there was a strong demand for clarity. This meant that the accessibility of words and symbols had to be taken into account. Corporations wanted international identification, and events such as the Olympics called for universal solutions, which the Typographic Style could provide.

However, the International Typographic Style began to lose its energy in the late 1970s. Many criticised it for being cold, formal and dogmatic. A young teacher in Basel, Wolfgang Weingart, experimented with the offset printing process to produce posters that appeared complex and chaotic, playful and spontaneous – all in stark contrast to what had gone before. Weingart's liberation of typography was an important foundation for several new styles. These ranged from Memphis and Retro to the advances now being made in computer graphics.
adapted from www.internationalposter.com

④ **Look at Questions 1–5 below.**

1 Decide what type of information you need to complete each gap.
2 What parts of the table help you quickly find the paragraphs that will give you the answers?
3 Read those paragraphs carefully and answer Questions 1–5.

Questions 1–5

Complete the table below.

*Choose **NO MORE THAN THREE WORDS** from the passage for each answer.*

Early Printing Methods

	Features	Problems
Metal type	• produced large print	• cost, weight and **1** .... difficulties • mixed styles
Wood type	• Darius's wood drill used in connection with another **2** .... • produced a range of letters	• lacked both **3** .... • mixed type
Lithography	• letters drawn by hand • design tool – a **4**	• had to use a mirror or **5** .... to achieve correct image

⑤ **Why were these answers to Questions 1–5 marked wrong?**

1 not enough letters
2 pantograph
3 colour
4 greasy crayon
5 paper

Exam advice   Table completion

• Check how many words you are allowed to use.
• Use the title to find the right part of the passage.
• Write answers exactly as they are spelled in the passage.

6 **Look at the flow chart and Questions 6–9 below.**

1 Decide what type of information you need to complete each gap.

2 Find the correct part of the passage, read it carefully and answer Questions 6–9.

Questions 6–9

Complete the flow chart below.

Choose **NO MORE THAN THREE WORDS** *from the passage for each answer.*

Jules Cheret

1860s – invention of 'three-stone lithographic process'

↓

combination of both **6** .... on coloured posters

↓

1870s – posters used for advertising and **7** .... in Europe

↓

1884–86 – Cheret's poster **8** .... and book on poster art

↓

1890s – posters represent **9** .... around the world

---

Exam advice *Flow-chart completion*

- Use the title of the flow chart to find the right part of the passage.
- Check how many words you will need to fill each gap.
- Underline the words you need in the passage and copy them exactly onto the answer sheet.

7 **Read Questions 10–13 in the next column.**

1 Underline the words in the questions, e.g. dates and names. Then scan and find the same or similar words in the passage.

2 Read those parts of the passage carefully and answer Questions 10–13.

Questions 10–13

Do the following statements agree with the information in the reading passage?

Write

TRUE *if the statement agrees with the information*

FALSE *if the statement contradicts the information*

NOT GIVEN *if there is no information on this*

10 By the 1950s, photographs were more widely seen than artists' illustrations on posters.

11 Features of the Typographic Style can be seen in modern-day posters.

12 The Typographic Style met a global need at a particular time in history.

13 Weingart got many of his ideas from his students in Basel.

Exam advice *True / False / Not Given*

- Quickly find the part of the passage that deals with each statement. You should be able to find this, even when the answer is 'NOT GIVEN'.
- The answers may all be located in one part of the passage or they may occur at different points across the whole passage.

8 **Work in pairs. Discuss these questions.**

1 Do you have any posters at home? What of?

2 What are your favourite posters? Why do you like them?

3 Who buys posters today? Will they be popular in the future?

Vocabulary

Collocations and phrases with make, take, do *and* have

❶ Complete these sentences from the passage using *make, take, do* **or** *have* **in the correct form.**

1 So printers .....*did*..... **their best** by mixing and matching styles.
2 ... the invention of the lithographic process .... little **impact** on posters until the 1860s ...
3 He quickly .... **advantage** of the public interest ...
4 It .... **use** of a mathematical grid, strict graphic rules ...
5 This meant that the accessibility of words and symbols had to be .... **into account**.
6 These ranged from Memphis and Retro to the **advances** now being .... in computer graphics.

❷ Copy the table below into your notebook and add these words and phrases to the correct column.

> a prediction (about/regarding)   an interest (in)
> someone aware (of)   a profit (from)   mistakes (with)
> a decision (about/regarding)   business (with)
> an influence (on)   an effect (on)   a choice (between)
> action (on)   someone better   an impression (on)
> better   advantages (for)   (into) consideration
> a result (on)   research (on)   damage (to)
> benefits (for)

make	take	do	have
use (of)	advantage (of)	your/	an impact
advances (in)	(into) account	their best	(on)

❸ Complete these sentences using phrases from Exercises 1 and 2 in the correct form.

1 My friend ...*is doing some research*... in order to find out more about Japanese art.
2 If I were to .... , I would say that more people will collect art in the future.
3 Living outside the city .... , and one of these is that I have my own workshop.
4 The recent storms .... to the modern sculpture on the seafront.
5 Although I have my own personal style, previous artistic styles .... on my work.
6 I don't know which course to take, but I do know I need to .... soon.
7 Last year, I .... in Egyptian art and bought a book on the subject.

Listening Part 4

❶ Work in small groups. You are going to hear a lecturer talking about Australian Aboriginal art. Before you listen, look at the photos at the bottom of the page and discuss these questions.

1 What sort of places in Australia do you think you might see examples of Aboriginal art?
2 What features do you notice in the paintings?
3 How do you think the way this art is produced has changed over the years?

❷ Work in pairs. Look at Questions 1–10 on page 45.

1 How is the lecture structured?
2 What type of information do you need for each gap?

❸ 🔊 Now listen and answer Questions 1–10.

❹ Work in small groups.

1 How important is modern art in your culture?
2 Is modern art less skilful/valuable than traditional art?
3 In what ways do modern art forms differ from traditional ones?

Questions 1–10

Complete the notes below.

*Write **NO MORE THAN TWO WORDS AND/OR A NUMBER** for each answer.*

Australian Aboriginal Art

ANCIENT ART

- Rock and bark painting
- Sand drawings
- 1 ....
- Decorations on weapons and tools

  Cave art

  - protected from 2 ....
  - styles include dot paintings (e.g. arrows, water holes and 3 ....) and naturalistic art
  - main function: 4 ....

  Use of ochre

  Reason

  - readily available
  - soil or rock contains 5 ....
  - produces many colours and shades of red
  - artist's palette found that is 6 .... old

  Preparation

  - ochre collected
    ↓
  - turned into a 7 ....
    ↓
  - fluid binder, e.g. tree sap or 8 .... added

MODERN ART

- Artists use acrylic colours and 9 ....
- Paint and decorate pottery and a range of 10 ....

Speaking Parts 2 and 3

❶ Look at this task for Speaking Part 2 and think of a piece of art to talk about.

> Describe an object you find particularly beautiful (e.g. a painting, sculpture, piece of jewellery/furniture, etc.).
>
> You should say
>
>   where the artwork is
>
>   how it was made
>
>   what it shows / looks like
>
> and explain why you find it particularly beautiful.

❷ Before you make notes on the task in Exercise 1, study these words and phrases and make sure you know what each of them means. Then, work in pairs and discuss what you could say to answer the task.

where artwork is	how made	what shows / looks like	why beautiful
located/ situated in/ on …	by hand	… in shape	admire the workmanship
hanging in gallery/ exhibition/ museum	using local materials	a ...... scene	so impressive/ stunning to look at
on display in/ at …	carved by/using …	a portrait of …	makes you think/feel …
installed in/ on …	decorated with …	life-like/ abstract	very eye-catching
at home / my grandmother's house	dates back to …	modern/ traditional	the level of detail/skill of the artist is incredible

❸ Work in pairs and take turns to give your talks. You should each speak for two minutes.

> *Exam advice*   Speaking Part 2
>
> - Choose a topic you can talk about for the full two minutes.
> - Use advanced topic-related vocabulary to support your points and improve your score.

- The examiner asks you a range of questions connected with the topic of Part 2; you express your opinions.
- This is the most challenging part, because you need to demonstrate your ability to discuss general, abstract and academic topics.
- This part lasts between four and five minutes.

❹ Work in pairs. Look at this Part 3 question and Lee and Majut's answers.

1 Which is a general answer to the question, and which is personal?
2 Which is a better approach to answering questions in Part 3?

> *How popular is art as a school subject?*

> *Well, in my primary school, children loved it – I loved making things, for example – and in my secondary school, students hated it – we couldn't see the point when we had so many other things to do.*

> *On the whole, I think most children enjoy art, although they do seem to go off it a bit when they get older. I guess that's to be expected.*

❺ Majut uses the phrase *on the whole* to introduce a general point that may not be true for everyone.

1 What phrase does she use to show that her point may not be true for all children? Write it in the second column of the table below.
2 What verb does she use to generalise? Write it in the third column.

introducing a general point	generalising about people /places, etc.	verbs to generalise
on the whole		

❻ Work in pairs. Ask and answer these Part 3 questions.

- How popular is art as a school subject?
- What can young children learn from doing art at school?
- Why do you think secondary schools give arts subjects a low priority?

❼ ⟨20⟩ Listen to Naresh, an IELTS candidate, answering the second and third questions in Exercise 6. As you listen, add any expressions that he uses to generalise to the table in Exercise 5.

▶ page 114 *Generalising and distancing*

❽ ⦿ IELTS candidates often make mistakes when they generalise or distance themselves from what they are saying. Find and correct the mistake in each of these sentences.

1 Artists tend to varied their style over the years.
2 Nowadays, artists are tendency not to use local materials as they did in the past.
3 I feel that, as a whole, a lot of art is just not very good these days.
4 People who are artistic also tends to being very expressive.
5 In the past, people seem to had more time for art than they do now.
6 Actually, majority of people don't appreciate art.

▶ Pronunciation: *Speech rate and chunking*

❾ Work in pairs. Take turns to ask and answer these questions.

Art and society

1 In what ways are artists important in society?
2 What should governments do to support the arts?
3 Why do styles of art change over time?
4 What can you learn about a culture from its art?

Art and archaeology

1 Where do archaeologists often find ancient art?
2 What can archaeologists learn from ancient art objects?
3 How can governments protect ancient sites?

Exam advice *Speaking Part 3*

- Listen carefully to the questions and try to give an extended answer that expresses several points or ideas.
- Talk about the subject in general, not about yourself.
- Use appropriate words and phrases to put across a general point of view.

Pronunciation
Speech rate and chunking

We divide our speech up into meaningful groups of words called chunks and pause between them. If we pause in the middle of a natural chunk, people will find us difficult to understand, so we tend to pause between chunks, either to choose what we want to say next or to breathe. Speaking too quickly or too slowly is often the result of poor chunking.

1 (21) – (23) **Listen to three students giving the same answer to a question. As you listen, decide which speaker – 1, 2 or 3 – is easiest to understand. Why?**

2 (24) **Listen to Naresh answering a question and mark / where he pauses. What do you notice about his speech rate?**

Well I think broadly speaking they can learn a great deal. The majority of pre-school children for example are incredibly creative and experiment with paints and all sorts of other art materials and they just love getting their hands dirty. Older students tend to be less enthusiastic but many of them still enjoy art and well I guess if you don't try it you won't know whether you're any good at it.

3 (25) **Work in pairs. Mark the places where you think Naresh will pause in his answer to this question. Then listen and check your answers.**

Why do you think secondary schools give arts subjects a low priority?

Well generally there are quite a few reasons. These days a lot of head teachers seem to be more concerned about exam results than giving the students an all-round education. That's obviously going to have an influence on how significant art is in the school curriculum. Another possible reason is that many educational institutions don't tend to have the money to provide all the materials you need for art courses. They seem to be more worried about buying technological equipment these days.

4 **Work in pairs. Take turns to read his answer aloud.**

5 **Write your own answer to this question and mark where you think you will pause.**

Should students learn traditional crafts in schools? Why? / Why not?

Writing Task 2

1 **Work in pairs. Read this Writing task and <u>underline</u> the points you must deal with in your answer.**

Write about the following topic.

> *Some educationalists argue that non-exam, arts-based subjects, such as music, drama, art and craft, should be compulsory in the secondary-school curriculum. They believe that activities such as these can improve overall academic performance.*
>
> *To what extent do you agree or disagree?*

Give reasons for your answer and include any relevant examples from your own knowledge or experience.

2 **Work in small groups. Brainstorm some ideas for and against the topic, then select your main ideas and complete this diagram.**

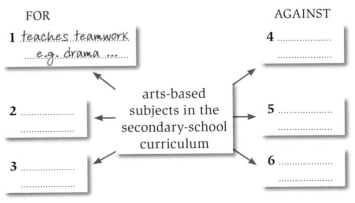

FOR
1 teaches teamwork e.g. drama
2 ....
3 ....

arts-based subjects in the secondary-school curriculum

AGAINST
4 ....
5 ....
6 ....

3 **Read the introductory paragraphs from three student essays. Then answer questions 1 and 2.**

Mika's essay

People have different views about the role of arts subjects in secondary-school timetables. Some people believe that they have a beneficial impact on students' learning, while others feel they are simply a form of creative relaxation. I agree with the former statement because I believe that they play a vital part in educational development.

Tom's essay

Obviously, success at school does not depend on study alone; it's true that arts subjects may help develop qualities in students that will further their educational achievement. However, non-exam subjects should never override the importance of academic subjects, such as maths and English.

Dhillon's essay

In today's world, the importance of academic subjects has grown. So I tend to feel that school time should be spent on things that help students achieve good grades and get to university, rather than on subjects that have no purpose within the school environment.

1 Underline the words each writer uses to introduce his/her view.
2 When you write your essay, you need to have a clear position throughout. Whose introduction:
   a agrees with the statement?
   b disagrees with the statement?
   c mentions both sides of the statement?

4 **Work in pairs. Read the second paragraphs from Mika's and Tom's essays. Then answer questions 1–3 in the next column.**

Mika's essay

It is generally thought that activities in the arts can help students learn how to work in a team. A student who takes part in a theatrical production has to co-operate with other members of the cast, with the aim of producing a successful final show. The same is true of musicians who play in an orchestra. They also have to work together to produce the best sound. I would suggest that experiences like these can enhance a student's ability to work with different types of people and participate successfully in a group project.

Tom's essay

People who value art lessons claim that it is important to exercise the imagination. This, they say, is likely to have a beneficial impact, due to the fact that students get a break from intellectual pursuits. On the other hand, others would argue that students have a lot of schoolwork to complete and they need to feel they have time to do this, otherwise they will get stressed. Art, it seems, can have a positive influence on students, but it could also undermine their sense of well-being.

1 Underline the sentences in each paragraph that state the main idea. Are the ideas the same as any of your ideas from Exercise 2?
2 Which sentences support the main idea in each paragraph? What type of support does each writer use: reasons or examples?
3 How is Mika's second paragraph different from Tom's?

▶ Key grammar: *Expressing purpose, cause and effect*

5 **Underline phrases in Mika's and Tom's paragraphs in Exercise 4 where they introduce their own and other people's opinions.**

▶ page 114 *Introducing arguments*

6 **⊙ IELTS students often make mistakes introducing arguments. Find and correct the mistakes in these sentences.**

1 Personally, I agree the view that music helps you relax.
2 Nowadays, as some teachers claimed, schools need arts subjects more than ever.
3 I'm tend to agree with the idea that dance helps children express themselves.
4 It is generally believe that drama activities should be provided for all students.

7 **Use phrases for introducing opinions to express agreement or disagreement with each of these views.**

1 Art helps children to make sense of the world.
   Many experts would argue that art helps children to make sense of the world.
2 Drama classes foster creativity and self-expression.
3 Classical music is more relaxing than modern music.
4 Actors are born, not made.
5 Formal education fails to encourage creative expression.

8 Write out Mika's third paragraph by re-ordering these sentences. Add one or two phrases to introduce the arguments.

 a It might be something concrete like a painting or object, or it might be something abstract like a piece of music.

 b This sense of achievement may then stimulate someone to achieve more in other subjects.

 c Another way in which the arts can help students is that they can improve self-confidence.

 d Both types of product need plenty of time and creativity and, as a result, can make someone feel very proud of the outcome.

 e This is because art is often about making a product.

9 Write a conclusion to Mika's essay.

10 Analyse, brainstorm, plan and write an answer to this Writing task. Take about 40 minutes and write at least 250 words.

> Write about the following topic.
>
> *Some modern artists receive huge sums of money for the things they create, while others struggle to survive. Governments should take steps to resolve this unfair situation.*
>
> *To what extent do you agree or disagree?*
>
> Give reasons for your answer and include any relevant examples from your own knowledge or experience.

Exam advice   Writing Task 2

- Your introductory paragraph should start with a general statement about the topic and state your position.
- Keep your position clear throughout your answer.
- Make sure the sentences in each paragraph follow a logical sequence.
- Support your main ideas with reasons, examples and consequences.
- Summarise your position in the final paragraph, but don't introduce new points or ideas.

Key grammar
Expressing purpose, cause and effect

1 <u>Underline</u> these words/phrases in Exercise 4 on page 48. Then put them in the correct column of the table below, according to whether they express a purpose, a cause or an effect.

with the aim of	due to	otherwise

purpose	cause	effect

2 Add these words/phrases to the table in Exercise 1.

as a result	because of	for	in order to	so that

3 Complete each of these sentences with the correct word/phrase from the table. Sometimes more than one answer is possible.

 1 The students study drama throughout their school lives. .... , they have high levels of self-confidence.

 2 The artist was awarded a government grant .... he could work on his project full time.

 3 You have to start with something easy .... develop your painting skills over time.

 4 Theatre audiences have been smaller over the past year .... the economic recession.

 5 People sometimes go to museums .... social purposes, such as to meet their friends.

 6 I have to feel that an artist has some talent, ... I don't have any respect for their work.

▶ page 113 *Expressing purpose, cause and effect*

4 ⊙ Choose the correct option in each of these sentences.

 1 The majority of people enjoy music *due to / because* it helps them relax.

 2 Working in a gallery is interesting *because / because of* the wide variety of customers.

 3 Governments should fund more courses *as a result / so that* there is greater choice.

 4 I strongly disagree with that statement *because of / for* the following reasons.

 5 Children use art to express themselves. *Otherwise / On the other hand*, adults use it to relax.

 6 The problem became worse and worse *as a result / so that* eventually it caused the system to fail.

Vocabulary and grammar review **Unit 3**

Vocabulary

❶ **Complete the collocations in each sentence using the verbs from the box in the correct form. Use each verb only once.**

> ~~challenge~~   determine   devise   gauge
> outline   overlook   promote

1   Medical experts often ..*challenge*.. the effectiveness of alternative treatments.
2   Some people believe that the amount of exercise you do .... your resistance to illness.
3   Arnica, a herbal remedy, is often used to .... faster healing after surgery.
4   The Internet provides a useful service to patients who wish to .... the overall success rate of a particular treatment.
5   When the data were analysed, the team realised that some critical factors had unfortunately been ....
6   Some hospitals have .... a new approach to patient care.
7   The director was asked to .... the reasons why his staff failed to adhere to guidelines.

❷ **Complete the sentences below using the words from the box in the correct form.**

> ~~aspect~~   incidence   level   number
> quantity   rate   type

1   Cost is one ...*aspect*... of the problem which the government needs to deal with.
2   Lower birth .... have led to a decline in primary-school enrolments.
3   There are many different .... of milk on supermarket shelves.
4   Some people say that if you want to lose weight, you should eat the same things as you normally do but in smaller ....
5   As well as staying healthy, it is important to maintain a certain .... of fitness.
6   Some cities have a considerable .... of specialist food stores.
7   As a result of health screening, the .... of stress-related illnesses has fallen.

Grammar

❸ **Circle the correct option in *italics* in these sentences.**

1   I (*wish*) / *dream* I could take part in an Olympic event, but I'm not good enough.
2   I often *dream / hope* of becoming a professional footballer.
3   I worry that if I take up running, I'm *likely / expecting* to become obsessive about it!
4   Having dieted for several weeks, I sincerely *wish / hope* I have lost some weight.
5   Unfortunately, I hadn't been *looking forward / expecting* to find the training so hard.
6   I'm taking swimming lessons because *I'd like / I'm likely* to improve my style.

❹ **Complete the sentences below describing data in the chart using words from the box. Sometimes two answers are possible.**

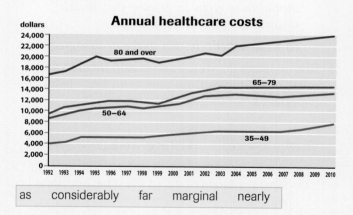

> as   considerably   far   marginal   nearly

1   The government spends ..*considerably/far*.. more on the 80+ age group than on any other group.
2   However, the amount spent on the over-80s was not .... as high in 1992 as it was in 2010.
3   The overall difference between the healthcare costs of the 65–79 age group and the 50–64 age group was .... during this period.
4   Although spending on the 35–49 age group was .... higher in 2010, the very elderly cost the government three times the amount of money .... the younger age group.

Vocabulary and grammar review **Unit 4**

Vocabulary

❶ Complete these sentences with the correct form of *make, take, do* or *have*.

1 There were a number of factors that needed to be ...*taken*... into consideration when deciding on the age of the painting.
2 Only the wealthy can expect to .... a profit from selling works of art.
3 I'm afraid that some sculpture these days .... very little impression on me.
4 An extensive amount of research .... on Mozart and his music.
5 Over the years, many artists .... a strong influence on the emerging world of advertising.
6 It's time we .... action to stop the forgery of famous artists' work.
7 It was my uncle's visit to a health spa that eventually .... him better.
8 Like many parents, I wish my children .... more interest in classical music when they were young.

❷ Complete these adverb phrases that writers use to generalise.

1 broadly ..*speaking*..
2 on .... whole
3 by and ....
4 .... a rule
5 in most ....
6 .... average

Grammar

❸ Rewrite these statements as arguments using the words in brackets and starting with the words in bold. You may need to change the form of the words in brackets.

1 Artists have a considerable impact on everyday life. (*can, argue*)
   It ...
2 People sometimes think artists are less talented than they used to be. (*think*)
   Artists ...

3 Wealthy people often purchase art for investment purposes. (*tendency*)
   The wealthy ...
4 I agree with people who say that graffiti is the most interesting modern art form. (*tend, view*)
   Personally, ...
5 One of the most influential figures in 20th-century art is Pablo Picasso. (*often said*)
   Pablo Picasso ...
6 Children are better able to express themselves through art than adults. (*seem*)
   Children ...
7 According to most historians, art has played a key role in cultural development. (*majority, claim*)
   The ...

❹ Circle the correct option in *italics* in these sentences.

1 *With the aim of /* (*In order to*) generate more money for restoration, visitors to the archaeological site were asked to make a small donation.
2 Technology has become very sophisticated, *with the result that / consequently* complex musical pieces can be produced without anyone playing an instrument.
3 The event had to finish early *owing to / because* an electricity failure.
4 It was fortunate that so many copies of the poster were made, *otherwise / as a result* it would have been lost forever.
5 Is there a way to upload photographs onto your website *so that / in order to* no one can copy them?
6 The torrential rain *has resulted in / has caused* all the chalk pictures on the pavements being washed away.
7 Soft music was playing in the background *so as to / with the intention of* encouraging shoppers to spend more money.

Stepping back in time

Starting off

❶ Work in small groups. Complete the captions to the photos with words from the box. Use each word only once.

> amber   artefacts   burial   creature   pots
> prehistoric   preserved   remains   ruins   shipwreck

❷ Who do you think made each of these discoveries, and what questions might they have asked about them?

Listening Part 3

❶ Work in pairs. You are going to hear two students discussing a talk by a palaeontologist (a fossil expert). First, discuss these questions.

1 Have you ever seen or found a fossil? If so, where?
2 How do you think fossils form?

The **1** .... of an ancient spa city in Turkey

Roman **2** .... found on an Indian **3** ....

Ancient Mayan **4** ....

Archaeological **5** .... found at a family **6** .... site

An insect **7** .... in **8** ....

The fossilised footprint of a **9** .... **10** ....

2 Look at Questions 1–5 and <u>underline</u> the key ideas in the questions (not the options).

3 🔊 (26) **Now listen and answer Questions 1–5.**

Exam advice   *Multiple choice*

• <u>Underline</u> key ideas in the questions and use them to help you follow the conversation.

• Listen carefully to everything the speakers say in relation to the key idea before you choose your answer.

• Although you may hear the words in the options, the speaker may be expressing the opposite idea.

• Listen for synonyms or paraphrases of the words in the question.

4 Work in pairs. Look at Questions 6–10.

  1 What is happening at each stage in the diagram?

  2 What type of information do you need to complete each gap?

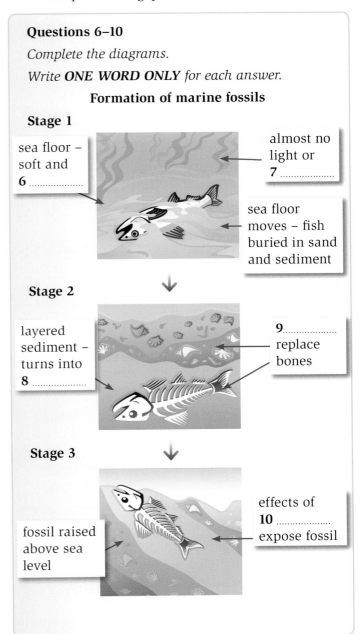
5 🔊 (27) **Now listen and answer Questions 6–10.**

Exam advice   *Labelling a diagram*

• Read the title to know what you are going to be listening about.

• If there is more than one diagram, compare the features in each one.

• Decide what information you need for each gap.

6 The speakers use a number of sequencers to describe the stages in the development of a fossil. Match the phrases in *italics* (1–7) with one or two of the meanings (a–g). Use the recording script on page 155 to help you.

1 … *as soon as* a fish dies, … c, g
2 … the fish *gradually* gets covered over …
3 … so *once* the fish gets buried …
4 … it gets heavier and heavier *until* it becomes hard rock …
5 … *during that time*, the bone in the skeleton is replaced …
6 … the rock may lift and *eventually* be above sea level.
7 *Meanwhile*, the surface of the rock wears away?

a slowly, over a period of time
b up to the time that
c from the moment when
d while something else is happening
e over that period
f in the end, especially after a long time
g immediately after

▶ page 121 *Using sequencers when describing processes*

7 Choose the correct opinion in *italics* to complete these paragraphs about underwater archaeology.

Underwater archaeology is most successful in areas where the currents are not strong enough to move a shipwreck. **1** *Once / Until* the depth of the water has been measured, a site plan can be drawn up. **2** *Whilst / As* doing this, divers swim around the shipwreck locating artefacts. **3** *Meanwhile / Gradually*, they also assess the site for ease of access and potential hazards.

In the next stage, divers use special tools to **4** *gradually / once* remove silt and sediment from the area of investigation. It is a long process, but **5** *eventually / during that time* the artefacts are ready to be taken up to the surface and transported to laboratories, where they will be carefully examined, but not **6** *as soon as / until* all the water has been removed.

8 Work in small groups.

Should people be allowed to keep ancient artefacts that they find, or should the artefacts be put in museums as part of the nation's heritage? Why?

Reading Section 2

1 Work in small groups. You are going to read a passage that describes some of the findings archaeologists have made about human species. Before you read, discuss these questions.

1 What do you think the work of an archaeologist involves?
2 What skills and abilities do you think an archaeologist needs?
3 Why might someone decide to become an archaeologist?

2 Work in pairs.

1 Read the title and subheading and discuss how they are connected.
2 Skim the passage, then say which of these statements best summarises the content.
   a How Homo sapiens eliminated other human species
   b Why Homo sapiens survived when other species died out

Last man standing

Some 50,000 years ago, Homo sapiens beat other hominids to become the only surviving species. Kate Ravilious reveals how we did it.

A Today, there are over seven billion people living on Earth. No other species has exerted as much influence over the planet as us. But turn the clock back 80,000 years and we were one of a number of species roaming the Earth. Our own species, Homo sapiens (Latin for 'wise man'), was most successful in Africa. In western Eurasia, the Neanderthals dominated, while Homo erectus may have lived in Indonesia. Meanwhile, an unusual finger bone and tooth, discovered in Denisova cave in Siberia in 2008, have led scientists to believe that yet another human population – the Denisovans – may also have been widespread across Asia. Somewhere along the line, these other human species died out, leaving Homo sapiens as the sole survivor. So what made us the winners in the battle for survival?

B Some 74,000 years ago, the Toba 'supervolcano' on the Indonesian island of Sumatra erupted. The scale of the event was so great that ash from the eruption was flung as far as eastern India, more than 2,000 kilometres away. Oxford archaeologist Mike Petraglia and his team have uncovered thousands of stone tools buried underneath the Toba ash. The mix of hand axes and spear tips have led Petraglia to speculate that Homo sapiens and Homo erectus were both living in eastern India prior to the Toba eruption. Based on careful examination of the tools and dating of the sediment layers where they were found, Petraglia and his team suggest that Homo sapiens arrived in eastern India around 78,000 years ago, migrating out of Africa and across Arabia during a favourable climate period. After their arrival, the simple tools belonging to Homo erectus seemed to lessen in number and eventually disappear completely. 'We think that Homo sapiens had a more efficient hunting technology, which could have given them the edge,' says Petraglia. 'Whether the eruption of Toba also played a role in the extinction of the Homo erectus-like species is unclear to us.'

C Some 45,000 years later, another fight for survival took place. This time, the location was Europe and the protagonists were another species, the Neanderthals. They were a highly successful species that dominated the European landscape for 300,000 years. Yet within just a few thousand years of the arrival of Homo sapiens, their numbers plummeted. They eventually disappeared from the landscape around 30,000 years ago, with their last known refuge being southern Iberia, including Gibraltar. Initially, Homo sapiens and Neanderthals lived alongside each other and had no reason to compete. But then Europe's climate swung into a cold, inhospitable, dry phase. 'Neanderthal and Homo sapiens populations had to retreat to refugia (pockets of habitable land). This heightened competition between the two groups,' explains Chris Stringer, anthropologist at the Natural History Museum in London.

D Both species were strong and stockier than the average human today, but Neanderthals were particularly robust. 'Their skeletons show that they had broad shoulders and thick necks,' says Stringer. 'Homo sapiens, on the other hand, had longer forearms, which undoubtedly enabled them to throw a spear from some distance, with less danger and using relatively little energy,' explains Stringer. This long-range ability may have given Homo sapiens an advantage in hunting. When it came to keeping warm, Homo sapiens had another skill: weaving and sewing. Archaeologists have uncovered simple needles fashioned from ivory and bone alongside Homo sapiens, dating as far back as 35,000 years ago. 'Using this technology, we could use animal skins to make ourselves tents, warm clothes and fur boots,' says Stringer. In contrast, Neanderthals never seemed to master sewing skills, instead relying on pinning skins together with thorns.

E A thirst for exploration provided Homo sapiens with another significant advantage over Neanderthals. Objects such as shell beads and flint tools, discovered many miles from their source, show that our ancestors travelled over large distances, in order to barter and exchange useful materials, and share ideas and knowledge. By contrast, Neanderthals tended to keep themselves to themselves, living in small groups. They misdirected their energies by only gathering resources from their immediate surroundings and perhaps failing to discover new technologies outside their territory.

F Some of these differences in behaviour may have emerged because the two species thought in different ways. By comparing skull shapes, archaeologists have shown that Homo sapiens had a more developed temporal lobe – the regions at the side of the brain, associated with listening, language and long-term memory. 'We think that Homo sapiens had a significantly more complex language than Neanderthals and were able to comprehend and discuss concepts such as the distant past and future,' says Stringer. Penny Spikins, an archaeologist at the University of York, has recently suggested that Homo sapiens may also have had a greater diversity of brain types than Neanderthals. 'Our research indicates that high-precision tools, new hunting technologies and the development of symbolic communication may all have come about because they were willing to include people with "different" minds and specialised roles in their society,' she explains. 'We see similar kinds of injuries on male and female Neanderthal skeletons, implying there was no such division of labour,' says Spikins.

G Thus by around 30,000 years ago, many talents and traits were well established in Homo sapiens societies but still absent from Neanderthal communities. Stringer thinks that the Neanderthals were just living in the wrong place at the wrong time. 'They had to compete with Homo sapiens during a phase of very unstable climate across Europe. During each rapid climate fluctuation, they may have suffered greater losses of people than Homo sapiens, and thus were slowly worn down,' he says. 'If the climate had remained stable throughout, they might still be here.'

adapted from Focus Magazine

❸ Work in pairs. Read Questions 1–5 and <u>underline</u> the key ideas that tell you what information you need to read for.

Questions 1–5

The Reading passage has seven paragraphs, **A–G**.

Which paragraph contains the following information?

1 <u>a comparison</u> of a range of <u>physical features</u> of Neanderthals and Homo sapiens

2 reference to items that were once used for trade

3 mention of evidence for the existence of a previously unknown human species

4 mention of the part played by ill fortune in the downfall of Neanderthal society

5 reference to the final geographical location of Neanderthals

❹ Now answer Questions 1–5 by reading each paragraph of the article carefully to see whether it contains the information for any of the five questions.

Exam advice   *Matching information*
- <u>Underline</u> the key ideas in each question.
- Start with Paragraph A and decide if it contains information which matches a question. If there is no match, go on to the next paragraph.

❺ Work in pairs.

1 Read Questions 6–9 below and quickly check what information you need.

2 <u>Underline</u> words in the questions which will help you to find the right place in the passage.

3 Answer Questions 6–9.

Questions 6–9

Complete the sentences below. Choose **NO MORE THAN THREE WORDS** *from the passage for each answer.*

6 Analysis of stone tools and .... has enabled Petraglia's team to put forward an arrival date for Homo sapiens in eastern India.

7 Homo sapiens used both .... to make sewing implements.

8 The territorial nature of Neanderthals may have limited their ability to acquire resources and ....

9 Archaeologists examined .... in order to get an insight into Neanderthal and Homo sapiens' capacity for language and thought.

Exam advice   *Sentence completion*
- <u>Underline</u> the key ideas in each question and scan the passage for the right place.
- Read that section of the passage carefully and choose your answer.

❻ Look at Questions 10–13.

1 <u>Underline</u> the key ideas in the questions.

2 Scan the passage for the name of each researcher and <u>underline</u> it.

3 Answer Questions 10–13 by reading around each name to decide whether what the researcher said at that point matches any of the statements.

Questions 10–13

Look at the following statements and the list of researchers, **A–C**, *below.*

Match each statement with the correct researcher.

10 No evidence can be found to suggest that Neanderthal communities allocated tasks to different members.

11 Homo sapiens may have been able to plan ahead.

12 Scientists cannot be sure whether a sudden natural disaster contributed to the loss of a human species.

13 Environmental conditions restricted the areas where Homo sapiens and Neanderthals could live.

List of Researchers
A Mike Petraglia
B Chris Stringer
C Penny Spikins

- <u>Underline</u> the key ideas in the statements.
- Scan the passage for the options (A, B, C, etc.) and <u>underline</u> every reference to them. (They are always in the same order in the passage as they are in the box.)
- Read around each option carefully and match it to the statement(s). If there are fewer options than statements, you will need to use some of them more than once. If there are more options than statements, do not use all the options.

❼ Work in pairs.

1 What factors might affect the future survival of the human species?
2 How do you think the human species might change or develop in the future?

Vocabulary
Word formation – negative affixes

❶ Complete each of these sentences from the passage by writing the correct form of the word in brackets in the gap.

1 After their arrival, the simple tools belonging to Homo erectus seemed to lessen in number and eventually .... completely. (*appear*)
2 But then Europe's climate swung into a cold, ... , dry phase. (*hospitable*)
3 They .... their energies by only gathering resources from their immediate surroundings … (*direct*)
4 They had to compete with Homo sapiens during a phase of very .... climate across Europe. (*stable*)

◗ page 114 *Negative affixes*

❷ Complete these sentences by adding an affix to the word in brackets and, where necessary, putting the word in the correct form.

1 Unfortunately, the researchers felt that the audience had ..*misinterpreted*.. their results. (*interpret*)
2 You cannot be .... if you work in the field of archaeology, as everything must be carefully categorised. (*organise*)
3 Although the coins looked valuable, they turned out to be .... (*worth*)
4 Some artefacts are so precious that if you lose them, they are .... (*replace*)

5 The speaker's sentences contradicted one another, making his overall statement .... (*logic*)
6 Eventually, the diggers had to agree that their chances of finding any artefacts were .... (*exist*)
7 The team was exhausted and had clearly .... the difficulties of working long hours in the desert. (*estimate*)
8 It is dangerous and .... for many people to view a burial site at the same time. (*practical*)
9 The soil in the local area had been .... by intensive farming practices. (*grade*)
10 The term '....................' is used to describe people who cannot read or write. (*literate*)

❸ Work in pairs. Complete these sentences in any way you like using one of the words with a negative affix from Exercise 2. You may need to add or change the suffix of the word.

1 One of the purposes of education is to …
… *eradicate illiteracy.*
2 Many experiments fail because …
3 Despite the demand for pills and creams that aim to make people look younger, …
4 Although many scientists have brilliant minds, …
5 Museums require expensive security systems, as …

Speaking Parts 2 and 3

❶ Look at this Speaking Part 2 task and Tibah's notes on page 58.

1 What do her notes consist of, how are they organised, and how will they help her do the task?
2 Take one minute to make your own notes for the task.

Describe something old that you or your family own and that you feel is important.

You should say:

what the item is and what it looks like

where it came from

what it is/was used for

and explain why you feel the item is important.

necklace - inheritance, Gran, 95

attic

market India

ancient/antique

blue beads, chipped

unfashionable

not eye-catching

my children

family treasure

2 (28) **Listen to Tibah. How has she used her notes?**

3 (28) **Listen again to Tibah doing the task in Exercise 1. She uses several strategies to help her keep going. As you listen, complete the extracts below by writing two or three words in each gap.**

strategy	extract
Gives a full introduction	Actually, there are **1** ...*a number of*... objects that I could talk about ...
Picks the point she can say the most about first	First, I think I'll **2** .... where it came from.
Speculates on the origins of the necklace	As **3** .... I know, *she'd* been given it ...
Includes a saying or quote	But as **4** .... says, you can't ...
Says what the item is not	I **5** .... that it's strikingly beautiful ...
Compares the item to others that she has	... not as **6** .... as the gold necklace that I got for my 21st birthday!
Makes a concession	... I don't really like beads, but, **7** .... that, I'll always keep them.

▶ page 60 Key grammar: *Speaking hypothetically*

4 **Work alone and think how you can use the phrases you noted down in Exercise 2 in your talk.**

Then work in pairs and, using your notes from Exercise 1, take turns to give your talks.

5 **Work in pairs. Discuss how you could answer this Part 3 question related to the Part 2 topic in Exercise 1. Make notes as you do this.**

> Why do you think some people like to keep old things, while others don't have any interest in doing this?

6 **Now look at Kenny's answer.**

> *Well, old things are full of memories, and I think that's the main reason why people keep them. Perhaps the most obvious example of this is photographs. I mean, although people often get rid of the ones that they don't like themselves in, they often keep others because they remind them of a special person or event.*

1 What reason does Kenny give, and how does he illustrate it?

2 What words does he use to introduce the reason and example? Write them in this table.

reasons	examples
I think that's the main reason why ...	

7 (29) **Listen to two students, Margarete and Johannes, answering the same question.**

1 Add the words/phrases that they use to introduce reasons and examples to the table in Exercise 6.
2 Is one answer better than the other? Why?

8 **Look at the notes you made in Exercise 5, then take turns to ask and answer the question.**

▶ Pronunciation: *Sentence stress 2*

9 **Look at the Part 3 questions below.**

1 List some possible ideas and vocabulary for answers.
2 Think of some reasons and examples you could include.
3 Work in pairs and take turns to ask and answer the questions.

Ancient objects

- What features distinguish modern-day objects from ancient ones?

- Why do some items increase in value as they get older, while others don't?

- What present-day items might be interesting to archaeologists in the future?

Our historical past

- Apart from keeping old objects, how else can we keep in touch with our past?

- How important is it for human beings to maintain their links with the past?

- In what ways can the events of the past help us to understand our future?

Exam advice   *Speaking Part 3*

- Listen carefully to the questions and try to give reasons and examples in your answer.

- Use stress to highlight important information.

Pronunciation
Sentence stress 2

Speakers use stress to emphasise certain elements in their speech, for example to:
a highlight a reference
b emphasise an aspect of their answer
c make a contrast.
Sometimes you need to stress a whole phrase to draw particular attention to it.

1 **Work in pairs. Look at Johannes's answer from Speaking Exercise 7. Why does he stress the words in bold? Choose from the reasons a–c above.**

Example: must – *(b) to emphasise this aspect of his answer (personality)*

I think it **must** be a question of personality …
and by **that** I mean, well, **some** people are **really** sentimental, so they don't like to throw away things like cards or presents – **even though** they don't want them any more. I guess, you know, **were** they to throw them away, they'd feel a sense of **loss**. Whereas **other** people, maybe, don't care that much – **they're** just happy just to focus on the **present**.

2 (30) **Listen to Kenny's answer from Speaking Exercise 6.**

Well, old things are full of memories, and I think that's the main reason why people keep them. Perhaps the most obvious example is photographs. I mean, although people might get rid of the ones that they don't like themselves in, they often keep others because they remind them of a special person or event.

1 Underline the words he stresses.
2 Why do you think he stresses these words?
3 Take turns to read Kenny's answer using the same stress.

3 **Write your answer to one of these questions, underlining the words you would like to stress.**

1 Has the type of item people keep changed over the past 20 years?
2 Should people be discouraged from keeping old things? Why?

4 **Work in pairs. Take turns to read your answers aloud to each other.**

Key grammar

Speaking hypothetically

❶ Complete these sentences from Tibah's talk by writing one word in each space. Then check your answers in the recording script on page 156.

1 I'd know its origins for certain .... I'd asked her.
2 You wouldn't realise how old it was .... you examined it closely.
3 If I .... to throw the beads out, I wouldn't be able to forgive myself.
4 It's funny to think, but if it hadn't been .... my granny's aunt, I wouldn't .... inherited that necklace.

❷ Look at the sentences in Exercise 1 again. Which sentences refer to:

a the present or future?
b the past?
c the past and the present?

▶ page 118 *Speaking hypothetically*

❸ Complete these sentences by putting the verb in brackets into the correct conditional form.

1 Children were allowed to view the fossils provided that they .... them. (*not touch*)
2 The climbers knew that if the rocks were .... , someone could get hurt. (*fall*)
3 Had there not been a storm, the divers .... the shipwreck. (*reach*)
4 If we .... a good scientist on the committee, we might not have made so many mistakes. (*have*)
5 Were it not for the aerial photos they took, they .... the ancient city's remains. (*never find*)
6 The site .... to the public on condition that visitor numbers were restricted. (*open*)
7 I wouldn't have walked around the ruins unless I .... it was safe! (*know*)
8 The walkers wouldn't have spotted the fossil had it .... for the exceptionally low tide. (*not be*)

❹ Work in small groups. Complete these sentences.

1 Were it not for the bad weather, …
2 Wouldn't it be amazing if …
3 If I were to change my career plans, …
4 Had it not been for my parents, …
5 Provided that I save some money, …
6 As a young teenager, I knew I wouldn't be allowed to go out unless …

Writing Task 1

❶ Work in pairs. Look at the diagram in the Writing task below.

1 In one sentence, say what the diagram shows, using your own words.
2 Decide on the following:
 a the key stages in the process
 b the changes in the process, and how they could be compared
 c some useful vocabulary for the introduction and the description of the diagram.
3 Discuss how you would organise your answer into paragraphs.
4 Decide what you would write in your overview.

> *The diagram below illustrates how fossils were exposed beneath a cliff as a result of coastal erosion.*
>
> *Summarise the information by selecting and reporting the main features, and make comparisons where relevant.*
>
> **Cliff erosion and fossil exposure**
>
>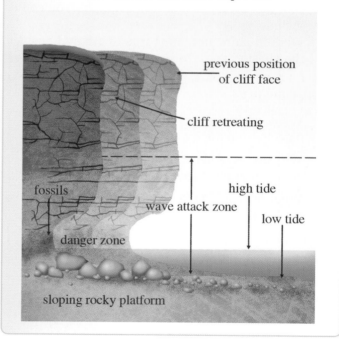

❷ Re-order the sentences on page 61 so that they produce a sample answer for the task in Exercise 1. Then divide the answer into paragraphs.

a Conversely, at high tide, the waves sometimes reached half-way up the cliff wall, beating on it with some force.

b Meanwhile, the overhanging cliff at the top cracked, creating a dangerous area beneath it.

c This meant that stones and boulders fell into the sea, and the cliff slowly retreated, exposing previously buried rock at low tide.

d Clearly, the fossils would have remained buried and the coastline unchanged if it had not been for the action of the sea.

e The diagram shows the changes that took place in a cliff face as a result of coastal erosion, and how this led to the discovery of fossils.

f As the waves hit the lower part of the cliff more frequently, this area eroded more quickly and became a hollow in the cliff wall where fossils could be found.

g Eventually, the power of these waves loosened and wore away the rock.

h At one time, the cliff stood much further out and, at low tide, the sea water did not touch the base of the rock.

❸ <u>Underline</u> the words and phrases in Exercise 2 that the writer uses to:

a mark the stages in the process
b compare aspects of the process.

❹ The writer uses participle clauses to express consequences. This is useful when describing processes and also helps build more complex sentences.

… the waves sometimes reached half-way up the cliff wall, **beating on it with some force**.

1 What is the subject of *beating*?
2 What do you notice about the punctuation?
3 <u>Underline</u> two more examples of this use in the sample answer. What is the subject of the *–ing* verb forms in these sentences?

▶ page 121 *Using participle clauses to express consequences*

❺ Use participle clauses to link these pairs of sentences.

1 Archaeology has become a highly computerised science. This has transformed our ability to analyse findings.

2 Fossil specimens can be CT-scanned. This reveals how creatures moved and walked.

3 The fossil could not be removed from the rock. This makes it hard to analyse it.

4 The wind will travel across the beach. This carries the sand to different parts of the coast.

5 Large rocks are thrown against the cliff wall. This produces a bed of pebbles and small stones.

❻ Work in pairs. Look at this Writing task. Quickly note down some vocabulary you could use to describe the key stages.

The diagrams below show the stages in the erosion of a headland.

Summarise the information by selecting and reporting the main features, and make comparisons where relevant.

Erosion of a headland

1 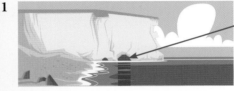 weak areas – rock eroded

2  cave becomes arch

e.g. Durdle Door, Dorset

3  water beats against roof

stack

4  headland retreating

stack

stump

❼ Write your answer to the task in at least 150 words.

Exam advice   **Writing Task 1**

• Describe key stages in the process in a logical order, making comparisons where appropriate.

• Use suitable words and phrases to structure and link the process clearly.

• Remember to include an overview summarising the main features of the process.

• Vary your vocabulary and use your own words as far as possible (e.g. do not lift long phrases from the task instructions).

Unit 6 IT society

Starting off

1 Work in small groups. Match the photos (1–6) with these uses of information technology (IT) (a–f).

a monitoring passenger movement
b finding directions
c working/studying
d providing entertainment
e managing personal finance
f purchasing goods

2 How has IT changed the way people do the things in the photos?

3 Choose one of the types of IT in the photos and discuss how it will change in the future.

Reading Section 3

❶ **Work in small groups. You are going to read a passage about an innovative approach to teaching maths. Before you read, discuss these questions.**

1 Did you enjoy studying maths at school?
2 What do you find particularly easy or difficult about working with numbers?

❷ **Work in pairs. Read the title and subheading of the article. What do you expect to read about in the article?**

❸ **Skim the passage quickly to find out what Khan Academy is, how it is changing education, and how people feel about it.**

The new way to be a fifth-grader

by Clive Thompson

Khan Academy is changing the rules of education.

I peer over his shoulder at his laptop screen to see the math problem the fifth-grader is pondering. It's a trigonometry problem. Carpenter, a serious-faced ten-year-old, pauses for a second, fidgets, then clicks on "0 degrees." The computer tells him that he's correct. "It took a while for me to work it out," he admits sheepishly. The software then generates another problem, followed by another, until eventually he's done ten in a row.

Last November, his teacher, Kami Thordarson, began using Khan Academy in her class. It is an educational website on which students can watch some 2,400 videos. The videos are anything but sophisticated. At seven to 14 minutes long, they consist of a voiceover by the site's founder, Salman Khan, chattily describing a mathematical concept or explaining how to solve a problem, while his hand-scribbled formulas and diagrams appear on-screen. As a student, you can review a video as many times as you want, scrolling back several times over puzzling parts and fast-forwarding through the boring bits you already know. Once you've mastered a video, you can move on to the next one.

Initially, Thordarson thought Khan Academy would merely be a helpful supplement to her normal instruction. But it quickly became far more than that. She is now on her way to "flipping" the way her class works. This involves replacing some of her lectures with Khan's videos, which students can watch at home. Then in class, they focus on working on the problem areas together. The idea is to invert the normal rhythms of school, so that lectures are viewed in the children's own time and homework is done at school. It sounds weird, Thordarson admits, but this reversal   line 40
makes sense when you think about it. It is when they are doing homework that students are really grappling with a subject and are most likely to want someone to talk to. And Khan Academy provides teachers with a dashboard application that lets them see the instant a student gets stuck.

For years, teachers like Thordarson have complained about the frustrations of teaching to the "middle" of the class. They stand at the whiteboard trying to get 25 or more students to learn at the same pace. Advanced students get bored and tune out, lagging ones get lost and tune out, and pretty soon half the class is not paying attention. Since the rise of personal computers in the 1980s, educators have hoped that technology could save the day by offering lessons tailored to each child. Schools have spent millions of dollars on sophisticated classroom technology, but the effort has been in vain. The one-to-one instruction it requires is, after all, prohibitively expensive. What country can afford such a luxury?

Khan never intended to overhaul the school curricula and he doesn't have a consistent, comprehensive plan for doing so. Nevertheless, some of his fans believe that he has stumbled onto the solution to education's middle-of-the-class mediocrity. Most notable among them is Bill Gates, whose foundation has invested $1.5 million in Khan's site. Students have pointed out that Khan is particularly good at explaining all the hidden, small steps in math problems—steps that teachers often gloss over. He has an uncanny ability to inhabit the mind of someone who doesn't already understand something.

However, not all educators are enamoured with Khan and his site. Gary Stager, a long-time educational consultant and advocate of laptops in classrooms, thinks Khan Academy is not innovative at all. The videos and software modules, he contends, are just a high-tech version of the outdated teaching techniques—lecturing and drilling. Schools have become "joyless test-prep factories," he says, and Khan Academy caters to this dismal trend.

As Sylvia Martinez, president of an organization focusing on technology in the classroom, puts it, "The things they're doing are really just rote." *Flipping* the classroom isn't an entirely new idea, Martinez says, and she doubts that it would work for the majority of pupils: "I'm sorry, but if they can't understand the lecture in a classroom, they're not going to grasp it better when it's done through a video at home."

Another limitation of Khan's site is that the drilling software can only handle questions where the answers are unambiguously right or wrong, like math or chemistry; Khan has relatively few videos on messier, grey-area subjects like history. Khan and Gates admit there is no easy way to automate the teaching of writing—even though it is just as critical as math.

Even if Khan is truly liberating students to advance at their own pace, it is not clear that schools will be able to cope. The very concept of grade levels implies groups of students moving along together at an even pace. So what happens when, using Khan Academy, you wind up with a ten-year-old who has already mastered high-school physics? Khan's programmer, Ben Kamens, has heard from teachers who have seen Khan Academy presentations and loved the idea but wondered whether they could modify it "to stop students from becoming this advanced."

Khan's success has injected him into the heated wars over school reform. Reformers today, by and large, believe student success should be carefully tested, with teachers and principals receiving better pay if their students advance more quickly. In essence, Khan doesn't want to change the way institutions teach; he wants to change how people learn, whether they're in a private school or a public school—or for that matter, whether they're a student or an adult trying to self-educate in Ohio, Brazil, Russia, or India. One member of Khan's staff is spearheading a drive to translate the videos into ten major languages. It's classic start-up logic: do something novel, do it with speed, and the people who love it will find you.

adapted from *Wired Magazine*

❹ Writers often use reference words/phrases (e.g. *it, such*) to avoid repetition and to link different parts of the text. Find these words and phrases in the passage and decide what the words in *italics* refer to.

1 work *it* out   a trigonometry problem
2 on *which* students
3 the next *one*
4 more than *that*
5 *such a luxury*
6 plan for *doing so*
7 among *them*
8 *this dismal trend*
9 grasp *it* better

⑤ Underline the key ideas in Questions 1–5 (not the options). Then scan the passage to find the relevant parts and read each part carefully to choose the correct options.

Questions 1–5

Choose the correct letter, A, B, C or D.

1 What do you <u>learn</u> about the <u>student</u> in the <u>first paragraph</u>?

   A He has not used the maths software before.

   B He did not expect his answer to the problem to be correct.

   C He was not initially doing the right maths problem.

   D He did not immediately know how to solve the maths problem.

2 What does the writer say about the content of the Khan Academy videos?

   A They have been produced in a professional manner.

   B They include a mix of verbal and visual features.

   C Some of the maths problems are too easy.

   D Some of the explanations are too brief.

3 What does *this reversal* refer to in line 40?

   A going back to spending fewer hours in school

   B students being asked to explain answers to teachers

   C swapping the activities done in the class and at home

   D the sudden improvement in students' maths performance

4 What does the writer say about teaching to the 'middle' of the class?

   A Teachers become too concerned about weaker students.

   B Technology has not until now provided a solution to the problem.

   C Educators have been unwilling to deal with the issues.

   D Students in this category quickly become bored.

5 Students praise Khan's videos because they

   A show the extent of his mathematical knowledge.

   B deal with a huge range of maths problems.

   C provide teaching at different ability levels.

   D cover details that are often omitted in class.

Exam advice   *Multiple choice*

• For referencing questions, read around the word(s) carefully to find what the reference refers to. The answer may come before or after the reference.

• For vocabulary questions, read before and after the word to understand the context.

---

⑥ Underline words in Questions 6–10 which will help you scan to find the relevant parts of the passage. Then read those parts of the passage and answer the questions.

Questions 6–10

Do the following statements agree with the claims of the writer in the reading passage?

Write

YES   *if the statement agrees with the claims of the writer*

NO   *if the statement contradicts the claims of the writer*

NOT GIVEN   *if it is impossible to say what the writer thinks about this*

6 Thordarson's first impressions of how she would use Khan Academy turned out to be wrong.

7 Khan wished to completely change the way courses are taught in schools.

8 School grade levels are based on the idea of students progressing at different rates.

9 Some principals have invited Khan into their schools to address students.

10 Khan has given advice to other people involved in start-up projects.

Exam advice   Yes / No / Not Given

- Find words in the passage that are the same as, or similar to, words in the question.
- The answers will be in passage order. They may be found in the same block of text or in different parts of the passage.

7 For Questions 11–14, <u>underline</u> key ideas in each of the options and use the names in the questions to find the relevant parts of the passage. Then read carefully to answer the questions.

Questions 11–14

Complete each sentence with the correct ending, A–G, below.

11 Bill Gates thinks Khan Academy

12 According to Gary Stager, Khan Academy

13 Sylvia Martinez regrets that Khan Academy

14 Ben Kamens has been told that Khan Academy

A is only suited to subjects where questions have exact answers.

B can teach both the strongest and the weakest pupils in a class.

C means the teaching of other school subjects will have to be changed.

D only prepares students to pass exams.

E could cause student achievement to improve too quickly.

F requires all students to own the necessary technology.

G is unlikely to have a successful outcome for most students.

Exam advice   Matching sentence endings

- <u>Underline</u> the key ideas in the options.
- Use names and other words in the questions to find the right places in the passage. (You will find them in the same order.)
- Read the completed sentences to check they make sense.

8 Work in small groups.

1 What IT or websites do you use to supplement your classwork or lectures?

2 What effect do you think IT will have on classrooms in the future?

Listening Part 4

1 Work in pairs. You are going to hear a media-studies lecturer talking about animation technology in the film industry. Before you listen, discuss these questions.

1 How did film makers make animated films before the invention of computers?

2 Why do you think both adults and children enjoy animated films?

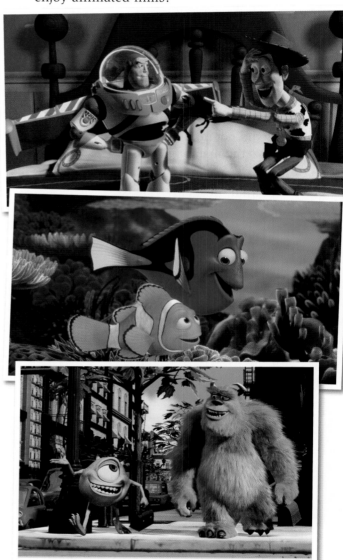

2 Work in pairs. Look at Questions 1–10 on page 67.

1 What main areas will the lecturer cover in her talk?

2 How does the organisation of the notes guide your listening?

3 What type of word (noun, verb, adjective, etc.) and what type of information do you think you need to complete each gap?

Questions 1–10

Complete the notes below.

*Write **NO MORE THAN TWO WORDS AND/OR A NUMBER** for each answer.*

Animation Technology

History

Thomas Edison:	first camera – 1889
J. Stuart Blackton:	first animated film technique – used many **1** .... of faces
Émile Cohl:	first animated scene – used cut-outs made of **2** ....
Walt Disney:	• first talking colour film – 1928 – used **3** .... slides
	• first full-length colour film – *Snow White and the Seven Dwarfs* – 1937

Pixar Animation Studios

Origins:	graphics group
Earnings:	Over **4** $.................... worldwide
Famous films:	1995 – *Toy Story* – first computer-animated film
	2001 – *Monsters, Inc.* – included **5** .... as a new animation feature
	Finding Nemo – new techniques in **6** ....
	The Incredibles – believable simulations of people and **7** ....

Future developments:

a   Digital humans: focusing particularly on skin and **8** ....

b   Speed: companies producing **9** .... will help

c   Colour: aim to preserve vibrancy

d   Styles of animation: a move from **10** .... to new concepts

❸ 🎧 Listen and answer Questions 1–10.

❹ Take a minute to prepare a short talk on a film you have seen that includes some computer-animated features. Then work in pairs and take turns to give your talks. You can use these questions to help you.

1   What was the film about and what happened during the film?

2   What computer effects did you see in the film?

3   What did you particularly like or dislike about the film?

❺ Change partners and give your talk.

Vocabulary

Adjective + noun collocations

❶ Look at these sentences. For each one, cross out the adjective that CANNOT be used with the noun in bold to form a collocation.

1   It was possible to build up a small scene, though a *large* / *~~big~~* / *considerable* **number** of cut-outs were required to do this.

2   Now it has become a Hollywood icon, with earnings of over 6.3 billion dollars and *numerous* / *plentiful* / *countless* **film awards**.

3   Many **features** of the film were seen as *outstanding* / *irreplaceable* / *excellent*.

4   It is still considered to be one of the most *extensive* / *significant* / *noteworthy* **achievements** in the history of film animation.

5   This helped to enhance the appeal of one of the film's *central* / *primary* / *main* **characters**.

6   Many scenes took place underwater and relied on a *certain* / *particular* / *sure* level of brilliance and clarity throughout.

7   Yet cinema audiences have increasingly *high* / *tall* / *great* **expectations**.

② Complete these sentences using collocations from Exercise 1 in the correct form.

1 If friends praise a film too much, your .... can be too .... when you go to see it.
2 Film directors know that audiences need to be able to identify with the .... in a film.
3 In my view, Leonardo DiCaprio's performance was the most .... of the film.
4 Producers now have a .... of animation techniques at their disposal.
5 Making a short animated film was a .... for me.

Speaking Parts 2 and 3

① Look at this Speaking Part 2 task and think about what you could say. Make some notes.

Describe a website that you like using.

You should say:

> **what this website is**
>
> **how people use it**
>
> **who uses it**

and explain why you like using this website.

---

② 🎧₂ Listen to Rosy doing the task.

1 Tick (✓) the things that she does.

1	introduces her topic	✓
2	introduces each point clearly	☐
3	paraphrases when she can't remember a word or phrase	☐
4	repeats some points	☐
5	rephrases to avoid hesitation	☐
6	uses a strategy to include something she forgot	☐
7	pauses unnecessarily	☐
8	ends her talk naturally within two minutes	☐

2 Look at the recording script on page 157 and check your answers, underlining the phrases Rosy uses for each function.

③ Work in pairs. In her talk, Rosy doesn't remember these words

1 amateur   2 music genre

Look at the recording script on page 157. Which of these strategies (a–d) does she use to explain what she means?

a saying what it is not
b explaining how it works
c giving a definition
d describing what it looks like

④ Work in pairs. If you had forgotten or did not know the words in bold in these sentences, how would you explain the idea?

1 What people do is they make a CD in a **recording studio** somewhere.
2 … some people set up the **recording equipment** in their own home, …
3 … though there's no **age limit** …
4 … they're usually talented musicians and **composers**.
5 … and they hope a **talent scout** will **spot** them on the website!
6 I love this website because you get to hear **original music** …

⑤ Work in pairs. Take turns to do the Speaking task in Exercise 1.

Exam advice   Speaking Part 2

- Use a range of strategies to express ideas when you can't think of the right word(s). Showing you can do this will improve your score.

---

⑥ 🎧₃–🎧₅ Listen to three candidates answering the questions below. Which question does each candidate answer?

A Katalina

B Obi

C Elicia

Children's use of the Internet

1 Some people say it isn't good for children to use the Internet a lot in their free time – what do you think?

2 Is it true that the Internet is sometimes an *unhelpful* tool when it comes to children's education?

3 Would you agree that the Internet has a positive effect on children's social lives?

---

7 <u>Underline</u> the phrases in the recording script on page 157 that each candidate uses to talk about advantages and disadvantages.

Example: *a significant advantage for anyone is ...*

8 IELTS candidates often make mistakes with prepositions when they describe advantages and disadvantages. Choose the correct preposition in these sentences. Then check your answers in the language reference.

1 One of the many advantages *for / of* teleworking is being able to work in your own home.
2 The students said that they benefited enormously *from / with* attending the performance.
3 There are several drawbacks *of / to* this type of behaviour.
4 *For / To* a technician, it is a significant advantage to have good equipment.
5 The outstanding features of this software give it many advantages *over / from* other packages.

▶ page 116 *Prepositions with advantages and disadvantages*

▶ Pronunciation: *Intonation 2*

9 Work in pairs. Take turns to ask and answer the questions in the task in Exercise 6 and the questions below.

Entertainment on the Internet

1 Would you say the Internet is a better form of entertainment than television? Why?
2 Would you agree that there are a lot of advantages to watching TV on the Internet? Why?
3 Some people say the Internet is a good place to be 'discovered' as an entertainer. What do you think? Why?

Exam advice ▸ *Speaking Part 3*
• Introduce positive and negative points clearly, using appropriate language.
• Use intonation to help signal agreement and disagreement.

Pronunciation
Intonation 2

Speakers use intonation to show that they are engaged in a discussion and to help the conversation flow. This is important when you introduce your arguments, particularly if you want to disagree with the examiner but maintain a friendly, interested tone.

1 (6) Work in pairs. Listen to two students responding to a Part 3 question.

a *Not really. It's convenient sometimes, but I don't think it's as enjoyable.*
b *Yeah – a lot of young people do that these days.*

1 Which speaker sounds more interested? Why?
2 How does the other speaker sound? Why?

2 (7) Listen to these questions and answers and mark where the students' voices rise and fall when responding. Then repeat the sentences.

1 A: Some people say it isn't good for children to use the Internet a lot in their free time – what do you think?
   B: That could be right – yeah, a lot of people would agree with that.
2 A: Would you agree that the Internet has a negative effect on children's social lives?
   B: Oh, well, actually, I think it has a positive one.

3 Work in pairs. Look at this question and the candidates' responses below. Discuss how you think the candidates might say these sentences to show they are interested and engaged in the discussion.

Some people say we've reached the point where technology is intruding on our private lives. Would you agree?

---

a Oh, completely. There are CCTV cameras everywhere.
b I don't think people notice really – they're just used to it.
c I would, yes. Everywhere you go, there are screens of one kind or another.
d Well, you can't stop it – new developments are happening all the time.
e I'm not sure. In some ways it's a nuisance, but in others it isn't.

4 (8) Listen to the exchanges from Exercise 3. Then take turns to repeat the answers.

Writing Task 2

❶ Work in pairs. Look at this Writing task and make a list of benefits and drawbacks.

> Write about the following topic.
>
> ***Information technology is changing many aspects of our lives and now dominates our home, leisure and work activities.***
>
> ***To what extent do the benefits of information technology outweigh the disadvantages?***
>
> Give reasons for your answer and include any relevant examples from your own knowledge or experience.

❷ Work in pairs. Read the sample answer in the next column (ignoring the underlining and bold for the moment) and answer these questions.

1 What is the writer's view, with regard to the question in the task?
2 How does the structure of the writer's answer reflect this view?
3 Has the writer referred to the three areas specified in the task?
4 How does the writer link paragraphs 2 and 3?
5 How does the writer link paragraphs 3 and 4?
6 How does the writer link paragraphs 4 and 5?
7 In what three ways is the last paragraph an effective summary?

Information technology has become an integral part of human life, and we are becoming increasingly dependent on it. But <u>while</u> it enhances certain aspects of our lives, I also think it may be having a detrimental effect on others.

One of the biggest drawbacks of information technology is that it can be incredibly time-consuming. People who work in international business have to read hundreds of emails every day, and children can spend hours chatting online. Some people would argue that **this time** could be better spent.

A related criticism is that it leads to unhealthy lifestyles. Rather than going out and taking regular exercise, for example, some people spend a lot of time sitting at their computers or with their smart phones. In the long term, **this lack of activity** does not do our bodies any good.

<u>Despite these drawbacks</u>, we cannot deny that technology has made many aspects of life more pleasurable. We all have instant access to entertainment and social connections are just a click away. Like many people, I use a networking site, which apparently has more than 800 million active users. **This type of statistic** illustrates just how popular this website is.

There are also huge benefits to using technology for study and work. The Internet is an invaluable resource for students of all ages, provided that it is used sensibly. Also, some areas of work have moved forward in leaps and bounds due to the huge amount of data that computers can store.

Clearly, there are some negative aspects to technology. <u>Having said that</u>, it is the way we use it that causes these. If it is used sensibly and people take regular breaks from their computers, there are only benefits that remain.

❸ With this type of question, it is important to present a balanced view.

1 The writer uses discourse markers such as *despite these drawbacks* as signposts to show that he is moving from one side of the argument to the other (or the counter-argument). Which of the <u>underlined</u> discourse markers has a similar function in the sample answer?
2 Which of the <u>underlined</u> discourse markers indicates that there will be a 'for' and 'counter-' argument in the same sentence?
3 What other linkers can you use to introduce counter-arguments?

▶ Key grammar: *Referencing*

4 Work in pairs. Complete these useful collocations from the sample answer by writing one word in each gap.

1 an *integral* part
2 a .... effect
3 one of the .... drawbacks
4 taking .... exercise
5 instant ....
6 .... benefits
7 an .... resource

5 Complete these sentences using collocations from Exercise 4 in the correct form.

1 Some medical experts are critical of the .... that computers have had on our health.
2 Working from home has .... for parents.
3 The website proved to be an .... when I wrote my media-studies essay.
4 Data processing is an .... of most business systems.
5 One of the .... of living in this area is that I do not always have .... to the Internet.
6 Although I have a sedentary job, I still make sure I ....

6 Work in pairs. Read the Writing task below.

1 Note down some advantages and disadvantages.
2 Discuss how you can present a balanced view.
3 Write an essay plan.

Write about the following topic.

Information technology enables many people to do their work outside their workplace (e.g. at home, when travelling, etc.).

Do the benefits of this mobility outweigh the disadvantages?

Give reasons for your answer and include any relevant examples from your own knowledge or experience.

7 Write your answer to the task in at least 250 words.

Exam advice   *Writing Task 2*
- When you write an essay evaluating advantages and disadvantages, present a balanced viewpoint, but make your own opinions clear.
- Use reference devices and discourse markers to make your essay clear and coherent.
- Use collocations to make your English sound natural and more persuasive.

Key grammar
Referencing

1 Complete this paragraph from the sample answer on page 70 by writing one word in each gap.

Clearly, there are some negative aspects to technology. Having said **1** .... , it is the way we use it that causes **2** .... If **3** .... is used sensibly and people take regular breaks from **4** .... computers, there are only benefits that remain.

2 What do the phrases in bold in the sample answer refer to?

▶ page 117 *Referencing*

3 ⊙ IELTS candidates often make mistakes by using or omitting reference words. Correct the mistakes in these sentences either by adding a missing reference word or changing an incorrect one.

1 Children ∧ grow up here have the best facilities at schools. *who*
2 ~~These~~ kind of educational material is available in most schools. *This*
3 Some training should be given to anyone who asks for.
4 Using this two types of educational material means we can learn things more quickly.
5 Many factors are involved in such kind of production.
6 When it comes to films, most of us can say we enjoy it.
7 Other drawback of computers is that people become too solitary.

4 Complete this paragraph by writing a suitable reference word in each gap.

It is often said that computer games are bad for children, but **1** .... argument is not based on any evidence. In fact, some experts have shown that **2** .... can have a positive impact on the mental processing of children suffering from attention-related disorders. It seems that, in **3** .... cases, there are positive effects on areas such as concentration. Nowadays, computers are an integral part of life, and not having access to **4** .... is a huge disadvantage. Having said **5** .... , it is up to parents to monitor children's computer use and ensure that **6** .... does not become excessive.

Vocabulary and grammar review **Unit 5**

Vocabulary

❶ Complete the text below using the sequencers from the box. Use each sequencer only once.

| after | eventually | first | following that |
| meanwhile | next | once | whilst |

A large number of seventh-century gold coins have been unearthed by a teacher in the UK. **1** ...After... 12 years of treasure hunting, he found the coins **2** .... searching farmland with a metal detector.

If you find objects that you believe to be treasure, you must **3** .... report your find to the appropriate authority. Otherwise you may face a £5,000 fine. **4** .... the find has been reported. and experts agree it is real treasure, the **5** .... stage involves determining its market value.

In England, valuation takes place at the British Museum. **6** .... , individual museums can bid for the treasure. Many finds are currently being assessed in this way.

7 .... , the teacher and the farmer on whose land the gold was found hope to **8** .... receive a reward for their find.

❷ Complete these sentences using the correct form of the words in brackets.

1 Even though our early ancestors were _uneducated_, they had remarkable survival skills. (*educate*)
2 Climate change has had .... consequences for certain species. (*reversible*)
3 It is important not to keep animals in .... conditions. (*crowd*)
4 The idea of protecting wildlife would have been .... to our early ancestors. (*meaning*)
5 The clerk admitted that he had .... the instructions and sent the artefact to the wrong address. (*understand*)
6 Those in the queue to enter the museum were becoming very .... (*patient*)
7 Although it is .... to remove your shoes when entering the building, most people do. (*necessary*)

Grammar

❸ Circle the correct option in *italics* in these hypothetical sentences.

1 The find would be considered a 'treasure' provided that it (was) / *had been* at least 300 years old.
2 The scientist *wouldn't have included* / *won't include* the data in his research unless he had double-checked it first.
3 If *I've* / *I'd* been told that the pot was valuable, I would never have touched it!
4 Had the object been in better condition, it *might have been* / *might be* worth more money.
5 Were it not for my uncle, *I'd never have become* / *I will not become* interested in history.
6 Had it not been for natural disasters, some ancient cities *might* / *may* still exist.
7 If some ancient humans *had* / *had had* better hunting techniques, they would have been more likely to survive.

❹ Rewrite each sentence / pair of sentences, using a participle clause to express the consequence.

1 In the south of the country, heavy rain fell for five consecutive days. This brought floods to many regions.
   In the south of the country, heavy rain fell for five consecutive days, bringing floods to many regions.
2 In order to safeguard the area, a sign was put up which encouraged walkers to take another route.
3 Predators ensure that they are well camouflaged. This enables them to take their prey by surprise.
4 The ship sank in extremely deep waters, which made it hard for divers to locate the wreck.
5 After the accident, oil leaked from the capsized ship, and the result was a treacherous zone for marine life.

Vocabulary and grammar review Unit 6

Vocabulary

❶ Complete the sentences below with the adjectives from the box to form noun–adjective collocations. In some cases, more than one answer is possible.

| able | convincing | first | high | innovative |
| ~~ordinary~~ | outstanding | private | | |

1 Most *ordinary* people expect to be entertained when they go to the theatre.
2 Like Khan Academy, there are other .... approaches to teaching maths.
3 My .... impressions of the play weren't good, but I ended up changing my opinion.
4 If my expectations hadn't been so .... , I would have enjoyed the lecture.
5 IT companies upgrade their technology in an effort to offer the most .... products.
6 Experts argue that .... students can help weaker students learn in mixed-ability classes.
7 The arguments in favour of individual tuition are too .... to ignore.
8 The media should show greater respect for the .... lives of celebrities.

❷ Complete these sentences with the correct prepositions. In some cases, more than one answer is possible.

1 A significant drawback *to/of* technology is that we can become too dependent on it.
2 There are benefits .... working from home, but a number of disadvantages too!
3 Being able to work at your own pace is one of the main advantages .... online study.
4 Many drivers these days benefit .... the use of GPS technology.
5 Being colour blind is a distinct disadvantage .... anyone who works in the film industry.
6 Children have an advantage .... many adults in that they adapt to new technology more quickly.
7 Online accounting software can be of great benefit .... people who struggle to manage their finances.

Grammar

❸ Replace the wrong word/phrase in each sentence with the correct one. In some cases, there may be more than one correct answer.

1 I hate vacuuming the floors and would love to have a robot to do ~~these~~ type of job for me. *this*
2 There are 50 computers on site, whereas a year ago we only had half such number.
3 Teachers play a very important role in primary education, as it can also assist in the personal development of children.
4 In 2000, the average household had one television downstairs and the other two upstairs.
5 Some of my relatives live in Australia, and the ones live here in Vancouver.
6 I've seen several films produced by James White, but neither was outstanding.
7 Before you download any music from the site, make sure you understand the legal implications of doing it.
8 Technology has become so widespread that it is impossible to imagine life without them.

❹ Complete the sentences below using the phrases from the box.

| other factors | ~~such a measure~~ | that success |
| this figure | this technique | this type of problem |

1 Mobile phones could be banned on trains, but *such a measure* would prove unpopular.
2 The sale of computer games in one store has increased to 1,000 per week, and .... is expected to double over the coming year.
3 Early animations were made using pictures of faces, but .... was very time-consuming.
4 The film *Snow White and the Seven Dwarfs* won several awards for Walt Disney, who was encouraged by .... to produce more films.
5 The company was forced to close due to their poor sales record, although .... also contributed.
6 Private information can quickly become public and it is hard to see how .... can be overcome.

Unit 7   Our relationship with nature

Starting off

❶ Work in pairs. Look at these photos and subheadings from five wildlife magazine articles. Match the photos (1–5) with the subheadings (A–E).

A

Wait for the action

B

In Zambia's Luangwa valley, rain and river create a wildlife stronghold

C

Sometimes survival means lying, stealing or vanishing

D

They are the Earth's pollinators and they come in more than 200,000 shapes and sizes

E

What's black and white and adored all over – and can cost a zoo more than three million dollars a year?

❷ Which article would you expect to focus on:

1 a natural habitat?
2 wildlife photography?
3 camouflage in the natural world?
4 conservation issues?
5 insect and plant relationships?

❸ Think of a suitable title for each article, then compare your ideas with the original titles on page 96.

❹ Which article would you be most interested in reading? Why?

Listening Part 3

1 Work in pairs. You are going to hear two students on an environmental studies course talking to their tutor about a photography assignment. First discuss these questions.

1 How does photographing nature differ from photographing people?
2 What makes a 'good' nature photograph?
3 Have you ever tried photographing animals? How easy or difficult was it?

2 Work in pairs. You are going to hear the first half of the students' conversation. Before you listen, read Questions 1–3, look at the map and answer these questions.

1 What does the map show?
2 How many woodland areas are there, where are they, and how do they compare in size?
3 What shape are the lochs? Explain in your own words where they are on the map.
4 How many rivers are there, and where are they?
5 Take turns to explain where each letter on the map is situated.

Questions 1–3

Label the plan below.

*Write the correct letter, **A–F**, next to questions 1–3.*

1 Oldest Scots pine trees ....

2 Red deer ....

3 Red squirrels ....

Loch Affric in Scotland

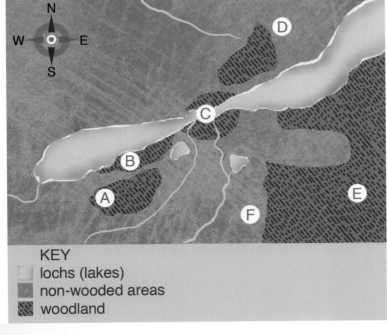

KEY
☐ lochs (lakes)
▓ non-wooded areas
▨ woodland

BBC Wildlife

---

3 Look at Questions 4–5 below and <u>underline</u> the key ideas.

Questions 4–5

Answer the questions.

Write **ONE WORD ONLY** for each answer.

4 What can cause someone to miss a good photograph?

5 What personal quality do wildlife photographers particularly need?

4 🔊 Now listen and answer Questions 1–5.

Exam advice

Labelling a plan

• Look at the location of each option on the map and think about how each one might be described.

• The answers will come in the same order as the questions.

• Listen for the things named in each question and follow the speaker's directions to locate them.

Exam advice

Short-answer questions

• <u>Underline</u> the key ideas in the question in order to focus your listening.

• Keep within the word limit.

• Check that you have spelled your answers correctly and not included unnecessary words.

⑤ Work in pairs. Look at Questions 6–10 below.

1 <u>Underline</u> the key ideas, then think of paraphrases that you might hear on the recording.
   Example: bad weather → mist / driving rain

2 What type of information is needed to complete each gap?

Questions 6–10

Complete the sentences.

*Write **NO MORE THAN TWO WORDS** for each answer.*

6 In <u>bad weather</u>, think more carefully about the ....

7 Take advantage of .... when photographing near water.

8 Use a piece of equipment called an 'angle finder' to avoid ....

9 Use the work of both artists and .... to generate ideas.

10 Think about .... issues when deciding on what to photograph.

⑥ ⑩ Now listen and answer Questions 6–10.

> *Exam advice* *Sentence completion*
>
> • The recording will use paraphrases or synonyms of the words in the questions, so you should focus carefully on the meaning of what the speakers are saying, rather than listening for identical words.
>
> • You will hear the exact word(s) you need to complete the sentences.
>
> • Read the completed sentences to check they make sense and reflect what you have understood.

⑦ Work in pairs. Take one minute to prepare, then take turns to tell each other about the best place to take photos where you live. Say where it is, what people can take photos of there, and how they can get there.

Vocabulary
Idiomatic expressions

❶ In order to achieve a high band score, you must be able to use some idiomatic expressions naturally. Complete these expressions from the Listening part using the words from the box.

account	bear	breath
experience	most	run	time

1 It's like anything, you have to **put it down to** ....

2 But suddenly something will **take your** .... **away** and you'll realise it's all been worth it!

3 Well, yes, but I wouldn't worry – **in the long** .... , you'll still get your pictures.

4 It does mean that you need to **take** the landscape **into** ....

5 I want to **make the** .... of all the stunning reflections in the water.

6 Just **take your** .... , and you might capture an amazing reflection.

7 It's just something to .... **in mind**.

❷ Find expressions in Exercise 1 which mean the following.

1 profit from in a positive way
2 you will learn from something, rather than get upset by it
3 be patient
4 eventually
5 surprise and amaze you
6 consider / think about (*two expressions*)

❸ Work in pairs. Discuss occasions when you might …

1 take someone's age into account.
2 need to take your time.
3 make the most of bad weather.
4 bear in mind a friend's preferences.
5 see something that takes your breath away.
6 be happy about the way things turned out in the long run.
7 put a mistake down to experience.

Reading Section 2

1 Circle the correct option in *italics* so that the sentences offer good advice for students doing the Reading test.

1 Do the sections in the order *in which they come / of your choice.*

2 Spend *a maximum of / more than* 20 minutes on each of the first two sections.

3 *Leave any tasks you do not like until last. / Do the tasks in the order they occur.*

4 Answers that consist of letters (e.g. A, B, C, D) *should also / need not* be written out in full.

5 If a question is too difficult, *leave a blank / guess the answer.*

6 You *must / need not* use correct spelling.

2 Work in pairs. You are going to read one of the articles whose titles you discussed in Starting off on page 74.

1 Spend two or three minutes skimming the article. Which letter – a, b or c – best describes the main topic?
   a where pollinators are most widely used
   b how honeybee losses have affected plant growth
   c why we need to encourage a wider range of pollinators

2 Take a quick look at the three task types in this Reading section (Questions 1–13). How long do you think you should spend on each task?

> **Exam advice** *Matching headings*
> • Familiarise yourself with the headings before you start reading.

3 Look at Questions 1–7 and <u>underline</u> the key ideas. Then read the passage and answer the questions.

> **Questions 1–7**
>
> The reading passage has seven sections, **A–G**.
>
> *Choose the correct heading for each section from the list of headings below.*
>
> | List of Headings |
> | --- |
> | i   Looking for clues |
> | ii   Blaming the beekeepers |
> | iii   Solutions to a more troublesome issue |
> | iv   Discovering a new bee species |
> | v   An impossible task for any human |
> | vi   The preferred pollinator |
> | vii   Plant features designed to suit the pollinator |
> | viii Some obvious and less obvious pollen carriers |
> | ix   The undesirable alternative |
> | x   An unexpected setback |
>
> 1 Section A ....
> 2 Section B ....
> 3 Section C ....
> 4 Section D ....
> 5 Section E ....
> 6 Section F ....
> 7 Section G ....

Gold dusters by Jennifer S. Holland

They are the Earth's pollinators and they come in more than 200,000 shapes and sizes.

A Row upon row, tomato plants stand in formation inside a greenhouse. To reproduce, most flowering plants depend on a third party to transfer pollen between their male and female parts. Some require extra encouragement to give up that golden dust. The tomato flower, for example, needs a violent shake, a vibration roughly equivalent to 30 times the pull of Earth's gravity, explains Arizona entomologist Stephen Buchmann. Growers have tried numerous ways to rattle pollen from tomato blossoms. They have used shaking tables, air blowers and blasts of sound. But natural means seem to work better.

B It is no surprise that nature's design works best. What's astonishing is the array of workers that do it: more than 200,000 individual animal species, by varying strategies, help the world's 240,000 species of flowering plants make more flowers. Flies and beetles are the original pollinators, going back to when flowering plants first appeared 130 million years ago. As for bees, scientists have identified some 20,000 distinct species so far. Hummingbirds, butterflies, moths, wasps and ants are also up to the job. Even non-flying mammals do their part: sugar-loving opossums, some rainforest monkeys, and lemurs in Madagascar, all with nimble hands that tear open flower stalks and furry coats to which pollen sticks. Most surprising, some lizards, such as geckos, lap up nectar and pollen and then transport the stuff on their faces and feet as they forage onward.

C   All that messy diversity, unfortunately, is not well suited to the monocrops and mega-yields of modern commercial farmers. Before farms got so big, says conservation biologist Claire Kremen of the University of California, Berkeley, 'we didn't have to manage pollinators. They were all around because of the diverse landscapes. Now you need to bring in an army to get pollination done.' The European honeybee was first imported to the US some 400 years ago. Now at least a hundred commercial crops rely almost entirely on managed honeybees, which beekeepers raise and rent out to tend to big farms. And although other species of bees are five to ten times more efficient, on a per-bee basis, at pollinating certain fruits, honeybees have bigger colonies, cover longer distances, and tolerate management and movement better than most insects. They're not picky – they'll spend their time on almost any crop. It's tricky to calculate what their work is truly worth; some economists put it at more than $200 billion globally a year.

D   Industrial-scale farming, however, may be wearing down the system. Honeybees have suffered diseases and parasite infestations for as long as they've been managed, but in 2006 came an extreme blow. Around the world, bees began to disappear over the winter in massive numbers. Beekeepers would lift the lid of a hive and be amazed to find only the queen and a few stragglers, the worker bees gone. In the US, a third to half of all hives crashed; some beekeepers reported colony losses near 90 percent. The mysterious culprit was named colony collapse disorder (CCD) and it remains an annual menace – and an enigma.

E   When it first hit, many people, from agronomists to the public, assumed that our slathering of chemicals on agricultural fields was to blame for the mystery. Indeed, says Jeff Pettis of the USDA Bee Research Laboratory, 'we do find more disease in bees that have been exposed to pesticides, even at low levels.' But it is likely that CCD involves multiple stressors. Poor nutrition and chemical exposure, for instance,

might wear down a bee's immunities before a virus finishes the insect off. It's hard to tease apart factors and outcomes, Pettis says. New studies reveal that fungicides – not previously thought toxic to bees – can interfere with microbes that break down pollen in the insects' guts, affecting nutrient absorption and thus long-term health and longevity. Some findings pointed to viral and fungal pathogens working together. 'I only wish we had a single agent causing all the declines,' Pettis says, 'that would make our work much easier.'

F   However, habitat loss and alteration, he says, are even more of a menace to pollinators than pathogens. Claire Kremen encourages farmers to cultivate the flora surrounding farmland to help solve habitat problems. 'You can't move the farm,' she says, 'but you can diversify what grows in its vicinity: along roads, even in tractor yards.' Planting hedgerows and patches of native flowers that bloom at different times and seeding fields with multiple plant species rather than monocrops 'not only is better for native pollinators, but it's just better agriculture,' she says. Pesticide-free wildflower havens, adds Buchmann, would also bolster populations of useful insects. Fortunately, too, 'there are far more generalist plants than specialist plants, so there's a lot of redundancy in pollination,' Buchmann says. 'Even if one pollinator drops out, there are often pretty good surrogates left to do the job.' The key to keeping our gardens growing strong, he says, is letting that diversity thrive.

G   Take away that variety, and we'll lose more than honey. 'We wouldn't starve,' says Kremen. 'But what we eat, and even what we wear – pollinators, after all, give us some of our cotton and flax – would be limited to crops whose pollen travels by other means. 'In a sense,' she says, 'our lives would be dictated by the wind.' It's vital that we give pollinators more of what they need and less of what they don't, and ease the burden on managed bees by letting native animals do their part, say scientists.

adapted from National Geographic Magazine

4 Look at Questions 8–11.

1 Underline the key idea in the question and decide what type of information you need to answer it.

2 Scan the passage to find where the key idea is dealt with and answer Questions 8–11.

Questions 8–11

*Complete the sentences below. Choose **NO MORE THAN THREE WORDS** from the passage for each answer.*

8 Both .... were the first creatures to pollinate the world's plants.

9 Monkeys transport pollen on their ....

10 Honeybees are favoured pollinators among bee species partly because they travel ....

11 A feature of CCD is often the loss of all the ....

---

5 Check your answers to Questions 8–11. Then look at these reasons (a–e) for losing marks in the Reading test. Which of the reasons might apply to Questions 8–11?

REASONS FOR LOSING MARKS

a writing a singular answer when it should be plural

b missing a double letter in a word

c missing out one of two answers

d repeating a paraphrased word from the passage

e leaving out an important word

Exam advice   *Sentence completion*
- Copy your answer from the passage exactly.
- Make sure you write all the words you need for a correct answer.
- Read the completed sentence to make sure it is grammatically correct and does not contain a word from the passage that has been paraphrased in the question.

6 Underline the key ideas in Questions 12–13 below. Then scan the passage to find the right places, read those parts carefully and answer the questions.

Questions 12–13

*Choose **TWO** letters, A–E.*

*Which **TWO** methods of combating the problems caused by CCD and habitat loss are mentioned in the article?*

A using more imported pest controllers

B removing microbes from bees' stomachs

C cultivating a wide range of flowering plants

D increasing the size of many farms

E placing less reliance on honeybees

Exam advice   *Pick from a list*
- The answers may come from one part or different parts of the passage.
- It doesn't matter which order you write the two answers in.

7 Work in small groups. Take turns to ask and answer these questions.

1 How important is farming in your country?

2 What problems do farmers in your country complain about?

3 How has human activity affected the natural world (for better or worse) where you live?

Speaking Parts 2 and 3

1 Work in pairs. Look at this topic and discuss what you could say, making notes as you speak.

Describe an animal or plant that is important in your country.

You should say:

where you can find it

whether people like or dislike it

what recent news there has been about it

and explain why this plant or animal is important.

2 🎧(11) **Listen to Daeng giving her talk.**

1 As you listen, complete these phrases using two words in each gap.

   a … they're an _integral part_ of Thai culture and history.

   b So Thai people are .... of elephants.

   c As you can tell, elephants ....

   d Basically, elephant numbers .... these days, and I think that's why there's been a lot of .... them recently.

   e … because they are such .... to us.

2 Which point on the task does each phrase relate to?

3 How do phrases a–e above help Daeng structure her talk?

3 🎧(11) **To achieve a high band score, you must use some advanced vocabulary related to the topic. Listen again, read the definitions and complete the phrases in _italics_ by writing one word in each gap.**

1	in a remote uninhabited area	_in the_ ....
2	not free	_in_ ....
3	main job	_primary_ ....
4	not cutting down so many trees	_less_ ....
5	earn money	_make a_ ....
6	best place	.... _environment_
7	taken measures against	_cracked_ .... _on_
8	improve knowledge/ understanding	_raise_ ....
9	animals	....

4 **Work in pairs. Look back at your notes from Exercise 1 and take a few minutes to think about how you can structure your talk.**

Then take turns to give your talks. Try to use some of the vocabulary from Exercise 3.

5 **Work in pairs. Look at these two sets of Part 3 questions and discuss how you could speculate about the future when you answer each one.**

a How is population growth likely to affect the world's flora and fauna?

b What are the potential benefits to people of animal conservation programmes?

c Is there any justification for continuing to keep animals in captivity?

d What benefits do you think will come from preserving the world's rainforests?

e What future role do governments have to play in the preservation of their country's wildlife?

f Is wildlife preservation a global or national issue?

6 🎧(12)–🎧(14) **Listen to Daeng, Per and Lucrecia answering three of the questions in Exercise 5. As you listen, complete these phrases about the future by writing one word in each gap.**

1 Looking .... , I can see a .... for …

2 There's a reasonable .... that …

3 It's highly .... that …

4 We may .... see …

5 There's .... possibility that …

6 As .... as I can see, …

7 There's very .... chance of …

8 In the .... future, …

▶ Key grammar: _Speculating and talking about the future_

7 🎧(12)–🎧(14) **Work in pairs. Listen to the speakers again and discuss what each student's views are and whether you agree or not.**

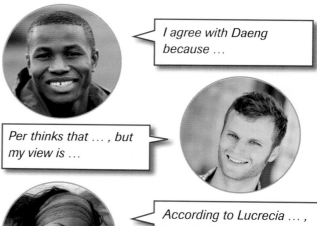

I agree with Daeng because …

Per thinks that … , but my view is …

According to Lucrecia … , but I don't agree with that.

▶ Pronunciation: _Word stress_

8 **Work in pairs. Take turns to ask and answer the remaining questions from Exercise 5.**

Exam advice   _Speaking Part 3_

Listen carefully to the questions in Part 3. You may have to speculate or hypothesise about the future. Use appropriate expressions to do this.

Pronunciation
Word stress

With words of more than one syllable, we stress one syllable more than the others. It is important to stress the correct syllable so that you can be understood.

1 (15) **Work in pairs. Look at this extract from Daeng's Part 3 answer.**

Also, <u>certain</u> <u>species</u> only <u>survive</u> if we <u>protect</u> them – like the <u>giant</u> <u>panda</u>.

1 Decide which syllables are stressed in the underlined words.

2 Listen and check your answers. Then complete this rule:

We often stress the **1** .... syllable in nouns and adjectives that do not have prefixes or suffixes, but the **2** .... syllable in verbs. (Words that don't follow this rule include *idea*, *ahead*, *handle* and *recognise*.)

2 (16) **Work in pairs. Look at this extract from Daeng's Part 2 talk.**

Although the elephants were in <u>captivity</u>, they used to be an <u>important</u> part of the <u>workforce</u> in the forests – that was their <u>primary</u> <u>occupation</u> – but as a result of <u>conservation</u> programmes, there's less logging <u>nowadays</u>.

1 Decide which syllables are stressed in the <u>underlined</u> words.

2 Listen and check your answers. Then complete these rules:

- With compound nouns (nouns formed from two separate words combined, e.g. *playground*), we often stress the **1** .... word.
- When a longer word is formed from a shorter word, by adding prefixes or suffixes (e.g. *gladly*, *incredible*), the stress usually stays on the **2** .... syllable (most prefixes are not stressed). However, when we add *–ion* or *–ic*, the stress always falls on the syllable that comes **3** .... the suffix (e.g. *production*).
- When we add *–ity*, the stress usually comes **4** .... syllables before the suffix (e.g. *productivity*).

Key grammar
Speculating and talking about the future

1 **Work in pairs. Look at these examples from Speaking Exercise 6.**

1 In the end, I think it's an issue that **will be handled** on an international level.

2 If we don't protect forests and other animal habitats now, we **may well** see a very steep decline in animal numbers …

3 Without new laws, **there's very little chance** of any real improvement in the foreseeable future.

In which of these sentences does the speaker think something in the future is:

a certain?

b probable?

c improbable?

2 **Work in pairs. Look at these sentences and classify the phrases in bold as a, b or c from Exercise 1.**

1 **It's highly likely that** we **will** find a cure for malaria.

2 As far as human cloning is concerned, I think **there is little likelihood of** this happening.

3 I **very much doubt whether** the world **will** ever become completely vegetarian.

4 The world's population **is bound to** exceed 8 billion in the next 15 years.

5 **There's a strong likelihood that** many more species will become endangered.

6 **There is unlikely to be** another ice age in our lifetime.

7 **There's no doubt that** scientists **will** one day come up with a 'food' pill.

8 It's **quite possible that** people **will** live to be over 150 in the future.

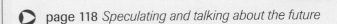

▶ page 118 *Speculating and talking about the future*

3 **Work in small groups and discuss which of the sentences in Exercise 2 you agree with and which you disagree with, and why. If you disagree, use one of the expressions in bold to make your own prediction about the future.**

Writing Task 1

❶ Work in pairs. Complete the sentences below with the words/phrases in the box so that they offer good advice for students doing Writing Task 1.

> ~~20 minutes~~   comparisons   diagram
> figures   grammar and spelling   key
> overview   paragraphs   task   words

1 Aim to write your answer in ..20 minutes.. .
2 Study the graph, chart or .... carefully first.
3 Use your own words rather than copying words from the ....
4 Make sure you have included all the .... points.
5 Always use .... to organise your points.
6 Make sure any .... you quote are accurate.
7 Make .... if they are appropriate and relevant.
8 Always include a clear ....
9 Leave time to check your ....
10 Don't lose unnecessary marks by writing too few ....

❷ Work in pairs. Look at the Writing task in the next column and answer these questions.

1 How are the two charts linked? How do the charts differ overall?

2 What are the key features of the charts?

3 Which categories on each chart could you combine? (You cannot mention every category.)

4 How many paragraphs would you write, and what would you include in each one?

5 What would your overview contain?

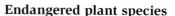

The charts below give information about endangered plants around the world.

Summarise the information by selecting and reporting the main features, and make comparisons where relevant.

Endangered plant species

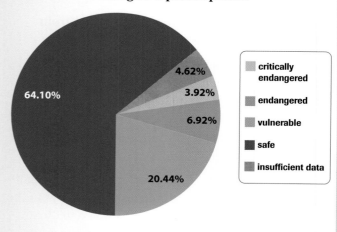

- critically endangered
- endangered
- vulnerable
- safe
- insufficient data

64.10%   4.62%   3.92%   6.92%   20.44%

Plant species at risk in different habitats

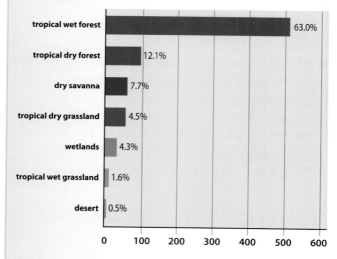

tropical wet forest	63.0%
tropical dry forest	12.1%
dry savanna	7.7%
tropical dry grassland	4.5%
wetlands	4.3%
tropical wet grassland	1.6%
desert	0.5%

0   100   200   300   400   500   600

❸ Read this sample answer. Divide it into paragraphs and insert the six missing commas.

The charts provide information on the proportion of plant species that are at risk, the levels of risk, and the different environments in which these plants grow. Although a lot of plants are safe about a third of all plant species around the world are under some kind of threat. For just over 10 percent of these species, the threat is severe, with 3.92 percent of plants likely to become extinct and over 25 percent being vulnerable to extinction. When you look at plant habitats the area with the greatest proportion of threatened species is tropical rainforest where 63 percent of species are threatened. In contrast desert areas have the lowest proportion of vulnerable plants at 0.5 percent. Forest grassland and wetland areas are also home to threatened species. However the danger is on a much smaller scale than in the tropics, with figures ranging between 12 and one percent. To conclude tropical areas of the world have more endangered plant species than others, and certain plants need immediate protection.

 page 121 *Using commas*

4 Study these two extracts from the sample answer on page 82. Then rewrite the sentences below using *with* to add supporting information to the opening statement.

a) *For just over 10 percent of these species, the threat is severe,* **with** *3.92 percent of plants* <u>likely to become</u> *extinct …*

b) *However, the danger is on a much smaller scale than in the tropics,* **with** *figures* <u>ranging</u> *between 12 and one per cent.*

1 The pollution levels will peak in 2015, and figures will reach 22 parts per million.
2 The figures increased fourfold in 2008, and costs went up from $200 to $800.
3 Bird-watching grew in popularity that year, and teenage groups became more involved in the hobby than any other group.
4 Cheetah populations are under threat, and numbers are predicted to continue to fall steadily in the future.
5 There were numerous complaints about the building project in 2006, and the highest number was recorded in September.
6 Extensive grazing is most marked in Europe, and 9.7 percent of land was over-used.

5 Compare the sample answer on page 82 with your ideas from Exercise 2.

6 When doing IELTS tasks, it is important to use your own words as far as possible and not repeat words from the task. Find the following in the sample answer.

1 two phrases that mean 'endangered'
2 an adjective that means 'critical'
3 a word that has been used to replace 'habitats'
4 a phrase that means 'the place where something lives'
5 a phrase that means 'a lot lower'

> **Exam advice**   Writing Task 1
> * Spend a few minutes planning the organisation of your answer and the content of each paragraph.
> * If there are large amounts of data, divide it into categories so that you express the main features, but not every detail.
> * Leave time to check your work for mistakes.

7 Work in pairs. Look at this Writing task and discuss how you would organise an answer into paragraphs, and what you would include in each one.

> *The graph and chart below give information about species extinctions and the threats to plant life.*
>
> *Summarise the information by selecting and reporting the main features, and make comparisons where relevant.*

Extinctions of plant and animal species – tropical forests

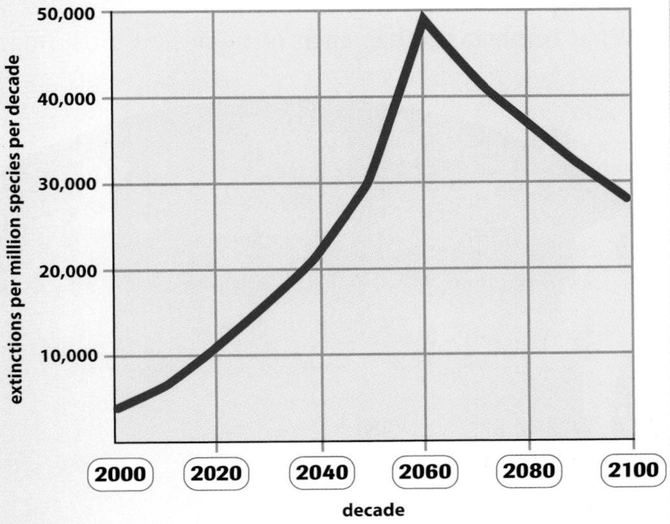

Threats to plant life

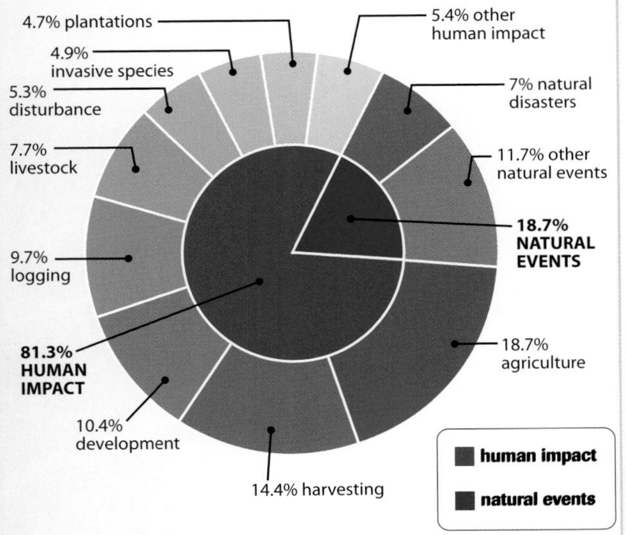

8 Now write your answer in 20 minutes. Write around 150 words. Leave a couple of minutes at the end to check for mistakes.

Unit 8 Across the universe

Starting off

❶ What aspect of space exploration does each of these photos show?

❷ What importance has each of them had for humanity?

Reading Section 3

1 Work in small groups. You are going to read a passage about an international charity called the Earth and Space Foundation. First discuss this question.

What are the advantages of international collaboration in space exploration?

2 Quickly glance through this section to see what types of questions you will have to answer.

3 Before you deal with the questions, spend two minutes skimming the passage to get an overview of the type of passage and its contents. When you have finished, compare your ideas with a partner.

The Earth and Space Foundation

The community that focuses its efforts on the exploration of space has largely been different from the community focused on the study and protection of the Earth's environment, despite the fact that both fields of interest involve what might be referred to as 'scientific exploration'. The reason for this dichotomous existence is chiefly historical. The exploration of the Earth has been occurring over many centuries, and the institutions created to do it are often very different from those founded in the second part of the 20th century to explore space. This separation is also caused by the fact that space exploration has attracted experts from mainly non-biological disciplines — primarily engineers and physicists — but the study of Earth and its environment is a domain heavily populated by biologists.

The separation between the two communities is often reflected in attitudes. In the environmental community, it is not uncommon for space exploration to be regarded as a waste of money, distracting governments from solving major environmental problems here at home. In the space exploration community, it is not uncommon for environmentalists to be regarded as introspective people who divert attention from the more expansive visions of the exploration of space — the 'new frontier'. These perceptions can also be negative in consequence because the full potential of both communities can be realised better when they work together to solve problems. For example, those involved in space exploration can provide the satellites to monitor the Earth's fragile environments, and environmentalists can provide information on the survival of life in extreme environments.

In the sense that Earth and space exploration both stem from the same human drive to understand our environment and our place within it, there is no reason for the split to exist. A more accurate view of Earth and space exploration is to see them as a continuum of exploration with many interconnected and mutually beneficial links. The Earth and Space Foundation, a registered charity, was established for the purposes of fostering such links through field research and by direct practical action.

Projects that have been supported by the Foundation include environmental projects using technologies resulting from space exploration: satellite communications, GPS, remote sensing, advanced materials and power sources. For example, in places where people are faced with destruction of the forests on which their livelihood depends, rather than rejecting economic progress and trying to save the forests on their intrinsic merit, another approach is to enhance the value of the forests — although these schemes must be carefully assessed to be successful. In the past, the Foundation provided a grant to a group of expeditions that used remote sensing to plan eco-tourism routes in the forests of Guatemala, thus providing capital to the local communities through the tourist trade. This novel approach is now making the protection of the forests a sensible economic decision.

The Foundation funds expeditions making astronomical observations from remote, difficult-to-access Earth locations, archaeological field projects studying the development of early civilisations that made significant contributions to astronomy and space sciences, and field expeditions studying the way in which views of the astronomical environment shaped the nature of past civilisations. A part of Syria — 'the Fertile Crescent' — was the birthplace of astronomy, accountancy, animal domestication and many other fundamental developments of human civilisation. The Foundation helped fund a large archaeology project by the Society for Syrian Archaeology at the University of California, Los Angeles, in collaboration with the Syrian government that used GPS and satellite imagery to locate mounds, or 'tels', containing artefacts and remnants of early civilisations. These collections are being used to build a better picture of the nature of the civilisations that gave birth to astronomy.

Field research also applies the Earth's environmental and biological resources to the human exploration and settlement of space. This may include the use of remote environments on Earth, as well as physiological and psychological studies in harsh environments. In one research project, the Foundation provided a grant to an international caving expedition to study the psychology of explorers subjected to long-term isolation in caves in Mexico. The psychometric tests on the cavers were used to enhance US astronaut selection criteria by the NASA Johnson Space Center.

Space-like environments on Earth help us understand how to operate in the space environment or help us characterise extraterrestrial environments for future scientific research. In the Arctic, a 24-kilometre-wide impact crater formed by an asteroid or comet 23 million years ago has become home to a Mars-analogue programme. The Foundation helped fund the NASA Haughton–Mars Project to use this crater to test communications and exploration technologies in preparation for the human exploration of Mars. The crater, which sits in high Arctic permafrost, provides an excellent replica of the physical processes occurring on Mars, a permafrosted, impact-altered planet. Geologists and biologists can work at the site to help understand how impact craters shape the geological characteristics and possibly biological potential of Mars.

In addition to its fieldwork and scientific activities, the Foundation has award programmes. These include a series of awards for the future human exploration of Mars, a location with a diverse set of exploration challenges. The awards will honour a number of 'firsts' on Mars that include landing on the surface, undertaking an overland expedition to the Martian South Pole, undertaking an overland expedition to the Martian North Pole, climbing Olympus Mons, the highest mountain in the solar system, and descending to the bottom of Valles Marineris, the deepest canyon on Mars. The Foundation will offer awards for expeditions further out in the solar system once these Mars awards have been claimed. Together, they demonstrate that the programme really has no boundary in what it could eventually support, and they provide longevity for the objectives of the Foundation.

adapted from Fostering links between environmental and space exploration: The Earth and Space Foundation, *Cockell, C., White, D., Messier, D. and Dale Stokes, M., Elsevier Science Ltd, 2002*

❹ **Work in pairs. Quickly look at Questions 1–9. You worked on 'Yes / No / Not Given' and multiple-choice questions in Units 3 and 6.**

1 What are the best techniques for dealing with these tasks in the exam?
2 How long should you spend on each of them?
3 Check your answers by reading the Exam advice on pages 32 and 65.
4 Now try to answer Questions 1–9 in the time you decided on above.

Questions 1–5

Do the following statements agree with the views of the writer in the reading passage?

Write

YES   *if the statement agrees with the views of the writer*

NO   *if the statement contradicts the views of the writer*

NOT GIVEN   *if it is impossible to say what the writer thinks about this*

1 Activities related to environmental protection and space exploration have a common theme.

2 It is unclear why space exploration evolved in a different way from environmental studies on Earth.

3 Governments tend to allocate more money to environmental projects than space exploration.

4 Unfortunately, the environmental and space exploration communities have little to offer each other in terms of resources.

5 The Earth and Space Foundation was set up later than it was originally intended.

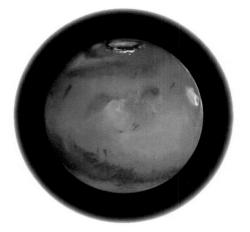

Questions 6–9

Choose the correct letter, A, B, C or D.

6 What was the significance of the 'novel approach' adopted in the Guatemala project?

   A It minimised the need to protect the forests.

   B It reduced the impact of tourists on the forests.

   C It showed that preserving the forests can be profitable.

   D It gave the Foundation greater control over the forests.

7 GPS and satellite imagery were used in the Syrian project to

   A help archaeologists find ancient items.

   B explore land that is hard to reach.

   C reduce the impact of archaeological activity.

   D evaluate some early astronomical theories.

8 One of the purposes of the Foundation's awards is to

   A attract non-scientists to its work.

   B establish priorities for Mars exploration.

   C offer financial incentives for space exploration.

   D establish the long-term continuity of its activities.

9 What is the writer's purpose in the passage?

   A to persuade people to support the Foundation

   B to explain the nature of the Foundation's work

   C to show how views on the Foundation have changed

   D to reject earlier criticisms of the Foundation's work

⑤ Work in pairs.

1 Quickly look at Questions 10–14.

2 Decide on the best techniques for dealing with this task in the exam, and how long the task should take you.

3 Check your answers by reading the Exam advice on page 34.

4 Answer Questions 10–14 in the time you decided.

Questions 10–14

Complete the summary using the words, A–I, below.

Field research: Applying the Earth's environment to the settlement of space

Some studies have looked at how humans function in 10 .... situations. In one project, it was decided to review cave explorers in Mexico who tolerate 11 .... periods on their own.

It is also possible to prepare for space exploration by studying environments on Earth that are 12 .... to those on Mars. A huge crater in the Arctic is the 13 .... place to test the technologies needed to explore Mars and gather other relevant 14 .... information.

A comparable	D ideal	G scientific
B extreme	E unexpected	H extended
C connected	F beneficial	I individual

⑥ Find these five phrases in the passage. What do they refer to, and which questions did they help you answer?

1 both fields of interest

2 this dichotomous existence

3 both communities

4 These collections

5 Together, they demonstrate

⑦ Work in small groups.

1 Why do you think Mars has become an important focus for space exploration?

2 If scientists found life on other planets, how would this change the way we see the world and ourselves?

Vocabulary

Verbs and dependent prepositions

1 Complete these extracts from the reading passage with the correct preposition.

1 The community that focuses its efforts .... the exploration of space has largely been different from ...

2 ... both fields of interest involve what might be referred to .... 'scientific exploration'.

3 The separation between the two communities is often reflected .... attitudes.

4 ... it is not uncommon for space exploration to be regarded .... a waste of money, distracting governments .... solving major environmental problems here at home.

5 In the sense that Earth and space exploration both stem .... the same human drive to understand our environment ...

6 Projects that have been supported by the Foundation include environmental projects using technologies resulting .... space exploration ...

2 Complete these sentences using the correct prepositions.

1 I do not believe .... spending money .... space exploration.

2 With regard to the rocket launch, the team agreed .... a six-hour delay.

3 Being away from family and friends for long periods must be hard to cope ....

4 The cloud cover prevented observers .... seeing the eclipse.

5 A team of experts will be involved .... setting up the space mission.

6 The astronaut said that he had devoted the past four years .... preparing himself for the mission.

7 Galileo is recognised worldwide .... having been an exceptional scientist.

3 Work in pairs. Complete the sentences any way you wish.

1 As a hobby, astronomy appeals ...
2 An interest in science can stem ...
3 The newspaper editor decided to devote the front page ...
4 People can be very divided ...
5 The course will provide me ...
6 Mars is often referred to ...
7 Journalists need to reflect carefully ...

Listening Part 4

1 Circle the correct option in *italics* so that the sentences offer good advice for students doing the Listening test.

1 Use the preparation time to *relax / decide what you need to listen for.*

2 If you lose your place, *wait for the next section to begin / listen for key ideas in the questions.*

3 It *matters / does not matter* how clearly you write your answers on the question paper, because you will transfer them to the answer sheet later.

4 Standard abbreviations (e.g. *km* for *kilometre*) are acceptable in answers; they *count / do not count* as words.

5 If you miss an answer, *leave a blank / make a guess.*

6 If you go over the word limit, you *will / will not necessarily* lose the mark for the question.

2 Work in small groups. You are going to hear a lecturer in physical sciences talking about space observation. Before you listen, discuss this question.

How has our understanding of the universe changed over the last 500 years?

❸ Work in pairs. Look at Questions 1–10. What are the best techniques for dealing with this task? (You practised it in Units 4 and 6.)

Questions 1–10

Complete the notes below.

*Write **NO MORE THAN TWO WORDS** for each answer.*

Space observation

Early days

First telescopes   –   started the **1** '...................'

Galileo's telescope –   moved the focus from **2** .... to the sky

First **3** ....   –   by John William Draper (1839)

Present day

Professional astronomers –aim to get **4** ....

Amateur astronomers   –aim to photograph beautiful images, e.g. **5** .... (Greece)

Contribution of amateur astronomers

Specialised knowledge

e.g. • recognise changes in the **6** .... of a space object

     • are able to produce **7** .... of space

Two main types of observation

a   new discoveries, e.g. an **8** .... or a comet

b   monitor the **9** .... of objects in space

Main advantages

• great patience and passion

• can conduct **10** .... observations

---

❹ ⒄ Now listen and answer Questions 1–10.

❺ Discuss these questions in small groups.

1   Would you like to travel into space one day? Why? / Why not?

2   What do you think the experience would be like?

Speaking Parts 2 and 3

❶ Circle the correct options in *italics* so that the sentences offer good advice for students doing the Speaking test.

1   Answers to Part 1 questions should be *very short / about two or three sentences long.*

2   You will *have / not have* a choice of topics in Part 2.

3   You should aim to speak for *just one minute / the full two minutes* in Part 2.

4   Part 3 is worth *more marks than / the same marks as* the other two parts.

5   Part 3 questions are about *personal / general and abstract* topics.

6   Pronunciation is *just as / not as* important as vocabulary, grammar and fluency.

7   You *will / will not* lose marks if you give irrelevant answers to questions.

❷ Take one minute to prepare your talk for this Part 2 topic.

Describe a story about space (real or fictitious) that you have read about or seen in a film or on TV.

You should say:

     when you read about or saw the story

     what happened in the story

     whether the story has any significance today

and explain how you felt about this story.

③ Work in pairs.

1 Complete this checklist with four more good things to do when answering Part 2. Then check your ideas by looking back at the Exam advice in previous units.

Did your partner …

☐ *introduce the topic clearly?*

☐

☐

☐

☐

2 Take turns to either give your talks or listen and complete the checklist. When your partner finishes, ask these short follow-up questions that an examiner might ask.

• Have you told other people about this story?
• Do other people that you know like this story?

3 Take turns to give each other feedback using the checklist.

④ Work in pairs. Read the questions below that a student, Pauline, answers in Speaking Part 3. For which question(s) is she likely to:

a compare the present with the past?
b speculate / make predictions about the future?
c give reasons and/or examples?

Attitudes towards space travel

1 What do you think fascinates humans about outer space?

2 Do you think that's why some stories about space travel have been so 'imaginative'?

3 How do you think people's attitudes towards space exploration have changed since the first Moon landings?

4 To what extent do you think governments will continue to fund projects in search of life on other planets?

---

⑤ ⑱ Listen to Pauline answering the questions in Exercise 4. In which answer(s) does she:

a compare the present with the past?
b speculate / make predictions about the future?
c give reasons and/or examples?

⑥ Read the recording script on page 160 and underline the phrases which:

a compare the present with the past.
b speculate / make predictions about the future.
c give reasons and/or examples.
d you would find useful when answering these questions yourself.

▶ Pronunciation: *Rhythm and chunking*

⑦ Work in pairs. Look back at the Exam advice in previous units to remind yourselves of the best approaches to this part. Add any ideas you wish to this checklist.

Did your partner …

☐ answer the question clearly and relevantly?
☐ use appropriate expressions to introduce points?
☐ include some reasons and examples?
☐ use some advanced vocabulary?

⑧ Work in pairs. Take turns to ask and answer the questions in Exercise 4 and these questions.

People and space

• What qualities do you think you need in order to be selected for a space mission?

• What considerations have to be made before sending humans into space?

• To what extent is it better to use robots rather than humans to explore space?

As you listen, prepare some feedback for your partner using the checklist in Exercise 7.

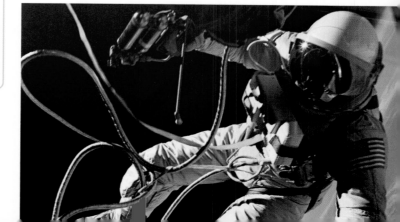

Pronunciation
Rhythm and chunking

Speakers divide their speech into groups of words, or chunks, and they deliver these with a natural-sounding rhythm. Some common phrases form natural 'chunks' and tend to be pronounced with a predictable rhythm.

❶ (19) Work in pairs. Listen to the rhythm of the phrases in bold which is produced by stressing the <u>underlined</u> words and syllables. Then take turns to read the phrases aloud.

As far as <u>I'm</u> con<u>cerned</u>, it's a <u>waste</u> of <u>money</u>.

❷ (20) Predict the rhythm in these phrases by <u>underlining</u> the stressed syllables. Then listen to check your answers.

1 I've no idea
2 What's the point?
3 make both ends meet
4 It's like the time when …
5 on the other hand
6 over the years

❸ Look at these extracts from another student's answers to Part 3 questions. <u>Underline</u> the syllables that you think will be stressed in the phrases in bold.

1 **Well, it's hard to say.** I think that, **over the decades**, people have **lost interest**.
2 **You know**, if you **go back to the time** of Galileo, no one even **thought about** travelling into space then.
3 **As far as space is concerned**, I don't think we have **any idea** what's out there.
4 **A lot of people say** 'What's the point in space exploration?', but **as far as I can see**, that's **a bit short-sighted**.
5 Actually, **I can't wait to see** what the Mars robot **comes up with**. I think **the whole space thing** is just **out of this world**!

❹ (21) Work in pairs. Take turns to read the extracts in Exercise 3 aloud, then listen to the recording and check your pronunciation.

Writing Task 2

❶ Work in pairs. Complete the sentences below using the words and phrases in the box so that they offer good advice for students doing Writing Task 2.

| ~~40 minutes~~ | grammar and spelling | main ideas |
| plan | questions | sentences | view | vocabulary |

1 Make sure that you leave ..40 minutes. to complete this task.
2 Study the task first and note how many .... you must address, and how many aspects of these you must cover to give a complete answer to the task.
3 Quickly brainstorm ideas and examples. Then spend a minute or two writing a rough .... where you organise your .... into paragraphs.
4 Make sure all the .... you write in a paragraph follow each other logically.
5 Use some advanced ....
6 End with a short conclusion that restates your personal ....
7 Leave two minutes at the end to check your ....

❷ Work in pairs. Look at the Writing task below.

1 How many questions do you need to cover in your answer, and what does each question require you to do?
2 What main ideas could you include for each question?

Write about the following topic.

A new generation of entrepreneurs believe that privately funded space tourism will be the next exciting development in space exploration.

How true do you think this is?

How would space tourism affect space exploration as we know it today?

Give reasons for your answer and include any relevant examples from your own knowledge or experience.

3 Work in pairs. Read this sample answer and write a brief plan to show the writer's main and supporting points.

I think it is very likely that space travel will become a popular activity in the private sector. There are wealthy people in the world who want to go into space, and there is the desire to take them there. All that these people need is the means to achieve their aims.

To a certain extent, that means is already available, and some wealthy business people have already paid millions of dollars to travel into space. If they have done it, others will follow. Human beings have a natural tendency to go beyond their limits; it is this desire to 'push the boundaries' that has motivated every explorer in the past.

In the same way, space is definitely where business people in the travel industry are setting their sights. In fact, newspapers say that millionaires like Richard Branson are in the process of doing test flights to the edge of space. So it is only a matter of time before space tourism becomes a reality for the population as a whole.

How that will change space exploration is an interesting question. As businesses will be concentrating on making profits and satisfying a general desire for adventure, it seems unlikely that they will have any influence on the work of space explorers. Essentially, the two activities are quite different; only by doing both would you make any link between them.

Having said that, if space tourism were to become popular, it is quite possible that it would raise extra money that could be channelled back into space exploration in the form of enhanced technology and communications systems. This, in turn, might speed up the process of space exploration.

4 Answer these questions.

1 How and where does the writer link the first question in the task to the second?
2 How does she link her main views across paragraphs?

5 Work in pairs. The answer in Exercise 3 lacks a conclusion.

1 Decide which of the conclusions below (1–3) is the best one, and say why.
2 Match the conclusions with the Teacher's comments (a–c) on page 96.

1 In general, I think space tourism will become a reality and, like everything, it will become cheaper and more accessible as time goes by. At the moment, it is only millionaires who would be able to afford it, but that will obviously change in the long run. Commercial flights to the Moon could become a regular occurrence, but I doubt whether I would ever take one.

2 Overall, space tourism seems an inevitable development. Whether or not it has an effect on the work of space explorers will depend on the level of success it has and the opportunities it opens up for scientific progress. Only time will tell.

3 In conclusion, I would argue that both questions are difficult to answer. While millionaires might go into space, it seems unlikely that ordinary people will be able to afford it. Even if they can, they will be seeking their own entertainment, not contributing to the work of space explorers.

6 Find words or phrases in the sample answer in Exercise 3 and the paragraphs in Exercise 5 which mean the following.

1 a method or way of doing something
2 an instinctive likelihood to behave in a certain way
3 go beyond the limits of something
4 deciding to achieve something
5 it will definitely happen at some point in the future
6 over the days/months/years
7 something that happens repeatedly in a fixed pattern
8 we will know whether or not something will happen at some point in the future
9 looking for
10 helping with

7 Use the phrases in Exercise 6 to complete these sentences. You may have to change the phrase slightly.

1 It is .... before we find life on another planet.
2 Adults, like children, often try to .... and do more than they are capable of.
3 Sometimes we have to control our .... to be over-optimistic about what we can achieve.
4 Richard Branson has .... operating a space-tourism venture.
5 Rocket technology provided us with .... to explore outer space.

▶ Key grammar: *Emphasising*

8 Work in pairs. Look at this task. Discuss your exam strategy for doing Writing task 2. Look back at the Exam advice in previous units. Then work alone and write your answer in at least 250 words.

Write about the following topic.

Some people argue that space exploration has had more to do with national pride than international effort.

To what extent do you agree with this?

How do you think space exploration will change in the future?

Give reasons for your answer and include any relevant examples from your own knowledge or experience.

Key grammar
Emphasising

1 Complete each of these sentences from the sample answer on page 92 with one word.

1 All that these people need .... the means to achieve their aims.
2 ... it is this desire to 'push the boundaries' .... has motivated every explorer in the past.
3 In the same way, space is definitely .... business people in the travel industry are setting their sights.

2 What is being emphasised in each sentence?

▶ page 112 *Emphasising*

3 Rewrite these sentences so that the underlined words and phrases are emphasised.

1 <u>Yuri Gagarin</u> was the first man in space, not Neil Armstrong.
   It was .... , not Neil Armstrong.
2 <u>The ISS shows</u> how successfully nations can co-operate.
   What ...
3 Some people consider <u>Mars</u> to be the most interesting planet.
   Mars is .... to be the most interesting planet.
4 I would find <u>the sense of weightlessness</u> rather unnerving.
   It is ...
5 Clearly we won't get a better <u>picture</u> than this.
   Cleary this picture ...
6 He <u>spends long hours</u> in his observatory.
   What ...
7 <u>Millionaires</u> are the only people who can afford to travel into space.
   It's ...

4 Write sentences about these topics using the words in brackets to help you.

1 a time when you were blamed for someone else's mistake (*it wasn't / it was*)
2 the most interesting person you know (*X is / what he/she does / is*)
3 the best way to prepare for a big change in life (*what you*)
4 an experience that you learned from (*what it taught me / X is the best way*)
5 something other people generally believe (*X is believed*)

Across the universe 93

Vocabulary and grammar review **Unit 7**

Vocabulary

1 Find nine more words connected with the natural world in this wordsearch puzzle.

B	J	C	L	O	U	D	E	R
T	U	A	N	T	S	U	A	S
R	S	L	I	S	L	I	O	U
E	C	R	L	D	N	O	F	N
E	A	A	L	B	L	T	H	E
S	T	K	O	G	R	E	E	N
I	N	W	G	O	P	R	E	Y
F	S	C	R	S	K	Y	E	A

2 Complete these idioms with six of the words you found in the wordsearch, then match each idiom (1–6) with the correct meaning (a–f) below.

1 give someone the ...*green*... light   c
2 take the .... by the horns
3 The .... is the limit.
4 Every .... has a silver lining.
5 can't see the wood for the ....
6 chase ....

a to be unable to see what is important in a situation because you are giving too much attention to detail
b to do something difficult in a determined and confident way
c to give permission for someone to do something
d to waste your time trying to get or achieve something impossible
e what you say when there is no end to what something or someone can achieve
f what you say when there is something good even in an unpleasant situation

3 Write sentences using these prompts.

1 The government / given / light / local council / build / new hospital
2 If / work hard / pass / exams / sky
3 There were / many / pages / report / we / see / wood

Grammar

4 Circle the correct options in *italics*.

1 Some experts deny that global warming is a direct cause of human activity, but I think there is (*every*) / *all* possibility that it is!
2 A young deer could *possible* / *probably* escape a lion attack if other deer distracted the pack.
3 There has been some negative publicity about eco-tourism recently, meaning that the industry *can* / *could* well suffer in the future.
4 The data indicate that the construction of buildings in the area is highly *certain* / *likely* to increase in the future.
5 Unless we act now to protect endangered wildlife, more species *are* / *will* bound to become extinct.
6 Experts doubt whether there *is* / *will be* a decline in deforestation in the area.
7 Our children's generation have a fair *chance* / *likelihood* of living in a more sustainable environment than we have now.

5 Insert nine more missing commas in this extract about ant colonies.

Ants, which form natural groups called ant colonies have much to teach us about group behaviour. As individuals ants are not the most intelligent of creatures. However, when they get into groups, they are seen to behave in very intelligent ways.

If you look at how ants gather food for example you can quickly see how the group mentality works. Rather than all rushing out at once a few foragers do the first trip. Having found food they return to the nest and send a signal to other ants to go out. Ants don't sit and decide how many foragers they need first which means that they can quickly adapt if a predator is around.

Ultimately, no one ant realises what it is doing on its own but each ant's actions are connected to those of other ants. Could such a lack of central control work in business? Definitely says one expert!

Vocabulary and grammar review **Unit 8**

Vocabulary

❶ Complete this paragraph by writing the correct preposition in each gap.

Being isolated in a space capsule for 520 days would certainly not appeal **1** ....*to*.... the majority of people. However, six men were carefully selected to do exactly that. The Mars 500 mission was designed to test how well human beings would cope **2** .... a return trip to Mars – although the capsule never left Earth. It was a simulated space flight during which the men were subjected **3** .... living together in a 550-cubic-metre space.

During the experiment, the men managed to distract their minds **4** .... their isolation by having a fixed work schedule and by celebrating events. The crew consisted **5** .... three Russians, two Europeans and a Chinese, so there were plenty of cultural traditions to focus **6** ....

Although the men were able to decorate their individual spaces **7** .... photos and other personal items, they said afterwards that they found it hard being separated **8** .... family and friends. However, their experience taught them a great deal about co-operation and teamwork, and they now see themselves **9** .... part of a bigger family.

❷ ⊙ Correct these top-ten spelling mistakes from the Cambridge Learner Corpus Bands 6–7.5.

1 goverment *government*
2 tempreture
3 oppotunities
4 countris
5 excercise
6 nowdays
7 competion
8 droped
9 happend
10 diffrent

❸ Complete the sentences below using a word/ phrase from the box in the correct form.

essentially	in the long run	push the boundaries
~~set your sights on~~	speed up	time will tell

As the Moon now seems to offer little more than a potential tourist resort, space agencies around the world have **1** ..*set their sights on*.. Mars. **2** .... , the 'red planet', as it is otherwise known, is still unexplored territory, but whether it will yield useful information or resources, only **3** .... One thing, though, seems clear: in space, as in other endeavours, human beings will continue to **4** ....

However, while the exploration of the Moon was characterised as a 'race', there seems to be less desire to **5** .... the first Mars landing. As time goes by, scientists are learning more and more about Mars, and this will only benefit everyone **6** ....

Grammar

❹ Rewrite these sentences in a more emphatic way, starting with the words in bold.

1 People want solutions to the problems on Earth.
   What …
2 The scientific study of the universe is astronomy, not astrology.
   Astronomy …
3 Humans have only ventured into space in the last hundred years.
   It …
4 Space travel fascinates me, even though it's risky.
   Regardless of …
5 We only needed a greater level of international co-operation to enhance our knowledge of the universe.
   All …
6 We stayed up all night observing the stars.
   What …

Additional material

Unit 1, Starting off, Exercise 1, page 8

Suggested answers

a You do things like read documents very carefully and focus on all the small points, checking their accuracy.

b You are able to think about something and come up with an original or unusual approach to it.

c When you come across something new, you are eager to learn or find out about it.

d You are able and willing to work with other people as part of a group in order, for example, to solve problems or develop new ideas.

e You can look ahead and plan how an organisation or company might best meet the needs of the future.

f You are friendly and energetic, and find it easy and enjoyable to be with others.

g You find it easy to exchange ideas with others; you listen well and can accurately put across your own ideas.

h You can look after and organise groups of employees so that they are performing in the best interests of the company.

Unit 7, Starting off, Exercise 3, page 74

A Photo masterclass

B Waiting for thunder

C The art of deception

D Pandas Inc.

E Gold dusters

Unit 8, Writing, Exercise 5, page 92

Teacher's comments

a The view presented in the conclusion is different from the ideas expressed in the main body of the essay.

b The conclusion focuses on one of the questions, but simply repeats ideas and adds a new point. There is no summary of views on the second question.

c The conclusion sums up the argument well and takes the reader back to the two key questions in the task.

Speaking reference

What to expect in the exam

The Speaking Test is normally held on the same day as the other tests. It is the last part of the exam.

- The Speaking Test lasts 11–14 minutes and has three parts.
- You do the test on your own.
- There is one examiner in the room who gives you the instructions, asks the questions and assesses your performance.
- It is recorded for administrative purposes.

Part 1: Introduction and interview

Part 1 lasts between four and five minutes. It consists of:

- a short introduction in which the examiner asks you your name and where you come from, and checks your identification;
- some initial questions about what you do or where you live;
- some questions on topics such as your hobbies and activities, places you know, family celebrations, holidays, etc.

You studied and practised Part 1 in Unit 1.

How to do Part 1

1 Listen carefully to each question the examiner asks you and consider the topic and the tenses that you need to use.

2 Give relevant replies and provide some reasons and examples for your answer.

3 Aim to answer each question in about two to four sentences.

4 Make sure you know the sort of topics that are often used in Part 1 and learn some advanced vocabulary related to these.

5 Speak clearly so that the examiner can hear and understand you.

6 Aim to appear confident and relaxed and look at the examiner when you are speaking.

7 Ask the examiner to repeat a question you do not understand or may have misheard: *I'm sorry, could you repeat the question, please?*

Topics and questions

1 Read these questions (1–12) and match them to a topic below (a–l).

1 How do you feel about using a mobile phone on public transport?

2 What job would you like to do in the future? Why?

3 In what ways are animals used to help people with their work in your country?

4 What forms of exercise did you do when you were at school?

5 What's the area like where you grew up?

6 Would you rather spend time with friends or family? Why?

7 How did you celebrate birthdays when you were a child?

8 What type of ancient objects do you find most interesting? Why?

9 How do you feel when you have a lot of things to do in a short space of time?

10 How important was painting to you when you were at primary school? Why?

11 Do you like the walls in your home to be light or dark? Why?

12 Would you ever want to be a celebrity? Why? / Why not?

Typical Part 1 topics

a Sport and health	g Special occasions
b History	h Colours
c Art and music	i Being busy
d Socialising	j Getting qualifications
e The world of entertainment	k Your home town or city
f Information technology	l Nature

2 Work in pairs. Ask and answer the questions in Exercise 1. Try to use some of these collocations and phrases in your answers.

an integral part	*make a decision (about/to)*
a considerable/huge number/amount	*take advantage (of)*
a wide range of	*do better/well*
many/few opportunities	*have an impact (on)*
outstanding feature(s)	*take an interest (in)*
key aspect(s)	*make the most of*

Part 2: Long turn

Part 2 lasts between three and four minutes. The examiner gives you a topic to talk about. The topic is written down and includes some bullet points to guide you. The examiner also gives you some paper and a pencil. You have one minute to prepare for the talk and two minutes to give the talk. When you have finished, the examiner may ask you a short *yes/no* question about the talk.

You studied and practised Part 2 in Units 2, 3, 4, 5, 6, 7 and 8.

How to do Part 2

1   Listen carefully to the instructions. The examiner will tell you how long you have to prepare and to talk. He/She will also read the first line of the topic to you, before giving you the written instructions.

2   Read the topic carefully, including all the bullet points, which help give you ideas and a structure for your talk.

3   Make full use of the minute's preparation time and write down some key points.

4   Introduce your talk at the start. Link your points together and use an appropriate ending.

5   Don't memorise a talk; the examiner will know if you do.

6   Speak for the full two minutes. You don't need to stop until the examiner says 'Thank you'.

7   If the examiner asks you a short question at the end, you only need to give a very brief answer.

Useful language

Introducing your talk

Well, I'm going to / I'd like to talk about …

The X I'm going to talk about is …

One of the best / most beautiful, etc. X that I've ever seen/heard, etc. is …

Giving a reason / a detail / an explanation

The reason (why) …

I think that's why …

As a result (of) …

In other words, …

What I mean is / By that I mean / That means that …

Plus …

What people do / happens is that …

Introducing a new point

So let me tell you …

The next thing …

As for when/where/who/what/how … , I …

In fact, …

Referring back to something you said earlier in the talk

As I mentioned before, …

As I said earlier, …

Avoiding hesitation

Let me see.

I'm afraid I can't remember.

I meant to say earlier, …

What else?

Future references

I like the idea of …

I wish I could …

Looking ahead, …

I just hope I'll …

As far as I know, …

Introducing an expression or saying

As the saying goes, …

As my mother/friend says, …

Ending the talk

So, all in all, …

In the end, …

So I guess that's …

Why did/do I …?

For me, well, …

Ultimately, …

Exercises

1   **In pairs, read the instructions and the sample topics on page 99 and discuss your ideas.**

2   **Choose a topic and spend a minute making notes on your own.**

3   **Take turns to give your talk. Make sure you talk for the full two minutes.**

Examiner's instructions

Now I'm going to give you a topic and I'd like you to talk about it for one to two minutes. Before you talk, you'll have one minute to think about what you're going to say. You can make some notes if you wish. Do you understand?

Here's a paper and pencil for making notes and here's your topic.

I'd like you to describe an important historical building that you have seen or heard about.

> **Describe an important historical building that you have seen or heard about.**
>
> **You should say:**
> > **what it looks like**
> >
> > **where it is**
> >
> > **what it is used for**
>
> **and explain why this building is important.**

> *I'd like you to describe your ideal home.*

> **Describe your ideal home.**
>
> **You should say:**
> > **what it would look like**
> >
> > **where it would be located**
> >
> > **how easy or difficult it would be to own**
>
> **and explain why it would be ideal for you.**

Part 3: Two-way discussion

Part 3 lasts between four and five minutes. The examiner leads a discussion that is based on the Part 2 topic. You have to give your opinions on general, abstract topics, not personal topics as in Part 1. This is your opportunity to show the examiner the full range of your language.

You studied and practised Part 3 in Units 4, 5, 6, 7 and 8.

How to do Part 3

1 Listen carefully to the instructions and questions. Consider what the examiner is expecting you to do, e.g. give reasons, explain something, compare two things, agree or disagree, speculate, etc.

2 Make sure your replies are relevant and give fully extended answers.

3 Don't use memorised answers, but make sure you know the sort of topics that come up in Part 3 (e.g. environmental issues, language and communications, human relationships, education and learning, etc.) and learn some advanced vocabulary and phrases related to them.

4 Speak clearly so that the examiner can understand you; try to answer the questions as you would in a natural discussion.

5 Remember that there are no right or wrong answers. The examiner is interested in hearing whether you can talk fluently about abstract topics and organise your points in a logical way.

Useful language
Generalising and distancing

I tend to think …

It seems to me …

On the whole, …

Generally/Broadly speaking, / In general, …

Most / The majority of people …

Giving reasons/explaining

The main reason why …

The most obvious example is …

By that I mean …

It's clearly a matter of …

It's all about …

To illustrate, …

Take for instance/example …

Comparing and contrasting (present and past)

Over the centuries, …

Back in (the last century), …

It's like the time when …

We've reached the point now where …

Unlike / In contrast to the situation X years ago, …

Advantages and disadvantages

One of the main advantages/disadvantages (of) …

There are several drawbacks (to) …

X can benefit (from) …

A significant advantage/disadvantage (of) …

X has numerous advantages over Y.

Talking about the future

Looking ahead, …

As far as I can see, …

In the near future, …

There's a slight/reasonable/good chance (that) …

It's quite/very/highly likely/possible (that) …

I have no doubt (that) …

There is every likelihood that …

X may well …

Exercises

1 In pairs, read these instructions and discuss the sample questions. Think about what sort of reply you need to give and write down some useful vocabulary.

> **Examiner's instructions**
>
> *We've been talking about an important historical building and I'd like to ask you one or two more general questions related to this. Let's consider first of all the importance of history.*

> - *How important do you think it is for people to have a sense of their country's history?*
> - *In what ways can schools ensure that children get some experience of their historical past?*

> - *Would you agree that older people tend to be more interested in history than young adults? Why?*

Let's move on to talk about discovering historical items.

> - *What sort of activities can lead to the discovery of historical items?*
> - *What skills or abilities do you think an archaeologist needs?*
> - *What sort of archaeological activities do you think governments should fund in the future?*

2 Ask each other the questions. Try to give extended answers.

How are you rated?

The examiner listens very carefully to your speech and gives you a Band Score from 1 to 9 for the whole test. This means that the three parts are not rated separately. However, there are levels of performance that you need to reach in order to achieve a certain band.

As the examiner is talking to you, he/she considers these questions:

1 Fluency and coherence
How long are your answers? How well can you link your ideas and structure your points?

2 Lexical resource
How varied is your vocabulary? How advanced and accurate is it?

3 Grammatical range and accuracy
How varied and complex are your grammatical structures, and how accurate are they?

4 Pronunciation
How well can you use standard features of pronunciation to enhance communication?

Exercise

Here are some things you should try to do in the Speaking Test. Match each of them (a–h) to one of the questions in the left-hand column (1–4).

a Produce many sentences that do not contain errors.

b Give extended answers in Part 3, without effort.

c Be easily understood, even though you may have an accent.

d Use a wide range of words and phrases, including some advanced collocations and idioms.

e Use a wide range of discourse markers with flexibility.

f Use intonation and stress appropriately.

g Paraphrase effectively when you cannot find the right word or phrase.

h Use a mix of simple and complex sentences.

Preparing for the Speaking Test

Part 1

- Build up a list of words, phrases and collocations that will help you to talk about the topics that are often used in this part of the test.
- Practise making statements about yourself in relation to Part 1 topics, e.g. talk about your likes, dislikes and preferences; your activities and when you do them; what you are studying and why; your favourite shop / animal / type of clothing; things you did as a child; where you would like to live/travel in the future, etc.
- Keep a list of topics and useful words and phrases in a Speaking notebook or file, and add to this list whenever you can.

Part 2

- Practise talking on your own on a topic for two minutes. There are plenty of examples of topics in IELTS practice materials. You can also use the topics in Units 2, 3, 4, 5, 6, 7 and 8 of this book, but think of a different idea from the one you used in the classroom.
- Make a collection of topics for your IELTS preparation. Brainstorm some ideas and vocabulary, and keep a record of this under a topic heading in your notebook.
- Study the model talks in the units. They will show you how to structure a Part 2 talk and how to link ideas. Make a note of any useful vocabulary and linkers.
- Record yourself and practise using some of the Useful language in this section. Also try to include some of the grammatical structures and functions that you have learned on this course, such as second conditionals, advanced comparatives, emphatic structures and

expressions of cause and effect, probability and certainty. When you first practise, allow yourself the time you need.

- As the test date approaches, use Practice Tests and try to spend only a minute preparing for your talk. When the test date is near, make sure you can readily speak for two minutes on a range of topics.

Part 3

- Build up a list of abstract Speaking topics in your notebook and note down some advanced vocabulary that you can use to talk about them. Start by re-reading the articles in this book and checking the relevant Vocabulary reviews. Topics like academic study, health, art, history, technology, the natural world, space, etc. are common Part 3 topics.
- Develop your ideas by reading some articles on international topics such as city life, pollution, psychology, crime, the rich and poor, etc.
- Practise expressing views on topical issues, using some of the structures on page 99. Write a list of questions, with a friend or classmate if possible, and then practise answering them, e.g.:
  1 How can governments encourage citizens to keep their town or city clean?
  2 What are the advantages of a 'home education'?
  3 What forms of pollution do you think will increase in the future?

For all parts, record yourself speaking and ask a teacher / native speaker to point out:

- how clearly you speak;
- whether you need to speak more quickly or slowly;
- any individual sounds or words that you don't pronounce clearly;
- how effectively you group words and phrases;
- how well you use stress to emphasise words;
- whether you need to use more or less intonation.

On the test day

Remember these important points because they may affect your mark.

- **Listen carefully to the examiner's questions and instructions**

  Each answer you give should be relevant. If you can't understand the examiner, ask him/her to repeat the question.

- **Smile at the examiner and look interested**

  Communication works better for everyone if people are interested in what they are saying.

- **Make sure the examiner can hear you**

  If you speak too softly, too quickly or not clearly enough, the examiner may mark you down for pronunciation and may be unable to judge your true language level.

- **Provide enough language for the examiner to assess**

  Examiners can only rate what they hear. Even if you know a lot of English, you won't get a high mark if you don't say enough to demonstrate your true language ability.

- **Use your imagination**

  There are no right or wrong answers to the questions. If you don't have any experience of the Part 2 topic, think about something you have read or seen on television, or make something up. Similarly, if you don't have a view on a Part 3 question, imagine one that someone else might have.

- **Be prepared and be confident**

  The Speaking Test materials are designed to help you talk as much as possible. During the test, the examiner will cover a number of different topics and will encourage you to speak. If you are well prepared, you should feel confident enough to do your best.

Writing reference

What to expect in the exam

The Writing Test is the third paper in the exam and it takes place after the Reading Test.

You do two tasks in one hour:

- Task 1 is a summary of one or more charts or diagrams on the same subject.
- Task 2 is a discursive essay. There is only one topic.

Task 1

In this task, you must summarise and compare information from a graph, chart, table or diagram, or a combination of these.

Your summary must be at least 150 words long. You may write more than this, but if you write less, you will lose some marks. You need to spend about 20 minutes on this task.

You should try to:

- include all the key points;
- include some details or data to support the key points;
- compare relevant features of the information;
- include an overview;
- organise your answer in a logical way;
- use relevant vocabulary;
- use your own words where possible, rather than copying from the question;
- write grammatically correct sentences;
- use accurate spelling and punctuation;
- write in a formal academic style (not bullet points or note form).

You studied and practised Writing Task 1 in Units 1, 3, 5 and 7.

How to do Task 1

1 Read the instructions and study the headings and information carefully. Find at least three key points and decide which features you should compare. (Allow between two and three minutes for this.)

2 Decide how many paragraphs to write and what to put in each one. Decide what will go in your overview. (Allow between two and three minutes for this.)

3 Write your answer, allowing a couple of minutes to check it through afterwards. (Allow 15 minutes for this.)

Graphs, charts and diagrams

There are different types of visual information that you will have to deal with.

1 Graphs that compare figures at different points in time

1 Look at the Writing task below and answer these questions.

1 What do the figures on the vertical axis represent?

2 What periods of time does the graph focus on?

3 How do the first two columns on the chart relate to the rest of the chart?

4 Find three key points that you can compare on the chart.

5 What tenses and verb forms would you use to write your answer?

The chart below gives information about the ageing population worldwide in 2000 and makes predictions for 2050.

Summarise the information by selecting and reporting the main features, and make comparisons where relevant.

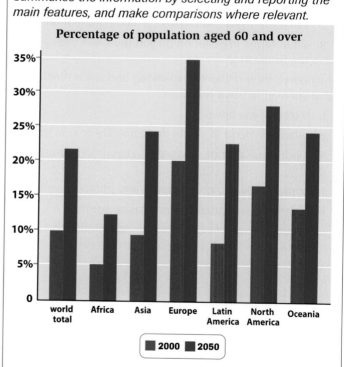

2 Read the sample answer below.

1 Underline the writer's key points.

2 Underline the comparative and superlative structures the writer uses.

> *Introduce the summary using your own words as far as possible.*

> *One approach is to summarise the main trend in one paragraph, then describe this in more detail in the next.*

> *The overview gives an overall picture of the information. It often comes at the end and forms the final paragraph.*

Sample answer

The graph shows how the size and distribution of the world's ageing population is likely to change over a 50-year period.

Overall, the proportions around the world are predicted to rise significantly. In 2000, just under ten percent of the world's population was over 60, but by 2050, this will more than double to approximately 22 percent.

A closer look at the data reveals that the ageing population is expected to rise more in some parts of the world than in others. In 2000, Europe had the largest group of ageing citizens, at 20 percent of its population. The second-largest group could be found in North America and the third in Oceania, while only 5 percent of Africa's population was in this category.

By 2050, Europe is still going to have by far the greatest percentage of over 60s, with figures likely to reach 35 percent. However, the biggest increases in this age group, relative to the rest of the population, are predicted to occur in Asia, Latin America and Africa. In Asia and Latin America, for example, figures will increase almost threefold to between 20 and 25 percent; in Africa, they will more than double.

Although Europe will maintain its lead in terms of its proportion of elderly citizens, the rate of increase in other parts of the world by 2050 will be much more significant.

3 Read the sample answer again and note the verb tenses and forms the writer has used to describe future trends.

2 Charts/tables/graphs that show related information

1 Look at the Writing task below and answer these questions.

1 How are the charts linked?

2 What are the key features of the charts?

3 How would you organise an answer? Why?

> *The table and charts below provide information about the destinations and employment of UK first degree holders.*
>
> *Summarise the information by selecting and reporting the main features, and make comparisons where relevant.*

Destinations of UK graduates by academic year (%)

	2007	2008	2009	2010
full-time employment	64	62	59	63
part-time employment and study	9	8	8	7
further study only	16	17	18	17
not employed	11	13	15	13

Salary bands for 2009/10 graduates in employment that year

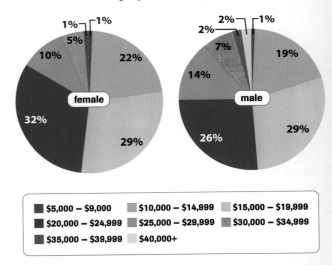

female: 1%, 1%, 5%, 10%, 22%, 32%, 29%

male: 2%, 2%, 1%, 7%, 14%, 19%, 26%, 29%

■ $5,000 – $9,000	■ $10,000 – $14,999	■ $15,000 – $19,999
■ $20,000 – $24,999	■ $25,000 – $29,999	■ $30,000 – $34,999
■ $35,000 – $39,999	■ $40,000+	

2 Read the sample answer on page 104.

1 Which sentence sums up the first key point?

2 Where is the overview?

Sample answer

The table and charts show the study and employment choices of UK graduates over a four-year period and the annual salaries of the 2009/10 group in full-time employment.

According to the table, the pattern in graduate destinations altered very little over this period. The largest category, comprising approximately two-thirds of graduates, found full-time jobs, while 7–9 percent opted for a mix of work and further study. Approximately twice this number continued their studies, while the percentage of graduates not working ranged from 11–15 percent.

Among those 2009/10 graduates who were employed in the UK, the majority were earning between £15,000 and £25,000 per year. Female graduates in the £20,000–£25,000 salary band formed the largest group at 32 percent, and a higher percentage of women than men were employed at lower salary levels. However, 14 percent of male graduates earned £25,000–£30,000 a year compared with only 10 percent of females, and this trend continued as salaries rose.

In summary, many first-degree holders secured jobs after graduation. However, women graduates tended to earn less, on average, than their male counterparts.

3 Read the sample answer again and find words/phrases that mean:

1 did not change much
2 group
3 chose
4 about
5 most
6 bands
7 got work

3 Graphs that show trends over time

1 Look at the Writing in the next column and answer these questions.

1 What are the key features of the data?
2 What comparisons could you make?
3 What should you mention in your overview?

The graph shows the impact of vaccinations on the incidence of whooping cough, a childhood illness, between 1940 and 1990 in Britain.

Summarise the information by selecting and reporting the main features, and make comparisons where relevant.

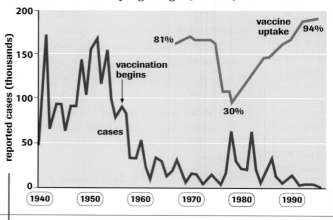

Cases of whooping cough (Britain) 1940–1990

2 Read the sample answer below.

1 How has the writer organised the information?
2 Where is the overview?
3 Which figures are included, and why?

Sample answer

The graph shows the changing number of cases of whooping cough in Britain from 1940 to 1990, and how the introduction and use of a vaccine for the disease affected the pattern. Clearly, there was a direct link between the administration of the vaccine and the number of cases of whooping cough among children during this period in history.

Overall, the number of cases fell from a high of 170,000 to almost zero. However, there were significant fluctuations in the trend. For example, just after 1940, there was a surge in the number of cases from 50,000 to approximately 170,000. Although the figure fell back in the next few years, it peaked again in the early 1950s and fluctuated considerably until the introduction of a vaccination in the late 1950s.

Following this, the number of cases dropped sharply to well below 20,000 in the mid-1970s, until a sudden fall in vaccinations, from 81 percent to 30 percent, resulted in a parallel rise in the incidence of the illness. Figures then went up again to 60,000 around 1980, but gradually fell back to their earlier level as vaccinations were resumed. By 1990, 94 percent of children were being vaccinated against whooping cough, and there were few, if any, cases.

3 Read the answer again and <u>underline</u> the words/ phrases the writer uses to:

1 introduce similarities and differences

2 describe events over time

3 link causes and effects.

4 Diagrams that show a process and/or how something works

1 Look at the Writing task below and answer these questions.

1 What are the key stages in the process? (Explain them to a partner.)

2 What vocabulary could you use in your answer?

3 What comparisons could you make?

4 What would you write in your overview?

The diagram shows the stages in the cultivation and management of a forest.

Summarise the information by selecting and reporting the main features, and make comparisons where relevant.

The life cycle of forest trees

2 Read the sample answer below and <u>underline</u> the words/phrases used to mark the stages in the process.

Sample answer

The diagram illustrates the stages in the creation of a man-made forest and the various uses of the wood that is produced.

> Note how the writer has used a mix of vocabulary from the diagram and original vocabulary.

Before planting can take place, the land must be cleared and prepared. Heavy machinery is used to turn over the soil and ensure that it is ready for young trees. Once this has been done, saplings that have been grown in a nursery are taken to the area and planted individually.

Over time, the young trees start to grow. As they reach a certain height, they are pruned by hand and the forest is thinned. Trees that have been cut down at this stage are used for firewood or to create posts for fences.

The remaining trees gradually reach maturity and are not removed until they are required for wood products. When this happens, individual trees are felled using electrical saws, and prepared for transport on site. The trunks are transported by lorry either to the pulp mill, where they are turned into paper or cardboard, or to the sawmill, where they are dried and cut into planks, to be used for floorboards and furniture. Meanwhile the cleared forest ground is prepared for the planting of new saplings.

Clearly, the agricultural process required to produce wood-based products consists of a number of well-defined stages that allow forest trees to reach a certain age before they are cut down and new forests are planted.

3 Read the answer again and <u>underline</u> the passive verb forms.

Useful language

Starting your answer / Introducing a key point

The graph/chart/table/diagram gives/provides/highlights information about / on / regarding / with regard to …

The graph/chart/table/diagram indicates that / provides a breakdown of …

The diagram illustrates …

According to the graph/chart/table/diagram, …

A closer / more detailed look at X reveals …

Comparing and contrasting

while / on the other hand / however

although

similarly / in contrast / in comparison / unlike …

the next most significant/important/marked

twice/three times as many

double / three times the number

Describing trends

(to experience) a(n) increase/decrease/rise/fall/drop in/of

to increase/decrease/rise/fall/drop by/from … to

to fluctuate

to undergo a change

to remain stable/steady

to stagnate

to dip

to peak

to increase twofold/threefold

to surge

a less/more marked increase/decrease, etc. (occurred / took place)

less/more significant / steady / especially strong growth

a parallel rise/fall

to expect/ predict / forecast

Describing figures

just over/under

a little below/above

slightly more/less than

approximately

not nearly as high/low as

to widen/narrow (e.g. a gap/difference)

Describing amount/extent/categories

a high/low level/incidence of

a large/small quantity of

one aspect/type of

a great/small proportion of

a slow/fast rate (of growth)

to a large/great extent

Summarising the stages in a diagram

after that / following that

before / prior to

once

as

meanwhile

over time / gradually

finally/lastly/eventually

Introducing the overview

Overall / Thus / Clearly / In summary / To summarise

Task 2

This task is in the form of a statement and question(s). There may be more than one part to discuss, and you need to give your own opinion.

Your answer must be at least 250 words long. You can write more than this, but if you write less, you will lose some marks. You need to spend about 40 minutes on this task. There are twice as many marks for Part 2 as for Part 1.

You should try to:

- discuss all the questions or issues in the task;
- present main ideas and provide some supporting ideas or examples;
- include relevant examples from your own experience;
- draw a logical conclusion;
- organise your answer into fully coherent paragraphs;
- link your ideas together in a logical way;
- use your own words where possible and avoid copying from the question;
- write grammatically correct sentences;
- use accurate spelling and punctuation;
- write in a formal academic style.

You studied and practised Writing Task 2 in Units 2, 4, 6 and 8.

How to do Task 2

1   Read the instructions carefully. Decide how many parts there are to the question and underline them. Decide what your view is on the topic. (Allow between two and three minutes for this.)

2   Quickly brainstorm some ideas and write a plan. Make sure you know how many paragraphs to write and what to put in each one. Decide what will go in your conclusion. (Allow between three and four minutes for this.)

3   Write your answer, allowing up to five minutes to check it through afterwards. (Allow about 34 minutes for this.)

Task 2 questions

In addition to writing about a single question or statement, there are other types of task you may have to deal with.

1 To what extent do you agree?

1 Read the Writing task below. What does the statement in the task mean?

a Graduates should get work before they do a second degree.

b Graduates should continue studying if they cannot find a job they want.

c Graduates with second degrees are usually over-qualified for their first jobs.

> *To what extent* means 'how much?'. You can agree completely or disagree completely, or you can present both sides of the argument.

> Write about the following topic.
>
> ***Graduates who cannot find work in their chosen field should be advised to do a second degree, rather than taking a job that does not interest them.***
>
> **To what extent do you agree with this statement?**
>
> Give reasons for your answer and include any relevant examples from your own knowledge or experience.

2 Read the sample answer on the right and complete this plan for the essay.

para. 1	introduction	• 1 Reasons why this happens • Depends on situation
para. 2	main idea supporting idea	• Paying for university • Supported by 2 _____ or a loan • Not good to continue like this
para. 3	main idea supporting idea	• Not enough 3 _____ • May have to wait or start at bottom of 4 _____ • Has advantages, e.g. my father
para. 4	main idea supporting idea	• A 5 _____ for some people • Good idea in today's 6 _____
para. 5	conclusion	• Difficult 7 _____ • Only good advice if part of your career 8 _____

Sample answer

These days, it can be difficult to get a good job when you leave university. Many more students are studying for degrees, so the job market is very competitive. Some people believe that it is better to take a second degree if you cannot secure suitable employment. But I tend to think it depends on your circumstances.

> State your position in the introductory paragraph.

The first consideration is finance. Universities charge high fees for their courses, and in some countries it can cost up to £25,000 to do a first degree. Although some students are fortunate in that their parents can fund their studies, many others have to borrow the money and then repay it when they start working. In my view, it is not a good idea to recommend that these students continue this situation, particularly if they have no real desire to study further.

> Make sure the sentences in each paragraph follow each other logically.

I think we now have to accept that there are not always enough jobs to go round. So the second consideration is that it might be better to be patient, start at the bottom and work your way up the career ladder. This is what my father did, and it definitely gave him a fuller understanding of his chosen field.

> Give a personal example if it is relevant to your main idea.

On the other hand, a second degree may be a natural progression for students who wish to enter a certain profession or to pursue a research-based career. If they can afford the course without getting into debt, it may be advisable for them to carry on with their studies, especially in the current economic climate.

Ultimately, the decision may be a difficult one. However, I feel that those who do not really want to continue studying or cannot afford it should not be encouraged to do so. Unless you had already planned to do a postgraduate course, it could turn out to be much better if you start working, whatever the status or salary.

> Write a final concluding paragraph that sums up your points and re-states your position.

3 Read the sample answer again.

1 How does the writer link the second and third paragraphs?

2 What discourse marker does the writer use to signal that he is moving on to a counter-argument?

4 **How does the writer express these ideas using more advanced vocabulary?**

1 get the right job

2 pay for someone's course

3 do not want to

4 take a low-level job

5 go into a particular type of work

5 **Find four phrasal verbs in the sample answer. What do they mean?**

2 Benefits and drawbacks

1 **Read the Writing task below and answer these questions.**

1 What two points of view are presented in the opening statement? <u>Underline</u> the key words.

2 Which point of view do you agree with most? Why?

> Write about the following topic.
>
> ***Some people believe that technological tools such as body scanners and CCTV have significantly enhanced our safety and security, while others feel that they have resulted in a loss of privacy.***
>
> ***Do the benefits of these items outweigh their disadvantages?***
>
> Give reasons for your answer and include any relevant examples from your own knowledge or experience.

2 **Read the sample answer below, then write a one-sentence summary of the writer's view. Is it the same as your view?**

Sample answer

Information technology has progressed in leaps and bounds over the past few decades. New devices are being designed and upgraded all the time, and it is inevitable that society will want to use them; what is important is how **they** are used. I believe that if they are employed for the right purposes, their benefits outweigh their drawbacks.

No one can deny that CCTV makes many public places safer for people. If youngsters need to travel by train or underground on their own, for example, their parents feel happier knowing that the public are being monitored on the platforms. **This type of surveillance** also reduces anxiety for those travelling in the evening, and has certainly been welcomed by staff working in shops and cafés at night.

Note the writer's use of reference words and phrases to avoid repetition.

Introduce main ideas clearly and then support these with examples and reasons.

Like CCTV, scanners are also used in many situations where the public welcome the heightened security that they provide. Flying is the form of travel that makes people most nervous, so body and luggage scanners can help ease **this concern**. Although **it** can be time-consuming, most passengers do not mind the additional wait as long as the process is efficient.

Having made these points, it is true that every invention receives some criticism, and perhaps **this** is a good thing. It is perfectly possible that the huge amounts of data gathered by CCTV and scanners could be misused by authorities or passed on to other organisations without people's knowledge. **Such uses** would amount to an abuse of personal privacy. If this were to happen, I would agree with the view expressed in the task.

In the end, it is up to us to ensure that technology is used wisely. Generally, **this is what happens**, and people who complain are often too impatient or too short-sighted to see the advantages that it offers. However, **that** does not mean that we should become complacent about it.

Use appropriate language to introduce your arguments.

3 **Read the sample answer again and <u>underline</u> the phrases the writer uses to introduce arguments.**

4 **What do the eight words/phrases in bold refer to?**

3 Two questions

1 **Read the Writing task below and answer these questions.**

1 What does *this* in the first question refer back to?

2 What issues are you likely to write about for each question?

> Write about the following topic.
>
> ***Recent research has confirmed that 'human activity has become the greatest threat to plant and animal life'.***
>
> ***Why do you think this has happened?***
>
> ***How can we reduce our impact on the natural world?***
>
> Give reasons for your answer and include any relevant examples from your own knowledge or experience.

You need to cover both questions, but you do not have to write the same number of words on each one

2 Read the sample answer below. In which paragraphs does the writer deal with each question in the task? How does the writer link his points across paragraphs?

Sample answer

There can be no doubt that human beings have been responsible for loss of wildlife. While we tend to exploit the natural world for our own purposes, some of our ancestors understood their relationship with other species much better. I would argue that it is this sense of harmony with nature that we need to **recapture**.

> Use discourse markers and/ or reference devices to your ideas across paragraphs.

One of the main reasons why certain species of wildlife have become threatened is loss of habitat. As the population of the world has grown, humans have claimed increasingly large areas of land for the construction of homes and cities. An inevitable result has been the removal of plants and trees and the destruction of animal territories.

Increasing urban development has, in turn, led to global warming, which is another contributing factor. Temperature and rainfall are critical to the survival of wildlife. Global warming has resulted in a **shift** in weather patterns, resulting in drought, flooding and heatwaves, all of which **have taken their toll** on the natural world.

> Aim to include some advanced phrases and words.

> A direct question can be a useful device for opening or closing a paragraph.

So what can be done? I believe that the problem has to be **tackled** on a number of levels. As individuals, we should ensure that we treat the countryside with respect, avoid activities that harm animal life and, if possible, participate in projects or donate to charities that work to protect the world around us.

However, it seems that the real work has to be done on a national and international level. What governments need to do in their own countries is to encourage sustainable building practices, limit urban growth and reduce human activities which contribute to global warming. But they also need to sign up to treaties that enable nations to **collaborate** in the protection of the world's diverse species. After all, we cannot live without our flora and fauna.

Many of the threats to plant and animal life are a direct result of human activity, so it is now time to **redress the situation**. If we do not do this, we may be the next species to become endangered.

3 Read the sample answer again and <u>underline</u> the emphatic devices that the writer uses.

4 What do you think the words and phrases in bold mean in the sample essay? Use a dictionary if you need to.

Useful language

Giving your opinions / expressing attitude

In my view/opinion, …

From my point of view, …

(Personally,) I tend to think/believe/feel that …

I would argue that / I tend to think that …

I am not sure I agree with/that …

I tend not to believe that …

As far as I'm concerned, …

Arguably / As a matter of fact / Interestingly / Clearly / To a certain extent, …

Introducing arguments

The main argument in favour of / against …

It is (certainly) true that …

It is (generally) believed/felt that …

The general view is / has been that …

Experts/Professionals would argue/say that …

Presenting reasons/examples

One of the main reasons why …

The main reason why …

There are a number of reasons why/for …

For this reason, …

Presenting a counter argument

Having said that / made this point / these points, …

Despite / In spite of this, …

Expressing purpose

with the aim of / in order to / so as to

Expressing cause and effect

due to / otherwise

as a result/consequence / with the result that / resulting in

Emphasising

What we/people/governments need to / should do is …

All that X needs to / should do is …

It is X that …

Drawing a conclusion

Overall, … / All in all, …

Ultimately, … / In the end, …

How are you rated?

The two tasks are rated separately, but Task 2 is worth twice as many marks as Task 1. The marks are combined to produce one Band Score from 1 to 9 for the whole test.

There are levels of performance that you need to reach in order to achieve a certain band.

The examiner considers the following questions:

Task 1

- Have you understood the task and the data/diagram?
- Have you highlighted all the key points/trends?
- Have you included important data?
- Is there an overview?

Task 2

- Have you understood the task?
- Have you covered all the parts/questions in the task?
- Is your position clear and consistent?
- Have you presented relevant main and supporting ideas?
- Have you drawn a logical conclusion?

Both tasks

- How well have you organised the answer into paragraphs? Is there a range of linkers and appropriate discourse markers? Have you used sufficient referencing devices?
- How advanced is your vocabulary, and how accurate is it?
- Can you use a range and variety of grammatical structures? How accurate are they?

Preparing for the Writing Test

- For Task 1, practise summarising the information in a range of different charts and diagrams. For Task 2, practise writing arguments on a range of different topics.
- Before you write, brainstorm some ideas and then organise them into paragraphs. The sample answers in the units and in this Writing reference have been written to show you how to structure an answer and how to link ideas.
- Try to use some of the advanced grammatical structures that you have learned on this course, e.g. second and third conditionals, clauses of purpose, cause and effect, emphatic structures, etc.

On the test day

Remember these important points because they affect your mark.

Task 1

- **Make sure you fully understand the data.**

  Study the task first and make sure you understand it.

  - If it is a graph or chart, look carefully at the axes, labels and any keys.
  - If it is a table, look at all the headings.
  - If it is a diagram, look at all the steps or stages and get a mental image of the process or structure.

- **Include the key points**

  Decide on at least three key points and make sure you highlight these in your answer.

- **Include data and make sure they are accurate**

  Make sure that the figures or details that you include to illustrate your key points are accurate.

- **Include an overview of the information**

  The overview is like a conclusion and it gives your reader a simple picture of what the graphic shows overall. It is not the same as the introduction, which states what the information is about. The overview usually goes at the end of the answer, but it doesn't have to. As long as it is there, you will get credit for it. If it is not there, you will lose marks.

Task 2

- **Make sure you understand the question**

  Take time to read the question very carefully. Underline the parts you have to write about and ask yourself:

  - What is the main topic?
  - How many parts are there?
  - Do I need to present arguments for and against?
  - What is my opinion?

- **Introduce your essay**

  The introduction sets the scene for your reader. It tells them what you are going to discuss, what the issues are, and often what your position is.

- **Make your opinion on the topic clear to the reader**

  Decide on your view and state this, either in the introduction or during the course of your essay. Keep your position clear and don't change it.

- **Include some main ideas**

  Decide on at least three main ideas and some supporting points. Build your paragraphs around your main ideas. Ideas can come from other people's opinions, your own opinions, facts, etc.

  Make sure the sentences in each paragraph follow on logically from each other. If they do not, you will lose marks.

  Make sure the paragraphs are linked to each other, using appropriate discourse markers or vocabulary.

- **Include some personal experience if it is relevant**

- **Draw a logical conclusion**

  At the end of your essay, you need to write one or two sentences that summarise your arguments and your point of view.

Language reference

Attitude adverbials

Attitude adverbials consist of a word or phrase which:

- is normally placed at the beginning of the sentence
- is normally followed by a comma (see *Using commas* on page 121)
- expresses the writer's attitude to what he/she is going to say in the sentence: **Surprisingly**, *many people believe that dogs cannot see colours.* (The writer is saying he finds it surprising that many people believe this.)

Attitude adverbials may express:

- a feeling or emotion:
  Sadly, *few students have applied for the grant.*
- a context:
  Generally speaking, *grants are only given to post-graduate students.*
  Of course, *this is not true in all cases.*
- an attitude:
  Frankly, *I think people should take more care of their pets.*
- an opinion:
  As far as I'm concerned, *all public buildings should be decorated in bright colours.*
- emphasis:
  As a matter of fact, *colour blindness is more common among men than women.*
  Actually, *it affects about 8% of men in North America, whereas only 0.5% of women are affected.*

Attitude adverbials can sometimes come between the object and the verb. Note the use of commas before and after the adverbial when it is not in the usual position in the sentence:

He was, **surprisingly**, *very upset* = **Surprisingly**, *he was very upset.*

Dependent prepositions

Many verbs, nouns and adjectives are followed by a particular preposition:

In his lecture, Dr Patel **focused on** *genetic variations in fruit flies.*

There are no clear rules to help you decide which preposition should follow a particular word; the best strategy is to learn the preposition with the word.

You should use a dictionary to check how words and prepositions are used. Look at this example from the *Cambridge Advanced Learner's Dictionary* (*CALD*):

> apologize, UK USUALLY apologise /əˈpɒl.ə.dʒaɪz/ /əˈpɑː.lə.dʒaɪz/ verb [I]
> to tell someone that you are sorry for having done something that has caused them inconvenience or unhappiness:
> *I must* **apologize to** *Isobel for my lateness.*
> *She* **apologized** *profusely* **for** *having to leave at 3.30 p.m.*

The examples show that you can apologise *for* something which went wrong. You apologise *to* the person you are addressing.

Remember: a preposition must be followed by a noun, noun phrase, pronoun or verb + *-ing*:

He apologised to me for damaging my car.

For a list of common verbs, adjectives and nouns and their dependent prepositions, see page 123.

Emphasising

We emphasise things to show that they are particularly important or worth giving attention to. Two common ways of emphasising are fronting and cleft sentences.

Fronting

We often place information at or near the beginning of a sentence to emphasise it. To do this, we have to alter the normal word order of the sentence. We can do this by:

- placing the complement or direct object of a verb before the subject. Compare these sentences:
  We know quite a lot about the Moon and Mars. We have less information about Venus.
  We know quite a lot about the Moon and Mars. Venus, we have less information about.
- placing the subordinate clause before the main clause. Compare these sentences:
  NASA has sent a spacecraft to Mars because they want to find out if there is life there.
  Because they want to find out if there is life on Mars, NASA has sent a spacecraft there.
- placing preposition and adverb phrases that are not part of another phrase before the subject of the sentence. Compare these sentences:
  There is a lot of interest in space exploration despite its cost.
  Despite its cost, there is a lot of interest in space exploration.

Cleft sentences

These are some ways of forming cleft sentences:

- *What* + subject + auxiliary verb + *is/was* + infinitive with/without *to*:
  The Chinese sent a probe to the Moon. → **What** *the Chinese* **did was to send** *a probe to the Moon.*

People don't think about the level of planning that is involved. → ***What** people **don't think** about **is** the level of planning that is involved.*

- *What + subject + main verb + is/was + infinitive with to:*
  Space explorers want to find water on other planets. → ***What** space explorers **want is to find** water on other planets.*

- *It + is/was + noun/noun phrase + (that):*
  The astronauts enjoyed the space walk most. → ***It was** the space walk **that** the astronauts enjoyed most.*

- *All (that) + subject + verb + is/was:*
  We only require political will to set up a permanent base on the Moon. → ***All (that)** we require to set up a permanent base on the Moon **is** political will.*

Expressing large and small differences
We can use words and phrases with comparative forms to express large and small differences.

Expressing large differences
We can say there is a large difference between one thing and another with the following patterns:

- *much/far/a lot/considerably + adjective/adverb + -er more + adjective/adverb:*
  *Scientists have found that eating fish is **far healthier** than eating red meat.*
  *Health risks for overweight people are **considerably more substantial** than for people whose weight is normal.*

- *not nearly as + adjective/adverb + as:*
  *The British do **not** eat **nearly as much** fish **as** the Spanish.*

Expressing small differences
We can express small differences between one thing and another using these patterns:

- *slightly / a bit / a little + adjective/adverb + -er/more + adjective/adverb:*
  ***Slightly lower** speed limits have led to considerable reductions in traffic accidents. Scientists have found that by eating **a little more slowly**, stress levels are significantly reduced.*

- *not quite as + adjective/adverb + as:*
  *The graph shows that consumption of chocolate was **not quite as high** in 2012 **as** in 1992.*

- *nearly/almost as + adjective/adverb + as:*
  *Coffee drinking was **nearly as** popular in 2011 **as** in 2010.*

Quantifying differences
We can quantify differences exactly using these patterns:

- *a quarter, one-and-a-half times, twice, three times, 30%, etc. + as much/many as:*

*A house in London may cost **twice as much as** a house in the north of England.*
*A house in the north of England may cost **half as much as** a house in London.*
*A house in the north of England may cost **50% as much as** a house in London.*

- three times, four times, 50%, etc. + more/greater, etc. than:
  *Fuel prices in Western Europe are on average **40% higher than** in North America.*

- a quarter, one-and-a-half times, double, three times, etc. + the number/amount + of + as:
  *The British import **three times the amount of** sugar **as** the Portuguese.*
  *The Portuguese import **a third the amount of** sugar **as** the British.*

Note the use of *as* not *than*:

Men can eat two-and-a-half times the number of calories ~~than~~ ***as*** *women.*

Saying things have no similarity
We can say that things have no similarity by saying:

- X *is completely/totally/entirely/quite different from/to* Y:
  *The Chinese medical system **is completely different from** the American one.*

- X *and* Y *are not the same at all* / X *and* Y *bear no similarity to each other*:
  *The Chinese and American medical systems **bear no similarity to each other**.*

Expressing purpose, cause and effect
We can use the following words/phrases to express or introduce:

- a purpose:
  - *with the aim/purpose/intention of ...:*
    *The law was introduced **with the intention of** encouraging more young people into higher education.*

  - *The aim/purpose/intention (of ...) is/was to ...:*
    ***The purpose of** the experiment **was to** see whether the disease had a genetic component.*

  - *so as to / in order to:*
    *The entrance was altered **so as to** make wheelchair access easier.*

  - *so / so that:*
    *He studies at night **so** (that) he can work during the day.*

- a cause:
  - *The cause of X is/was ...:*
    ***The cause of** children's failure to learn maths is often poor teaching at school.*

  - X *is/was caused by ...:*
    *The increase in unemployment **has been caused by** the financial crisis.*

- *due to / owing to / because of*:
  *Some people argue that children are neglected **due to** their parents working long hours.*
- an effect:
  - *with the effect/result/consequence that …*:
    *The Tate Gallery held an exhibition of Bardega's work **with the result that** it instantly became more valuable.*
  - *consequently / as a consequence / in consequence*:
    *The cave paintings were discovered 20 years ago, and **in consequence**, the whole area now attracts more tourists.*
  - *result in + noun/verb + -ing*:
    *The large numbers of people visiting the cave **have resulted in** the paintings **fading** and **losing** their fresh, bright colours.*

We can use *otherwise* to express an alternative effect to the one which occurs/occurred. It is often used with:

- an order or suggestion in the future:
  *You'd better fill up with petrol, **otherwise** we won't get there.*
- a second or third conditional (see *Speaking hypothetically* on page 118): *Fortunately, the hotel had a free room, **otherwise** we **would have had** to sleep in the railway station.*

(See also *Using participle clauses to express consequences* on page 121.)

Generalising and distancing

We have a number of ways of talking in general, or making general points that may not be true for every case. These may also soften your tone and distance you from the argument. (This is considered good academic style.)

We can use:

- attitude adverbials (see page 112), e.g. *on the whole, in general, broadly speaking, generally speaking, generally, by and large, as a rule, in most cases, on average*:
  ***By and large**, artists don't make much money from their art.*
  ***As a rule**, art is a greater part of the curriculum in primary schools than in secondary schools.*
- verbs and phrases, e.g. *tend, seem, appear, have a tendency, be liable, are likely + infinitive*:
  *Small children **tend to be** more creative than adults.*
  *Art works **have a tendency to increase** in price when the artist dies.*
  *Children **are liable to get** frustrated when they can't express their feelings.*

Introducing arguments

Introducing other people's ideas/arguments

We can introduce ideas and arguments which we do not necessarily agree with using these phrases:

- It can be argued that:
  ***It can be argued that** sport is more important than art in the school curriculum.*
- It is (generally/often/usually/sometimes, etc.) claimed/ suggested/argued/said that:
  ***It is often suggested that** young children have more facility for learning languages than adults.*
- … is/are (generally/often/usually/sometimes, etc.) believed/felt/understood/claimed/thought to be:
  *Women **are often thought to be** better at multi-tasking than men.*
- Some / Many / Most / The majority of people/teachers/ experts, etc. argue/suggest/believe/claim/say/agree/ think/feel/take the view that:
  ***Most experts agree that** children should start their formal education from the age of three.*

Note how the modals, verbs and adverbs in these examples soften the writer's tone and make the argument more thoughtful and less assertive. This is good academic style.

Introducing our own arguments and opinions

We can introduce our opinions using these phrases (we can use *personal/personally* to emphasise that the opinion may not be shared by other people):

I (personally) (tend to) think/feel/believe that …

I (personally) agree with X that …

In my (personal) opinion / From my point of view, …

My (personal) feeling / belief / opinion / view / point of view is that …

I (personally) (would) take the view that …

My (personal) opinion is that …

I (personally) would argue/suggest that …

I (personally) (would) agree with the view/idea/suggestion that …

***I personally would suggest that** adults are just as capable of learning languages as children if they make enough effort.*

Note: unlike other people's arguments, personal arguments have a very strong tone in an essay and should, therefore, not be used too often.

Negative affixes

Affixes are letters or groups of letters added to the beginnings or ends of words to form other words. Affixes added at the beginning of a word are called prefixes. Those added at the end of a word are suffixes.

Note: when we add a negative affix, we do not normally change the spelling of the original word. For example, when we add *dis-* to the adjective *satisfied*, the new word is *dissatisfied*. When we add *-less* to *hope*, the new word is *hopeless*.

We can add these affixes to give words a negative meaning:

affix	meaning	examples
anti-	opposed to, against	*anti-social, anti-virus*
de-	the opposite of, remove, reduce	*decaffeinated, decelerate*
dis-	added to words to form the opposite	*disadvantage*
in- *il-* (before *l*) *im-* (before *b, m* and *p* *ir-* (before *r*)	lacking, not, the opposite of	*inexact* *illegal* *impatient* *irrelevant*
-less	without	*meaningless, careless*
mal-	badly, wrongly	*malfunction, malpractice*
mis-	badly, wrongly	*mispronounce, misinterpret*
non-	not, the opposite of	*non-fiction, non-existent*
over-	above, more than, too much	*overflow, overcrowded*
un-	not, lacking, the opposite of	*untidy*
under-	not enough	*underestimate*

Past simple, present perfect simple and past perfect simple

We use the past simple tense to describe:

- something that happened at a specific time in the past:
  *Alexander Fleming **discovered** penicillin in 1928.*

- a state at a specific time in the past:
  *At the time of the American Declaration of Independence, the United States **consisted** of just 13 states.*

- things which happened over a period of time in the past, but not now:
  *The number of overseas students in Canadian universities **rose** between 2008 and 2011.*

- actions or events which happened one after the other:
  *They **dug** the foundations, then they **built** the walls and finally they **put** on the roof.*

When we use the past simple, the past time is usually stated (*yesterday, while he was a student, in the 18ᵗʰ century, etc.*) or clear from the context (*Did you give your tutor that essay?* (i.e. when you saw him)).

We use the present perfect tenses to describe:

- past events, if we do not say exactly when they happened, or if the past time is not implied by the speaker:
  *Brazil **has won** the World Cup several times.*

- a past event which has a result in the present:
  *Scientific research **has led** to the discovery of an important new antibiotic.*

- something which started in the past and is still happening now:
  *The authorities **have been working** on this project for six months* (and they're still working on it).

We use the present perfect with time adverbs that connect the past to the present, *e.g. just, already, lately, since, so far, up to now, yet*:
*Figures **have risen since** 2005.*
***So far**, little **has been done** to improve the situation.*
*There **has been** a lot in the news about this issue **lately**.*

The past perfect simple tense is used:

- to indicate that we are talking about an action which took place, or a state which existed, **before** another activity or situation in the past (which is described in the past simple):
  *When I **got** to the lecture theatre, the class **had** already **started**.*
  (Compare this with *When I **got** to the lecture theatre, the class **started**.* This indicates that the class started when I arrived.)

- typically with time expressions like: *when, as soon as, after, before, it was the first time, etc.*:
  *The number of students went up for ten consecutive years. **It was the first time** I'd ever **flown**.*

- with *by* + a time:
  ***By 2010**, it **had risen** to over 15,000.*

- with these adverbs: *already, just, never*:
  *Dimitri **had already done** a degree in biology when he decided to study medicine.*

Phrasal verbs

Phrasal verbs are formed from:

1 verb + adverb particle, e.g. *read on* (continue reading):
  *After you've read the introduction, you need to **read on** till you find the answer.*

2 verb + preposition, e.g. *get into* (enter):
  *You'll need high grades to **get into** university.*

3 verb + adverb particle + preposition, e.g. *come up with* (suggest or think of an idea or plan):
  *It was Einstein who **came up with** the theory of relativity.*

Phrasal verbs often have meanings which are not clear from their component parts:

get over = recover from

1 Verb + adverb particle

These verbs may be:

a intransitive, i.e. they don't have an object:
*She doesn't earn a lot of money, but she **gets by**.* (manages to live)

b transitive, i.e. they have an object:
*You should **back up** your ideas with examples.* (support)
(Here, *your ideas* is the object.)

With transitive verbs, when the object is:

- a noun, the noun can come between the verb and the adverb particle:
*You should **back your ideas up** with examples.*

- a pronoun, it **must** come between the verb and the adverb particle:
*My ideas are unconventional, but I know you'll **back them up**.* Not: ~~I know you'll back up them.~~

2 Verb + preposition

These verbs are always transitive, i.e. they always have an object. The object (noun or pronoun) always comes after the preposition:
*I always **go over** my notes at the end of lectures.* (check)
Not: ~~I always go my notes over at the end of lectures.~~

3 Verb + adverb particle + preposition

These three-part phrasal verbs are always transitive, i.e. they have an object. The object always comes after the three parts:
*Let's **get down to work**.* (start to direct your efforts towards something)

A good learner's dictionary will tell you which type of phrasal verb each is. Look at these extracts from the *CALD*:

> **go down** (BE REDUCED) phrasal verb
> to be reduced in price, value, amount, quality, level or size:
> *The temperature went down to minus ten.*

No object is indicated in the definition, so this phrasal verb is type 1a (verb + adverb particle, intransitive).

> **note sth down** phrasal verb
> to write something so that you do not forget it:
> *I noted down his phone number.*

The object (*sth* = something) is placed between the verb and the adverb particle, so this is type 1b (verb + adverb particle, transitive). *I noted his phone number down* is also correct.

> **deal with sth** (TAKE ACTION) phrasal verb
> to take action in order to achieve something or in order to solve a problem:
> *How do you intend to deal with this problem?*

The object (*sth* = something) is placed after the two parts of the verb, so this is type 2 (verb + preposition).

> **put up with sth/sb** phrasal verb
> to accept or continue to accept an unpleasant situation or experience, or someone who behaves unpleasantly:
> *I can put up with the house being untidy, but I hate it if it's not clean.*

This definition has an adverb particle and a preposition before the object (*sth/sb* = something or somebody), so this is a three-part phrasal verb (type 3).

Note: transitive phrasal verbs can have a noun/noun phrase as an object, or in many cases verb + -*ing*:
*The majority of young smokers **give up smoking** in their 30s.*

An exception to this is *turn out*, which is followed by the infinitive:
*The charity event **turned out to be** much more successful than the organisers had hoped.*

Prepositions with advantages and disadvantages

We can express advantages and disadvantages with these words and dependent prepositions:

- **advantage/disadvantage**
  - **of** a situation/circumstance/action
  - **for** someone/something affected by the advantage/disadvantage
  *The **advantage for** young people of knowing how to drive is that they are more independent.*
  *For dancers, the **disadvantage of** having big feet is that you may step on other people's toes.*

- **give/have an advantage over** someone/something:
  *Cycling **has several advantages over** driving; for example, you don't have to find somewhere to park the car.*

- **benefit** (noun)
  - **of** a situation/circumstance/action
  - **to/for** someone/something affected by the benefit
  *The **benefit of** work experience to young people is that they learn things they wouldn't learn at college.*

- **benefit** (verb) **from** a situation/circumstance/action
  *Francesca's health has **benefited from** the fresh sea air.*

- **be of benefit to** someone/something affected by the benefit (expression)
  *I hope this book will **be of benefit to** you.*

- **drawback**
  - **of** a situation/circumstance/action
  - **for** someone/something affected by the drawback
  *The **drawback of** modern medicine for governments is its high cost.*

Note: The phrases *pros and cons* and *ups and downs* are informal and best avoided in written work.

Referencing

We can use referencing devices to refer to things mentioned earlier and in this way avoid repeating them. Good writers make use of a mix of reference devices and linkers.

Pronouns

- We use *they/them* for people in the singular when we are talking in general about males and females, but we cannot specify their gender:
  *When a **child** plays a computer game, ~~he/she~~ **they** are often training ~~his/her~~ **their** reflexes.*

- We use *it, this, that, they, these, those, such* to refer to the things last mentioned:
  ***Technology companies are continually innovating** to stay ahead of the competition. **This** means that any device you buy is likely to be obsolete quite soon.*

Which pronoun: it, this *or* that?

We use *it, this* and *that* (in the plural *they, these* and *those*) to refer to something we have already mentioned. Often more than one of them is correct in the context. However:

- we use *it* when we are not making any emphasis:
  The participants found the introduction to the experiment rather unclear. It didn't really help them understand what they had to do.

- *this* and *that* are more emphatic in drawing attention to the thing just mentioned:
  *A new system of tagging was devised, and **this** gave the researchers a much better picture of the birds' migration patterns.*

- we often use *this* when:
  - we still have something more to say about the thing we are referring to: *We've recommended opening an office in Belgrade. **This** will be discussed at the Board meeting next month.*

    *Many of our staff have been off sick this month. **This** has meant that we have fallen behind with our orders.*

    *Scientists have come up with a new feature for the space probe. **This** will be demonstrated next month.*

    *Leaders have been unable to agree on the best strategy. **This** has delayed proceedings.*

  - we refer to the second of two things mentioned in the previous sentence. Compare:
  1 *The severe drought has resulted in a poor harvest. **This** has led to famine in certain parts of the country.* (this = a poor harvest)
  2 *The severe drought has resulted in a poor harvest. **It** has also affected livestock.* (it = the severe drought)

- we often use *that* in conditional sentences:
  *It would be good to experience both lifestyles if **that** were possible.*

- *That* is often used when giving reasons:
  ***The children spent all day in front of the television** and **that's** why we decided to throw it away.*

Note: we use *this, that, they, these, those, such* + collective noun/noun phrase to refer back to something previously mentioned:
*People feel the new software is expensive and hard to navigate. **Such** criticisms are seriously affecting sales.* (criticisms = expensive and hard to navigate)

*The children showed courage and compassion during the experiment. **These** qualities were considered unusual for students of such a young age.* (qualities = courage and compassion)

One, another, the ones, the other, the others, both, neither, all, none

- We use *one* to refer to singular countable nouns from a group:
  *There are **a lot of good tablet PCs** on the market now. **The one** I use is quite expensive but very versatile.*

- We use *a(n)/the … one* with an adjective:
  *There are several modern word-processing programmes, so I don't know why they're still using **an old one**.*

- We use *another* to refer to the second, third, etc. singular countable noun from a group:
  ***One app** gives you a weather forecast, while **another** brings you your favourite radio station.*

- We use *ones* to avoid repeating a plural noun:
  *She has **several mobile phones** and she keeps **the ones** she's not using in a drawer in the kitchen.*

- We use *the other* when referring to the second of two things/people already mentioned:
  *Pam has two cars: **one** is a Ferrari and **the other** is a Rolls.*

- We use *the others* when referring to the rest of a number of things/people already mentioned:
  ***Three of my classmates** went abroad to study, whereas **the others** stayed in my country.*

- We use *both* and *neither* to refer to two things/people:
  *He's got **two houses**. **Both** are by the sea; **neither** was very expensive.*

- We use *all* and *none* to refer to more than two things/people:
  *Tanya has **three computers**. **All** of them are old and **none** of them works.*

Using so

- We use *so* to avoid repeating a clause:
  *'Have you met my brother, Joe?' 'I think **so**.'* (= I think I've met him.)

- We use *do(ing) so* to avoid repeating a verb + the words which follow:
  *City planners decided to widen the highway without considering the disadvantages of **doing so**.* (= widening the highway)

Speaking hypothetically (including overview of conditionals)

We can talk about hypothetical situations and events – i.e. ones which are imaginary, theoretical or contrary to the facts – by using the second and third conditionals, or a combination of both.

	form	refers to
2nd conditional	*If* + past tense, *would/could/might* + infinitive without *to*: **If** the necklace **wasn't** so old, it **wouldn't** be valuable. (The necklace is old, and for that reason it is valuable.)	present time
3rd conditional	*If* + past perfect, *would/could/might* + *have* + past participle: **If** my aunt **hadn't travelled** to India, she **would** never **have acquired** the necklace. (My aunt did travel to India, and for that reason she acquired the necklace.)	past time

Note: we can combine second and third conditionals if one part of the sentence refers to the present and the other part refers to the past:

        3rd conditional   2nd conditional

If she **had passed** *the exam last summer, she* **would be** *at university now.*

     2nd conditional   3rd conditional

If I **couldn't speak** *French, I* **wouldn't have been given** *the job.*

These are sometimes called **mixed conditionals**.

Other ways of expressing second and third conditionals

- We can use these more formal phrases instead of *if*: *on (the) condition (that), providing/provided (that)*:

  She would only accept the position **on condition that** *she was given the contract in writing.*

- To be more emphatic, we can use *as long as* or *even if*:
  Consumers would always buy a second-hand car **as long as** *it hadn't been in an accident.*

  Even if *there were fines, people would still drop litter.*

- Instead of *if* + negative, we can use *unless*:
  As a child, I **wouldn't go** *swimming* **unless** *the sea was warm.*

Second conditionals – alternative constructions

We can use these constructions to express second conditionals:

- To express an unlikely conditional:
  If /Unless + subject + *were* + infinitive:

  If I were to sell *the necklace, I'd probably get a lot of money.*

- To say 'if someone/something didn't exist':
  If it were not for + noun:

  If it weren't for *my smart phone, I'd never keep in touch with all my friends.*

- To emphasise 'if someone/something didn't exist':
  Were it not for + noun:

  Were it not for *Julie, we'd never finish the project.*

Third conditionals – alternative constructions

- To emphasise a third conditional:
  Had + subject + (*not*) + past participle:

  Had *we* **had** *more time, we would have been able to finish the work.*

  Had *he* **not called** *the office, he wouldn't have found out about the meeting.*

- To say 'if someone/something hadn't existed':
  if it hadn't been for + noun:

  I couldn't have written the article **if it hadn't been for** *his research.*

- To emphasise 'if someone/something hadn't existed':
  Had it not been for + noun:

  Had it not been for *Saleem's help, I wouldn't have known how to address the problem.*

Speculating and talking about the future

- We can use the phrases in the table on page 119 to express our thoughts and opinions about the future and how certain we feel about them.
- Note carefully the adjective and adverb collocations (e.g. we say *highly unlikely* but not *high likelihood*) which are used with each phrase.

	phrase	example
very certain	• It's highly/very/extremely likely/unlikely that ... • There's little/no doubt that ... • I very much doubt whether/that ... • There's every / a strong likelihood that ... • ... is bound to ... • It's very possible/probable that ...	**It's highly unlikely that** we'll be able to prevent the Arctic ice from melting. **There's little doubt that** the climate is changing. **I very much doubt that** we shall be able to reverse the process of global warming. **There's every likelihood** that man will return to the Moon in the near future. Space travel **is bound to** continue. **It's very probable that** tigers will become extinct in the wild.
moderately certain	• ... is (quite) likely to ... • ... may/might/could well ... • It's quite/fairly likely/unlikely that ... • ... will probably ... • There's a strong possibility that ... • There's a good/fair/reasonable chance that ...	Governments **are likely to** reach a new agreement on carbon emissions in the future. In 20 years, all cars **may well** be electric. **It's fairly unlikely** that the Antarctic ice cap will melt completely. Space tourism **will probably** become quite common. **There's a strong possibility that** environmental policies will dominate politics in the future. **There's a fair chance that** severe storms will become more common.
neither certain nor uncertain	• ... may/might/could (possibly) ... • There's a possibility/chance that ...	We **could possibly** experience the coldest winter on record next winter. **There's a chance that** sea levels won't rise very much.
very uncertain	• There's little / almost no chance/ likelihood of/that ... • There's a slight possibility that ...	**There's little likelihood of** western societies abandoning consumerism. **There's a slight possibility that** the whole environmental situation will improve one day.

Superlative forms

We form superlatives by adding:

- *the* + adjective/adverb + *-est* to one-syllable adjectives and adverbs and two-syllable adjectives ending in *–y*, *-le*, *-er*, *-ow*:
  *They all work hard, but René works **the hardest**.* (adverb)
  *Mateu is **the cleverest** student in my class.* (adjective)

- *the most* to all other two-syllable adjectives, all adjectives with more than two syllables and all adverbs with two or more syllables:
  *Fleming made one of **the most important** discoveries of the 20th century.*

To say something is less than everything else, we use *the least* with all adjectives and adverbs:
The least dangerous *animal on the chart is the rhinoceros.*

Note: we use *least* with amounts, but *lowest* with numbers:
*The 60–75 age group ate **the least** amount of food.*

*Men in their 70s engaged in **the ~~least~~ lowest** number of calls.*

We can make comparisons using superlatives by using *the second*, *the third*, *the fourth*, etc.:

*The chart shows that **the second most important** reason for emigrating is work.*

To express a big difference between the largest, most important, etc., we use *by far*, *much*:
*Getting useful qualifications is **by far the most important** reason for studying abroad.*

*The job was **much harder** than I expected.*

To say something is a little less than the largest, most important, etc., we use *nearly*, *almost*, *not quite*:
*It is **not quite the oldest** university in the country.*

To say something is part of a group of the largest, most important, etc., we use *one of* and *among*:
*Abba is **one of my least favourite** groups.*

*The Komodo dragon is **among the largest** reptiles in the world.*

Note: we say *least favourite* to mean the opposite of *favourite*, but we do not use *most* with this adjective:
~~most~~ *favourite*.

Talking about ambitions and aspirations

- To talk about things we have wanted to do very much for a long time, we can use *dream of*:
  *He **dreams of** becoming a top medical researcher.*

- To say we feel pleased or excited about something we think is going to happen, we can use *look forward to* (three-part phrasal verb):
  *I'm **looking forward to** my summer holidays.*

- To talk about something good that we think will happen in the future, or that we feel confident will happen in the future, we can use *hope*:
  *Kioshi **hopes** to study medicine in Brisbane next year.*
  *I **hope** that I will be able to work abroad after I graduate.*

- To say we think something will happen, we can use:
  - *expect*:
    *Anita **expects** to be promoted at the end of the month.*
  - *be likely to*:
    *The job **is likely to** be quite challenging.*

- To say what we want for the future, we can use:
  - *want*:
    *I **want** to become a doctor.*
  - *would like*:
    *Pandora **would like** to get a place at Yale.*

- To say there is something we want for the future, but which we think is unlikely or impossible, we can use *I wish I could / I wish you/he/she/they would*:
  *I **wish I could** study at Harvard, but I cannot afford it.*
  *I **wish they would** increase student grants.*

  Note that *wish* is followed by *would* or *could*, whereas *hope* is followed by the infinitive or a present, future or past tense.

- To say we do not think something will happen, we can use:
  - *don't expect*:
    *I **don't expect** to finish in the first three in the race.*
  - *unlikely*:
    *She's **unlikely** to be elected to the student council.*

Use and non-use of articles

The indefinite article a/an

We use *a/an* with something general or non-specific, or when we refer to something for the first time:
*Can I borrow **a** pen? (= any pen)*
*Dr Sykes gave **a** lecture on 19th-century porcelain.*

We also use *a/an* to:

- refer to someone's job or function:
  *She's **a** physiotherapist.*

- mean *one*:
  *The flat has **a** sitting room and two bedrooms.*

The definite article the

We use *the*:

- when we know what is being discussed, e.g. it may be something specific, it may have been mentioned before, or there may be only one of it:
  ***The** university is holding **the** seminar next Wednesday.*
  (= the university we study at, the seminar we have already mentioned)

- with plural countable nouns to refer to something known, something specific or to something that has been mentioned before:
  *An experiment was carried out on 500 school children. **The** children were divided into two groups.*

- with superlative and other similar adjectives:
  ***The** most surprising result was also the most significant.*
  *We didn't know what would happen until **the** final moment.*

- in *the … the* comparative structures:
  ***The** harder you study, **the** more you'll learn.*

- with the following names:
  - a few countries:
    ***the** United States, **the** Netherlands.*

  Note: Most countries are used without articles: *England, China.*

  - rivers, seas and oceans, island groups, mountain ranges and deserts:
    ***the** Amazon, **the** Black Sea, **the** Pacific, **the** Bahamas, **the** Alps, **the** Sahara*

  Note: individual islands and mountains have no article: Majorca, Everest.

No article

We don't use an article:

- with plural countable nouns and uncountable nouns with a general meaning or when we are generalising:
  ***Behaviour** is very influenced by colour.*
  ***People** generally react unconsciously to it.*

- in certain expressions connected with places, institutions or situations:
  *Did you go to **university**? (= Were you a student?)*
  *What did you do in **class** today? (= What did you learn?)*

Used to and would

We use *used* + the infinitive to talk about past states and past habits or repeated activities which no longer happen in the present:
*It **used to be** a technical college, but now it's a university.*
(a past state)

She **used to call** her mother every day when she was in Australia. (past habit or repeated activity)

The negative is *did not use* + infinitive:
Katya **didn't use to be** a nurse.

The question form is *Did … use* + infinitive …?:
Did you **use to play** the piano?

Note: *used* + infinitive is only used in the past. It cannot be used in other tenses.

We use *would* to talk about past habits or repeated activities:
Every day, he **would** get up early and go for a run.
Note: we cannot use *would* for past states:
The price of oil ~~would~~ used to be much lower.

We use *be/become/get used to* + noun/noun phrase/ pronoun/verb + *-ing* to mean 'be/become/get accustomed to':
You'll soon **get used to living** in Toronto.

Note: *be/become/get* can be used in any tense:
He **wasn't** used to the cold weather.
I**'ve become** more used to city life now.

Using sequencers when describing processes

When we describe processes, we can use a number of words/phrases to explain when different stages of the process happen in relation to each other.

- To indicate the start of the process:
  first, firstly, in/at the beginning, to begin with:
  When a fish dies, **at the beginning** its body just sinks into the soft mud.

- To show the next stages in the process:
  after that / some time, (some time) later, when (that has happened), next, the next thing which happens is (that), following that:
  After some time, the fish's skeleton becomes covered by a thick layer of mud.

- To show stages which happen very soon afterwards:
  as soon as, immediately (after / after this), once:
  Once the fish is completely covered, no oxygen reaches it, so it stops decomposing.

- To show stages which happen at the same time:
  meanwhile, during that time / this stage in the process, while/whilst/as this happens / is happening:
  Meanwhile, the pressure of the ocean converts the layer of mud into rock.

- To show things which happen slowly over a period of time:
  gradually, little by little, progressively:
  The skeleton of the fish is **progressively** transformed into a similar, lighter-coloured rock by the same pressure.

- To show when a stage stops:
  until, up to the moment/point when:

The fish's skeleton is transformed **up to the point** when no organic matter remains.

- To show the last stage in the process:
  finally, lastly, eventually*, in the end*:
  Eventually, tectonic movements thrust the sea bed to the surface, and the fossil is uncovered.

* Note: *eventually* and *in the end* are used to mean 'after a long time' / 'after a long process'. *At last* is not correct in this context. *At last* implies that you were impatient for something to finish:
At last she's answered my email!

Using participle clauses to express consequences

- We can express a consequence like this:
  Copernicus realised that the Earth revolves around the Sun, and this changed the way people saw the Universe.

- This can also be expressed using a verb + *-ing*:
  Copernicus realised that the Earth revolves around the Sun, changing the way people saw the Universe.

- Note:
  - Use a comma to separate the main clause (*Copernicus realised that the Earth revolves around the Sun*) and the consequence (*changing the way people saw the Universe*).
  - The subject of the verb + *-ing* is the whole of the main clause.

Using commas

We use commas:

- after subordinate clauses* when they come before the main clause:
  Although great efforts are being made to protect endangered species, many are in danger of extinction.
  Note: when the subordinate clause comes after the main clause, a comma is not necessary.

- with non-defining relative clauses*:
  The Ngorogoro Crater, which is in Kenya, is one of the most-visited game reserves in Africa.

- before co-ordinate relative clauses*:
  The course will not start till mid-October, which is quite late for most students.

- to separate items on a list, except for the last two items when they are separated with *and*:
  The chart shows figures for plants, mammals, reptiles and birds in New Zealand.

- after adverbs/adverbial phrases at the beginning of sentences:
  However, I do not agree with this point of view.
  In contrast, 87% of women say they do housework regularly.

- before *but* and *or* (when *or* is used to join two sentences):

  It is difficult to understand such large changes, but we have to try.

  We have to solve the problems caused by insecticides, or farmers will be unable to grow their crops.

- when we put more than one adjective before a noun (unless they are all short, common adjectives):

  a simple, long-term solution

  a little old man

- when two nouns/noun phrases are together and one describes the other; the commas go before and after the second noun/noun phrase:

  One ocean liner, the Titanic, has been the subject of numerous films and books.

- before and after adverbs which are in an unusual place in the sentence:

  Folk music, however, is more popular with people over 40. (*However* is normally placed at the beginning of the sentence.)

- in numbers, to separate hundreds and thousands and thousands and millions:

  1, 550, 444.

  Note: you can also leave a space instead of a comma between hundreds, thousands and millions. Dots are used to indicate decimals.

  * Subordinate clauses are clauses introduced by words/ phrases such as *when, while, as soon as, before, after, because, although, since, whereas, if, unless,* etc.

  Non-defining relative clauses are clauses which give extra information when you already know what is being talked about.

  Co-ordinate relative clauses are relative clauses which start with *which*, come at the end of the sentence and refer to the whole of the sentence.

Appendix: words + dependent prepositions

Here are some common words and their dependent prepositions. You should check exactly how each is used in a dictionary.

Verb + preposition

account for
accuse of
accustom to
agree with/about
amount to
apologise to/for
appeal to
apply to
approve of
attach to
attend to
attribute to
base on
believe in
belong to
blame for
charge for
comment on
compare to/with
compete with
concentrate on
congratulate on
connect with
consider as
consist of
contrast with
cope with
count on
deal with
dedicate to
depend on
devote to
differ from
disapprove of
discourage from
distinguish from
distract from
divert from
divide into
dream of
exclude from
experiment on
focus on

help with
hinder from
hope for
impress with
include in
insure against
interfere with
invest in
involve in
link to/with
listen to
long for
object to
operate on
participate in
persist in
prepare for
prevent from
prohibit from
protest against
provide for/with
react to/against
recognise as
recover from
refer to
reflect in/on
regard as
relate to
rely on
remind of
resort to
result in
search for
separate from
spend on
stem from
subject to
suffer from
think about/of
warn about/against
worry about

Adjective + preposition

afraid of
angry with/about
anxious about
available to/for
capable of
confident of
delighted with
dependent on
different to/from
disappointed with
frightened of
good/bad/clever at
independent of/from
interested in
involved in
kind to
pleased with
prejudiced against
proud of
relevant to
responsible to/for
shocked at/by
sorry about/for
suitable for
suited to
surprised at/by
tired of
upset about

Noun + preposition

attention to
belief in
capacity for
confidence in
criticism of
difference of
difficulty in/with
discussion about
experience of
information on/about
problem of/with
reputation for
trust in

Word lists

Abbreviations: *n/np* = noun / noun phrase; *v/vp* = verb / verb phrase; *adj/adjp* = adjective / adjective phrase; *adv/advp* = adverb / adverb phrase; *pv* = phrasal verb; T/I = transitive / intransitive; C/U = countable / uncountable

The numbers indicate the page on which the word or phrase first appears. RS indicates that the word or phrase appears in the recording script.

Unit 1

automated *adj* (13) done by machines and not people

base something on something *vp* [T] (11) If you base something on facts or ideas, you use those facts or ideas to develop it.

bring people together *vp* [T] (11) If an organisation or activity brings people together, it causes people to do something as a group.

by the time *phrase* (14) at the point when

channel resources into something *vp* [T] (12) to use energy and effort for a particular purpose

a common desire *np* [C] (11) a strong feeling of wanting to achieve or have something, felt by all the members of a group

concentrate on something *vp* [T] (12) to use most of your time and effort to do something

crucial *adj* (12) necessary to make something succeed

down-to-earth *adj* (11) practical and realistic

discipline *n* [C] (11) a particular subject of study

everyday *adj* (11) normal and used every day

extraordinary *adj* (11) very unusual, special or surprising

facilities *plural n* (10) buildings, equipment or services that are provided for a particular purpose

field *n* [C] (RS) an area of study or activity

get to the top *phrase* (RS) to succeed in getting one of the most important jobs in a particular career

go on to do something *vp* (12) to do something after first doing something else

growth rate *np* [C] (16) the speed at which something increases

high achiever *np* [C] (9) a very successful person who achieves a lot in their life

highly gifted *adj* (11) extremely intelligent, or having a natural ability to do something extremely well

human potential *np* [U] (11) people's ability to develop and achieve good things in the future

inspire *v* [T] (11) to make someone feel enthusiastic about a subject and give them the idea to do something

institute *n* [C] (11) an organisation where people do a particular kind of scientific or educational work

interact with someone/something *vp* [T] (11) If two people or things interact with each other, they speak or do things with each other.

master *v* [T] (11) to learn how to do something very well

obtain *v* [T] (17) to get something that you want

recruitment program(me) *np* [C] (RS) a series of actions intended to get people to join an organisation or work for a company

remain unchanged *vp* (17) to stay the same, not changing in any way

responsible for something *adj* (11) being the person who causes something to happen

sensors *plural n* (11) pieces of equipment that can find heat, light, etc.

take something for granted *phrase* (11) to use something all the time, without thinking how useful it is or how lucky you are to have it

telecoms *n* [U] (9) short for *telecommunications*, the process or business of sending information or messages by telephone, radio, etc.

thus *adv* (16) in this way

a vast range (of) *np* [C] (11) a very large number of different things

visible *adj* (11) able to be seen

vocational training *np* [U] (9) the learning of skills that prepare you for a job

Unit 2

bold *adj* (26) describes a colour which is bright and strong

camouflage *n* [U] (23) when the colour or pattern on something is similar to the area around it, making it difficult to see

colour scheme *np* [C] (25) a combination of colours that has been chosen for the walls, furniture, etc. of a particular room or building

comprise *v* [T] (20) to have as parts or members, or to be those parts or members

concept *n* [C] (20) an idea or principle of something that exists

confirm *v* [T] (20) to prove that a belief or an opinion which was previously not completely certain is true

consistent *adj* (20) always behaving or happening in a similar, especially positive, way

cue *v* [T] (20) to give someone a signal to do something

decoration *n* [U] (18) the style and colour of paint or paper on the walls of a room or building

distinguish *v* [T] (19) to recognise the differences between two people, ideas or things

draw someone to something *vp* [T] (25) to attract someone to a thing or person

entities *plural n* [C] (20) things which exist apart from other things, having their own independent existence

give someone a taste of something *phrase* (RS) to allow someone to see or experience a little of something

give someone an idea of something *phrase* (RS) to allow someone to see or experience a little of something

haphazard *adj* (19) not having an obvious order or plan

house *v* [T] (RS) to contain or provide a space for something

hypothesise *v* [I] (19) to suggest an explanation for something which has not yet been proved to be true

in an effort to *phrase* (19) trying to

in such a way that *phrase* (26) If you do something in such a way that something happens, you do it in order to make that thing happen.

in the course of *phrase* (19) during

incompetence (at) *n* [U] (19) lack of ability or skill to do something successfully or as it should be done

interactive displays *plural n* (23) collections of objects for people to look at which react when people use them and instruct them to do particular things

make predictions *vp* (19) say what will happen in the future

master *v* [T] (19) to learn how to do something well

novel *adj* (20) new and original, not like anything seen before

occupants *plural n* (26) the people who live in a building

occupy *v* [T] (26) to live in a building

one by one *advp* (20) separately, one after the other

overwhelmingly *adv* (19) very strongly or completely

parental *adj* (20) connected with parents or with being a parent

pastel colours / pastels *plural n* (26) light colours that are not strong

play a role in something *phrase* (26) to be involved in something and have an effect on it

property *n* [C] (19) a quality in a substance or material, especially one which means that it can be used in a particular way

repertoire *n* [C] (19) all the words that you know or can produce

shade *n* [C] (18) one form of a colour, especially a darker or a lighter form

striking *adj* (RS) easily noticed and unusual

systematic *adj* (20) using a fixed and organised plan

to all intents and purposes *phrase* (RS) used when you describe the real result of a situation

to some degree *phrase* (20) partly

unique *adj* (19) being the only existing one of its type or, more generally, unusual or special in some way

Unit 3

absenteeism *n* [U] (38) when someone is frequently not at work or at school

behind the scenes *phrase* (33) If something happens behind the scenes, it happens secretly, or where the public cannot see.

breakdown *n* [C] (38) a way of presenting information in which things are separated into different groups

clinical trial *np* [C] (33) a test of a new medicine in which people are given the medicine

comb through something *vp* [T] (33) to search something very carefully

condition *n* [C] (33) an illness

conversely *adv* (33) used to introduce something that is different from something you have just said

cure *v* [T] (30) to make someone with an illness healthy again

demographics *n* [U] (37) the quantity and characteristics of the people who live in a particular area, for example their age, how much money they have, etc.

empathy *n* [U] (33) the ability to imagine and understand how someone else feels in their situation

evaluate *v* [T] (31) to consider something carefully and decide how good or important it is

fall behind (someone) *vp* [I/T] (32) to make less progress than other people who are doing the same thing

high stakes *plural n* (33) great advantages that could be gained in a situation and great disadvantages that could also be the result

hinge on something *vp* [T] (33) to depend completely on something

inoculate *v* [T] (30) to give a weak form of a disease to a person or an animal, usually by injection, as a protection against that disease

joint *n* [C] (30) a place in your body where two bones meet

to make matters worse *phrase* (32) used before you describe something bad that happened, making a bad situation even worse

medication *n* [C/U] (33) medicine that is used to treat an illness

open the door to something *phrase* (33) If one thing opens the door to another thing, it makes it possible for that second thing to happen.

parallel *adj* (37) happening in a similar way

pharmaceutical *adj* (32) relating to the production of medicines

plaster cast *np* [C] (30) a hard covering that is put over a broken bone in order to support and protect it while it heals

(good/bad) posture *n* [U] (RS) If someone has good posture, their back and shoulders are straight when they stand and sit; if someone has bad posture, their back and shoulders are curved and not straight.

prescribe *v* [T] (33) to say what medical treatment someone needs

receive physiotherapy *vp* [T] (30) to get treatment for an injury which involves doing special exercises and movements

rehabilitation *n* [U] (RS) when someone who has been ill or injured is cured and can do what they used to do before their illness or injury

relieve *v* [T] (30) to make pain or a bad feeling less severe

sedentary activities *plural n* (RS) activities which involve sitting and not being physically active

sleep patterns *plural n* (39) Someone's sleep patterns are their sleeping habits, for example, how much they usually sleep and when they usually sleep.

sports injury *np* [C] (30) damage to your body caused by doing a sport

substantially *adv* (37) by a large amount

symptoms *plural n* (33) physical feelings or problems which show that you have a particular illness

therapeutic *adj* (33) helping to cure a disease or improve your health

therapy *n* [C/U] (31) a type of treatment for an illness or injury

treat *v* [T] (30) to give medical care to someone for an illness or injury

undergo *v* [T] (34) to experience something, for example, a medical treatment

a wave of something *np* [C] (33) a period in which there is an increase in a particular type of activity

well-being *n* [U] (33) A feeling or sense of well-being is a feeling of being healthy, happy and comfortable.

Unit 4

accessibility *n* [U] (42) how easy something is to understand

all shapes and sizes *phrase* (41) of many different shapes and sizes

call for something *vp* [T] (42) to need or deserve a particular action or quality

clarity *n* [U] (42) the quality of being clear and easy to understand

decorative *adj* (41) intended to be attractive rather than having a use

dogmatic *adj* (42) not willing to accept other ideas or opinions because you think yours are right

dominant *adj* (41) main or most important

durable *adj* (RS) remaining in good condition over a long time

enhance *v* [T] (48) to improve something

exert an influence *vp* [T] (42) to have an effect

format *n* [C] (41) the way something is designed, arranged or produced

foster *v* [T] (48) to encourage something to develop

give someone an opportunity *vp* [T] (41) to allow someone to have the chance to do something

grind *v* [T] (RS) to keep rubbing something between two rough, hard surfaces until it becomes a powder

in stark contrast to *phrase* (42) used to show that someone or something is completely different from someone or something else

indigenous people *np* [C] (RS) people who have lived in a place for a very long time, before other people moved to that place from different parts of the world

make advances in something *phrase* (42) to make something develop or progress

make use of something *phrase* (42) to use something that is available

meet a need for something *phrase* (43) to provide what is necessary for something

nuance *n* [C] (41) a very slight difference

override *v* [T] (48) to be more important than something else

palette *n* [C] (RS) a board used by an artist to mix their paints on while they are painting

passionate about something *adj* (RS) very enthusiastic about something

pigment *n* [C] (RS) a substance that gives something colour

prior to something *adj* (41) before something

produce *v* [T] (42) to create something

remarkable *adj* (41) very unusual or noticeable in a way that you admire

share the spotlight with something/someone *phrase* (42) to receive less attention because someone or something else has started to be noticed too

spectrum *n* [C] (41) a range of something

stimulate *v* [T] (48) to give someone the interest and excitement to do something

take advantage of something *phrase* (41) to use a situation to get something good

take hold *phrase* (41) to become popular

take off *vp* [I] (RS) to suddenly become successful

take steps to do something *phrase* (49) to take action in order to solve a problem

to this day *phrase* (41) even now, after a long period

trace *v* [T] (41) to copy a picture by putting transparent paper on top and following the outer line of the picture with a pen

a vehicle for something / doing something *phrase* (41) a way of making something happen, often a way of communicating ideas

visual art form *np* [C] (RS) something that someone has made to be beautiful or to express their ideas which can be seen, for example a painting or a sculpture

wash away *vp* [T] (RS) If water washes something away, it removes that thing.

when it comes to something / doing something *phrase* (RS) used to introduce a new idea that you want to say something about

work of art *np* [C] (40) a very beautiful and important painting, drawing, etc.

Unit 5

allocate *v* [T] (56) If you allocate a task to someone, you give them that particular task.

artefacts *plural n* [C] (52) objects, especially very old objects, of historical interest

barter *v* [I/T] (55) to exchange goods or services for other goods or services, without using money

be a question of something *phrase* (59) to be related to something

burial site *np* [C] (52) an area of land where dead bodies are buried

catch up on something *vp* [T] (53) to do something that you did not have time to do earlier

erode *v* [I/T] (61) If soil, stone, etc. erodes or is eroded, it is gradually damaged and removed by the sea, rain or wind.

coastal erosion *np* [U] (60) the gradual disappearance of cliffs, beaches, etc. as a result of the action of the sea

come about *vp* [I] (55) to happen or start to happen

compact *v* [T] (RS) to press something together so that it becomes tight or solid

current *n* [C] (54) the natural flow of water in one direction

die out *vp* [I] (54) to become more and more rare and then disappear completely

division of labour *singular n* (55) a way of organising work so that different people are responsible for different tasks

entomb *v* [T] (RS) to bury something or someone in something so they cannot escape

exceptionally *adv* (60) unusually

fault lines *plural n* (RS) breaks in the Earth's surface

fossilisation *n* [U] (RS) the process of becoming a fossil (= part of an animal or plant from many thousands of years ago, preserved in rock)

give someone or something the edge *phrase* (55) to give someone an advantage over someone else

heritage *n* [U] (54) the buildings, paintings, customs, etc. which are important in a culture or society because they have existed for a long time

immediate surroundings *plural n* (55) Your immediate surroundings are the area that is closest to you.

implement *n* [C] (55) a tool

imply *v* [T] (55) to suggest or show something

inheritance *n* [C/U] (58) money or possessions that you get from someone when they die

an insight into something *np* [C] (56) a way of understanding what something is really like

keep themselves to themselves *phrase* (55) If a group of people keep themselves to themselves, they stay with that group and do not spend time with other people.

lead someone to do something *vp* (54) to cause someone to do or think something

lessen *v* [I/T] (55) to become less, or to make something less

lobe *n* [C] (55) one of the parts of the brain

maintain links with something *phrase* (59) to keep a connection with something

mimic *v* [T] (RS) to have the same behaviour or qualities as something else

plummet *v* [I] (55) If an amount or level of something plummets, it suddenly becomes very much lower.

predator *n* [C] (RS) an animal that kills and eats other animals

refuge *n* [C] (55) a place where you are protected from danger

robust *adj* (55) strong and thick

sediment *n* [C/U] (53) a layer of sand, stones, etc. that eventually forms a layer of rock

sentimental value *np* [U] (RS) importance that an object has because it makes you remember someone or something and not because it is worth a lot of money

silt *n* [U] (54) sand and clay that has been carried along by a river and is left on land

stocky *adj* (55) having a wide, strong body

trait *n* [C] (55) a quality in someone's character

turn the clock back *phrase* (55) to go back in time

wear away *vp* [I/T] (61) to disappear after a lot of time or use, or to make something disappear in this way

wear someone/something down *vp* [T] (55) to make someone or something gradually lose their strength

widespread *adj* (55) existing in a lot of places

Unit 6

the advent of something *phrase* (RS) the start or arrival of something new

advocate of something *np* [C] (64) someone who supports a particular idea or way of doing things

anything but (sophisticated) *phrase* (63) If someone or something is anything but a particular quality, they are the opposite of that quality.

break new ground *phrase* (RS) to do something that is different from anything that has been done before

by and large *phrase* (64) generally

cater to someone/something *vp* [T] (64) to give people what they want, usually something that people think is wrong

convincing *adj* (RS) able to make you believe that something is true or right

enamoured with someone/something *adj* (64) liking or approving of someone or something very much

engage in something *vp* [T] (69) to take part in something

the extent of something *phrase* (65) the level, size or importance of something

feature film *np* [C] (RS) a film that is usually 90 or more minutes long

film sequence *np* [C] (RS) a part of a film that deals with one event

generate *v* [T] (63) to cause something to exist

get stuck *phrase* (63) to not be able to continue doing something because there is something you cannot understand or solve

gloss over something *vp* [T] (64) to avoid discussing something, or to discuss something without any details in order to make it seem unimportant

icon *n* [C] (RS) a person or thing that is famous because it represents a particular idea or way of life

identify with someone *vp* [T] (68) to feel that you are similar to someone, and can understand them or their situation because of this

in essence *phrase* (64) relating to the most important characteristics or ideas of something

in leaps and bounds *phrase* (70) If progress or growth happens in leaps and bounds, it happens very quickly.

in vain *phrase* (63) without any success

instant access *np* [U] (70) the opportunity to use or see something immediately

mediocrity *n* [U] (64) the quality of being not very good

modify *v* [T] (64) to change something in order to improve it

overhaul *v* [T] (63) to make important changes to a system in order to improve it

pace *singular n* (63) the speed at which something happens

phenomena *plural n* (RS) things that exist or happen, usually things that are unusual

pioneer *v* [T] (RS) to be one of the first people to do something

prove to be something *v* (71) to show a particular quality after a period of time

reach the point *phrase* (70) to get to a particular situation

require someone to do something *v* [T] (66) to need someone to do something

rote *n* (64) a way of learning something by repeating it many times, rather than understanding it

save the day *phrase* (63) to do something that solves a serious problem

scroll up/down/back/forward, etc. *v* [I] (63) to move text or an image on a computer screen so that you can look at the part that you want

simulation *n* [C/U] (67) when you do or make something which behaves or looks like something real but which is not real

supplement *v* [T] (66) to add an extra amount or part to something

supplement *n* [C] (63) an extra amount or part added to something

tailor *v* [T] (63) to make or change something so that it is suitable

technique *n* [C/U] (64) a particular or special way of doing something

tune out *vp* [I] (63) to stop giving your attention to what is happening around you

unambiguously *adv* (64) clearly having only one meaning

Unit 7

absorption *n* [U] (78) the process by which something is taken in and becomes part of something else

at risk *phrase* (82) being in a situation where something bad is likely to happen

blow *n* [C] (77) a shock or disappointment

bolster *v* [T] (78) to make something stronger by supporting it or encouraging it

check something out *vp* [T] (RS) to get more information about something by examining it or reading about it

cloning *n* [U] (81) the process of making an exact copy of a plant or animal by removing one of its cells

clue *n* [C] (77) a sign or piece of information that helps you to solve a problem or answer a question

culprit *n* [C] (78) something that is responsible for a bad situation

cultivate *v* [T] (78) to grow plants in large numbers

do/play your part *phrase* (78) to perform an important function

distinct *adj* (78) separate

diversity *n* [U] (78) when many different types of things or people exist

flora and fauna *phrase* (80) The flora and fauna of a place are its plants and animals.

forage *v* [I] (78) to move about searching for things you need, especially food

frighten someone off *vp* [T] (RS) to make a person or animal afraid so that they go away

fungal *adj* (78) caused by or relating to a fungus (= a type of organism which gets its food from decaying material or other living things)

go back to something *vp* [T] (77) to go back to a time in the past

greenhouse *n* [C] (77) a building made of glass for growing plants in

justification for something *np* [U] (80) a reason for something

longevity *n* [U] (78) living for a long time

menace *n* [C] (78) something that is likely to cause harm

microbes *plural n* (78) very small organisms, often bacteria that cause disease

monocrops *plural n* (78) single plants grown for food

numerous ways *phrase* (77) many different ways

on an international/global/national level *phrase* (78) If something is dealt with on an international/global/national, etc. level, it is dealt with by all the countries of the world or by a whole country.

parasite infestations *plural n* (78) when animals or plants that live on or in another type of animal cause problems by being somewhere in large numbers

pathogens *plural n* (78) small living things that can cause disease

read up on something *vp* [T] (RS) to read a lot about a subject in order to get information

setback *n* [C] (77) a problem that makes something happen later or more slowly than it should

stunning *adj* (76) very beautiful

tease something apart *vp* [T] (78) to separate different things

tempt *v* [T] (RS) to make you want to do or have something

thrive *v* [I] (78) to grow very well, or to become very healthy or successful

toxic *adj* (78) poisonous

under threat *phrase* (82) If something is under threat, it is in danger.

vicinity *singular n* (78) the area near a place

viral *adj* (78) caused by or relating to a virus (= infectious organism)

Unit 8

allocate *v* [T] (86) to give money, time, space, etc. to be used for a particular purpose

astronomer *n* [C] (89) someone who scientifically studies stars and planets

astronomy *n* [U] (85) the scientific study of stars and planets

build a picture of something *phrase* (86) to gain an understanding of something

chiefly *adv* (85) mainly

comet *n* [C] (86) an object in space that leaves a bright line behind it in the sky

continuity *n* [U] (87) the state of continuing for a long period of time without changing or being stopped

cult following *np* [C] (RS) a group of people who very much like a particular thing that most people do not know about

distract someone from something *vp* [T] (85) to take someone's attention away from something

divert something from something *vp* [T] (85) to take someone's attention away from something

domain *n* [C] (85) a particular subject or activity that someone controls or deals with

early/ancient/modern, etc. civilisations *plural n* (85) the cultures and ways of life of societies at particular times

the end result *singular n* (RS) the result of an activity

evolve *v* [I/T] (85) to develop

for the purpose(s) of something *phrase* (85) in order to do something

found *v* [T] (85) to start an organisation, especially by providing money

galaxy *n* [C] (RS) a very large group of stars held together in the universe

geologist *n* [C] (86) someone who studies rocks and soil and the physical structure of the Earth

gravitational force *np* [U] (RS) the force that makes objects fall to the ground or that pulls objects towards a planet or other body

in collaboration with someone *phrase* (85) working together with someone

in the sense that *phrase* (85) in the way of thinking that

in turn *phrase* (92) as a result

intrinsic merit *np* [U] (85) If something has intrinsic merit, it has qualities itself.

introspective *adj* (85) thinking a lot about your own thoughts and feelings and not communicating these to other people

launch *n* [C] (88) the sending of a spacecraft into the sky

lens *n* [C] (RS) a curved piece of glass in cameras, glasses and scientific equipment used for looking at things

magnify *v* [T] (RS) to make an object look larger than it is by looking through special equipment

make a contribution to something *phrase* (85) to do something that helps something to develop or succeed

means *n* [C] (92) a way of doing something

minimise *v* [T] (97) to reduce something to the least amount or level

needless to say *phrase* (RS) as you would expect

obsessed with someone/something *adj* (RS) extremely interested in something

physiological *adj* (86) relating to how the bodies of living things work

primarily *adv* (85) mainly

realise *v* [T] (85) to achieve something

solar eclipse *np* [C] (RS) an occasion when the Moon passes between the Sun and the Earth, and the Moon blocks the light from the Sun

the solar system *singular n* (86) the sun and planets that move around it

sustain *v* [T] (RS) to allow something to continue

it is not uncommon for *phrase* (85) If you say it is not uncommon for something to happen, you mean it quite often happens.

undertake *v* [T] (86) to be responsible for a project or task that will take a long time or be difficult

the universe *singular n* (84) everything that exists, including stars, space, etc.

want nothing more than *phrase* (RS) to want most of all to do something

IELTS practice test

LISTENING

🎧 PART 1

Questions 1–5

Complete the form below.

*Write **NO MORE THAN ONE WORD AND/OR A NUMBER** for each answer.*

Lake Pane Campground, US
Bookings

Example	*Answer*
Length of stay:	5 nights

Date of arrival: **1** ....

Family name: **2** ....

Contact number: **3** ....

Camp facilities: **4** .... , water and **5** ....

Questions 6–10

Complete the notes below.

*Write **NO MORE THAN TWO WORDS AND/OR A NUMBER** for each answer.*

Site code: **6** ....

Location: Drive past the offices and **7** .... Keep going until you reach the **8** .... Then turn left.

Remember: Do not leave **9** ....

Return the **10** ....

🎧 PART 2

Questions 11–14

What does the speaker say about the following natural food colourings?

Write the correct letter, A–F, next to questions 11–14.

A	It is made using another food product.
B	The ingredients are difficult to find.
C	It is also used to dye cosmetics.
D	Sales fell then increased.
E	It can be used to give processed food a uniform colour.
F	It is less popular than other dyes.

11	green
12	brown
13	red
14	blue

Questions 15–17

Choose the correct letter, A, B, C or D.

15 When we buy new clothes, our
    A   friends may not like the colours we choose.
    B   choice may be based on the colours we see.
    C   ideas about fashion may not be up to date.

16 Colourists are people who
    A   decide which colours suit us best.
    B   create the dyes that are used to make clothes.
    C   predict which colours will be fashionable in the future.

17 What does the speaker say about the colours we wear?
    A   The colours we like change as we get older.
    B   Most people prefer light colours to dark ones.
    C   We worry too much about the colour of clothes.

Questions 18–20

Complete the sentences below.

*Write **ONE WORD ONLY** for each answer.*

18 Both a product and its .... must appeal to consumers.
19 Green indicates that businesses care about the ....
20 Blue helps people to think in a more .... way.

🎧(24) **PART 3**

Questions 21–26

Complete the table below.

Write ONE WORD ONLY for each answer.

International student mobility

Questions	Findings
What is the total number?	• about 3 million • Not every country uses the same **21** .... for an international student. • Figure may be much higher.
What is the global **22** .... ?	• Figures may be inaccurate. • **23** .... organisations may be ignored.
Where do students come from?	Big increases in figures for North America and **24** ....
Are student **25** .... changing?	• more **26** .... • a spirit of exchange

Questions 27 and 28

Choose TWO letters, A–E.

When choosing a course, which TWO factors did students consider important?

A   how expensive the course is
B   the reputation of the institution
C   the distance from home
D   the qualifications of the tutors
E   how useful the qualification will be

Questions 29 and 30

Choose TWO letters, A–E.

Which TWO incentives would encourage graduates to return home?

A   scholarships for higher degrees
B   research grants
C   special housing
D   lower tax rates
E   special work zones

(25) **PART 4**

Questions 31–40

Complete the notes below.

Write NO MORE THAN TWO WORDS for each answer.

LIONS

Lion history

- Found today in Africa and a **31** .... in India
- Have lived on every continent apart from Antarctica and **32** ....
- Killed by early humans:
  - **a)** in competition for food
  - **b)** for **33** ....

Cave paintings

- **34** .... confirms European lions much bigger than African lions
- Date of first appearance of mane **35** ....

Purpose of mane

- Mane is comparable to **36** .... in some ways
- Researchers first believed mane used for **37** .... during fights

The lion expert's study

- Made some **38** .... with different manes
- **39** .... manes attracted female lions
- Conclusion: mane is a **40** ....

READING

READING PASSAGE 1

*You should spend about 20 minutes on **Questions 1–13**, which are based on Reading Passage 1 below.*

Dino discoveries

When news breaks of the discovery of a new species of dinosaur, you would be forgiven for thinking that the scientists who set out in search of the fossils are the ones who made the find. The reality tells a different story, as Cavan Scott explains.

The BBC series *Planet Dinosaur* used state-of-the-art computer graphics to bring to life the most impressive of those dinosaurs whose remains have been discovered in the past decade. One of these is *Gigantoraptor erlianensis*. Discovered in 2005, it stands more than three metres high at the hip and is the biggest bird-like dinosaur ever unearthed. Yet its discoverer, Xu Xing of Beijing's Institute of Vertebrate Palaeontology and Paleoanthropology, was not even looking for it at the time. He was recording a documentary in the Gobi Desert, Inner Mongolia.

'The production team were filming me and a geologist digging out what we thought were sauropod bones,' says Xu, 'when I realised the fossils were something else entirely.' *Gigantoraptor*, as it later became known, turned out to be an oviraptorid, a therapod with a bird-like beak. Its size was staggering. The largest oviraptorid previously discovered had been comparable in size to an emu; the majority were about as big as a turkey. Here was a creature that was probably about eight metres long, if the bone analysis was anything to go by.

Sometimes it is sheer opportunism that plays a part in the discovery of a new species. In 1999, the National Geographic Society announced that the missing link between dinosaurs and modern birds had finally been found. Named *Archaeoraptor lianoingensis*, the fossil in question appeared to have the head and body of a bird, with the hind legs and tail of a 124-million-year-old dromaeosaur – a family of small theropods that include the bird-like *Velociraptor* made famous by *Jurassic Park* films.

There was a good reason why the fossil looked half-bird, half-dinosaur. CT scans almost immediately proved the specimen was bogus and had been created by an industrious Chinese farmer who had glued two separate fossils together to create a profitable hoax.

But while the palaeontologists behind the announcement were wiping egg off their faces, others, including Xu were taking note. The head and body of the fake composite belonged to *Yanornis martini*, a primitive fish-eating bird from around 120 million years ago. The dromaeosaur tail and hind legs, however, were covered in what looked like fine proto-feathers. That fossil turned out to be something special. In 2000, Xu named it *Microraptor* and revealed that it had probably lived in the treetops. Although it couldn't fly, its curved claws provided the first real evidence that dinosaurs could have climbed trees. Three years later, Xu and his team discovered a closely related *Microraptor* species which changed everything. '*Microraptor* had two salient features,' Xu explains, 'long feathers were attached not just to its forearms but to its legs and claws. Then we noticed that these long feathers had asymmetrical vanes, a feature often associated with flight capability. This meant that we might have found a flying dinosaur.'

Some extraordinary fossils have remained hidden in a collection and almost forgotten. For the majority of the 20th century, the palaeontology community had ignored the frozen tundra of north Alaska. There was no way, scientists believed, that cold-blooded dinosaurs could survive in such bleak, frigid conditions. But according to Alaskan dinosaur expert Tony Fiorillo, they eventually realised they were missing a trick.

'The first discovery of dinosaurs in Alaska was actually made by a geologist called Robert Liscomb in 1961,' says Fiorillo. 'Unfortunately, Robert was killed in a rockslide the following year, so his discoveries languished in a warehouse for the next two decades.' In the mid-1980s, managers at the warehouse stumbled upon the box containing Liscomb's fossils during a spring clean. The bones were sent to the United States Geological Survey, where they were identified as belonging to *Edmontosaurus*, a duck-billed hadrosaur. Today, palaeontologists roam this frozen treasure trove searching for remains locked away in the permafrost.

The rewards are worth the effort. While studying teeth belonging to the relatively intelligent *Troodon* therapod, Fiorillo discovered the teeth of the Alaskan *Troodon* were double the size of those of its southern counterpart. 'Even though the morphology of individual teeth resembled that of *Troodon*, the size was significantly larger than the *Troodon* found in warmer climates.' Fiorillo says that the reason lies in the *Troodon*'s large eyes, which allowed it to hunt at dawn and at dusk – times when other dinosaurs would have struggled to see. In the polar conditions of Cretaceous Alaska, where the Sun would all but disappear for months on end, this proved a useful talent. 'Troodon adapted for life in the extraordinary light regimes of the polar world. With this advantage, it took over as Alaska's dominant therapod,' explains Fiorillo. Finding itself at the top of the food chain, the dinosaur evolved to giant proportions.

It is true that some of the most staggering of recent developments have come from palaeontologists being in the right place at the right time, but this is no reflection on their knowledge or expertise. After all, not everyone knows when they've stumbled upon something remarkable. When Argentine sheep farmer Guillermo Heredia uncovered what he believed was a petrified tree trunk on his Patagonian farm in 1988, he had no way of realising that he'd found a 1.5-metre-long tibia of the largest sauropod ever known to walk the Earth. *Argentinosaurus* was 24 metres long and weighed 75 tonnes. The titanosaur was brought to the attention of the scientific community in 1993 by Rodolfo Coria and Jose Bonaparte of the National Museum of Natural Sciences in Buenos Aires. Coria points out that most breakthroughs are not made by scientists, but by ordinary folk. 'But the real scientific discovery is not the finding; it's what we learn from that finding.' While any one of us can unearth a fossil, it takes dedicated scientists to see beyond the rock.

Questions 1–6

Do the following statements agree with the information in Reading Passage 1?

Write

TRUE	*if the statement agrees with the information*
FALSE	*if the statement contradicts the information*
NOT GIVEN	*if there is no information on this*

1 Xu Xing went to the Gobi Desert to check fossil evidence of the existence of *Gigantoraptor erlianensis*.

2 The announcement made by the National Geographic Society in 1999 was based on false evidence.

3 Like *Gigantoraptor*, *Yanornis martini* was first discovered in China.

4 The bones originally discovered by Robert Liscomb changed the attitude of palaeontologists towards north Alaska.

5 According to Fiorillo, the name *Troodon* means 'wounding tooth'.

6 Guillermo Heredia had suspected that his find was a dinosaur fossil.

Questions 7–13

Complete the labels on the diagrams below.

Choose **NO MORE THAN TWO WORDS** *and/or* **A NUMBER** *from the passage for each answer.*

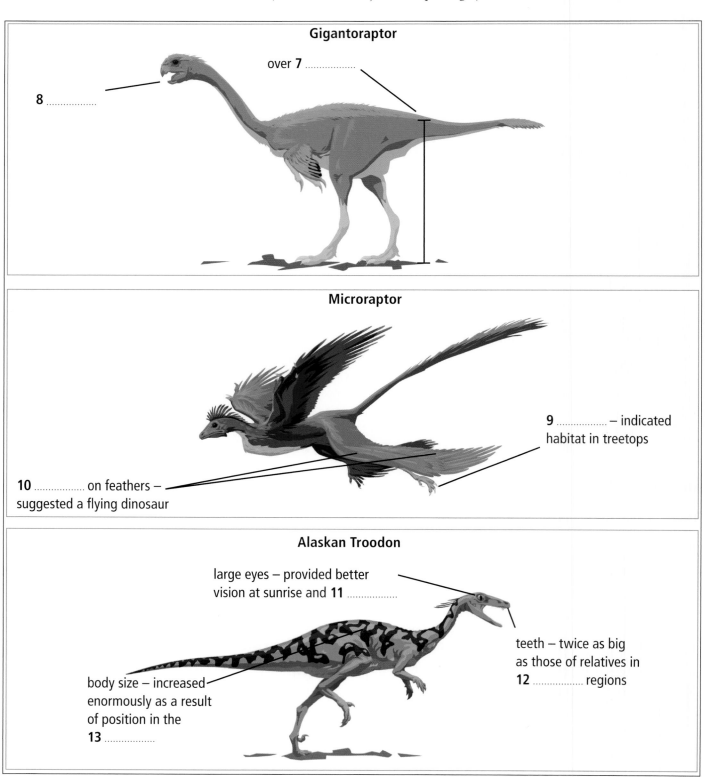

Gigantoraptor

over **7** ....

8 ....

Microraptor

9 .... – indicated habitat in treetops

10 .... on feathers – suggested a flying dinosaur

Alaskan Troodon

large eyes – provided better vision at sunrise and **11** ....

teeth – twice as big as those of relatives in **12** .... regions

body size – increased enormously as a result of position in the **13** ....

READING PASSAGE 2

*You should spend about 20 minutes on **Questions 14–26**, which are based on Reading Passage 2 below.*

Art to the aid of technology

What caricatures can teach us about facial recognition, by Ben Austen

A Our brains are incredibly agile machines, and it is hard to think of anything they do more efficiently than recognize faces. Just hours after birth, the eyes of newborns are drawn to facelike patterns. An adult brain knows it is seeing a face within 100 milliseconds, and it takes just over a second to realize that two different pictures of a face, even if they are lit or rotated in very different ways, belong to the same person.

B Perhaps the most vivid illustration of our gift for recognition is the magic of caricature—the fact that the sparest cartoon of a familiar face, even a single line dashed off in two seconds, can be identified by our brains in an instant. It is often said that a good caricature looks more like a person than the person themselves. As it happens, this notion, counterintuitive though it may sound, is actually supported by research. In the field of vision science, there is even a term for this seeming paradox—the caricature effect—a phrase that hints at how our brains misperceive faces as much as perceive them.

C Human faces are all built pretty much the same: two eyes above a nose that's above a mouth, the features varying from person to person generally by mere millimetres. So what our brains look for, according to vision scientists, are the outlying features—those characteristics that deviate most from the ideal face we carry around in our heads, the running average of every "visage" we have ever seen. We code each new face we encounter not in absolute terms but in the several ways it differs markedly from the mean. In other words, we accentuate what is most important for recognition and largely ignore what is not. Our perception fixates on the upturned nose, the sunken eyes or the fleshy cheeks, making them loom larger. To better identify and remember people, we turn them into caricatures.

D Ten years ago, we all imagined that as soon as surveillance cameras had been equipped with the appropriate software, the face of a crime suspect would stand out in a crowd. Like a thumbprint, its unique features and configuration would offer a biometric key that could be immediately checked against any database of suspects. But now a decade has passed, and face-recognition systems still perform miserably in real-world conditions. Just recently, a couple who accidentally swapped passports at an airport in England sailed through electronic gates that were supposed to match their faces to file photos.

E All this leads to an interesting question. What if, to secure our airports and national landmarks, we need to learn more about caricature? After all, it's the skill of the caricaturist—the uncanny ability to quickly distil faces down to their most salient features—that our computers most desperately need to acquire. Clearly, better cameras and faster computers simply aren't going to be enough.

F At the University of Central Lancashire in England, Charlie Frowd, a senior lecturer in psychology, has used insights from caricature to develop a better police-composite generator. His system, called EvoFIT, produces animated caricatures, with each successive frame showing facial features that are more exaggerated than the last. Frowd's research supports the idea that we all store memories as caricatures, but with our own personal degree of amplification. So, as an animated composite depicts faces at varying stages of caricature, viewers respond to the stage that is most recognizable to them. In tests, Frowd's technique has increased positive identifications from as low as 3 percent to upwards of 30 percent.

G To achieve similar results in computer face recognition, scientists would need to model the artist's genius even more closely—a feat that might seem impossible if you listen to some of the artists describe their nearly mystical acquisition of skills. Jason Seiler recounts how he trained his mind for years, beginning in middle school, until he gained what he regards as nothing less than a second sight. 'A lot of people think that caricature is about picking out someone's worst feature and exaggerating it as far as you can,' Seiler says. 'That's wrong. Caricature is basically finding the truth. And then you push the truth.' Capturing a likeness, it seems, has less to do with the depiction of individual features than with their placement in relationship to one another. 'It's how the human brain recognizes a face. When the ratios between the features are correct, you see that face instantly.'

H Pawan Sinha, director of MIT's Sinha Laboratory for Vision Research, and one of the nation's most innovative computer-vision researchers, contends that these simple, exaggerated drawings can be objectively and systematically studied and that such work will lead to breakthroughs in our understanding of both human and machine-based vision. His lab at MIT is preparing to computationally analyze hundreds of caricatures this year, from dozens of different artists, with the hope of tapping their intuitive knowledge of what is and isn't crucial for recognition. He has named this endeavor the Hirschfeld Project, after the famous New York Times caricaturist Al Hirschfeld.

I Quite simply, by analyzing sketches, Sinha hopes to pinpoint the recurring exaggerations in the caricatures that most strongly correlate to particular ways that the original faces deviate from the norm. The results, he believes, will ultimately produce a rank-ordered list of the 20 or so facial attributes that are most important for recognition: 'It's a recipe for how to encode the face,' he says. In preliminary tests, the lab has already isolated important areas—for example, the ratio of the height of the forehead to the distance between the top of the nose and the mouth.

J On a given face, four of 20 such Hirschfeld attributes, as Sinha plans to call them, will be several standard deviations greater than the mean; on another face, a different handful of attributes might exceed the norm. But in all cases, it's the exaggerated areas of the face that hold the key. As matters stand today, an automated system must compare its target faces against the millions of continually altering faces it encounters. But so far, the software doesn't know what to look for amid this onslaught of variables. Armed with the Hirschfeld attributes, Sinha hopes that computers can be trained to focus on the features most salient for recognition, tuning out the others. 'Then,' Sinha says, 'the sky is the limit'.

Questions 14–19

Reading Passage 2 has ten paragraphs, A–J.

Which paragraph contains the following information?

You may use any letter more than once.

14 why we have mental images of faces that are essentially caricatures
15 mention of the length of time it can take to become a good caricaturist
16 an example of how unreliable current security systems can be
17 reference to the fact that we can match even a hastily drawn caricature to the person it represents
18 a summary of how the use of multiple caricatures has improved recognition rates in a particular field
19 a comparison between facial recognition and another well-established form of identification

Questions 20–23

*Look at the following statements and the list of people, **A–C**, below.*

Match each statement with the correct person.

20 A single caricature can be recognised straight away if the parts of the face are appropriately positioned.
21 An evaluation of the work of different caricaturists will provide new information about how we see faces.
22 People misunderstand what is involved in the design of a caricature.
23 When given a choice, people will have different views regarding which caricature best represents a particular person's face.

List of People
A   Charlie Frowd
B   Jason Seiler
C   Pawan Sinha

Questions 24–26

Complete the summary below.

*Choose **NO MORE THAN TWO WORDS** from the passage for each answer.*

Sinha's Project

Sinha's aim in the project is to come up with a specific number of what he terms ......**24**...... that are key to identification purposes. He hopes these can be used to enable an ......**25**...... to identify faces more quickly and more accurately. In order to do this, his team must examine the most frequently ......**26**...... features in a large number of cartoon faces.

READING PASSAGE 3

You should spend about 20 minutes on **Questions 27–40**, *which are based on Reading Passage 3 below.*

Mind readers

It may one day be possible to eavesdrop on another person's inner voice. Duncan Graham-Rowe explains

As you begin to read this article and your eyes follow the words across the page, you may be aware of a voice in your head silently muttering along. The very same thing happens when we write: a private, internal narrative shapes the words before we commit them to text.

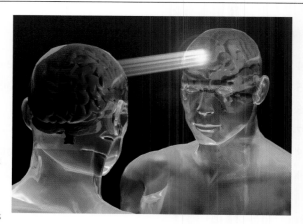

What if it were possible to tap into this inner voice? Thinking of words does, after all, create characteristic electrical signals in our brains, and decoding them could make it possible to piece together someone's thoughts. Such an ability would have phenomenal prospects, not least for people unable to communicate as a result of brain damage. But it would also carry profoundly worrisome implications for the future of privacy.

The first scribbled records of electrical activity in the human brain were made in 1924 by a German doctor called Hans Berger using his new invention – the electroencephalogram (EEG). This uses electrodes placed on the skull to read the output of the brain's billions of nerve cells or neurons. By the mid-1990s, the ability to translate the brain's activity into readable signals had advanced so far that people could move computer cursors using only the electrical fields created by their thoughts.

The electrical impulses such innovations tap into are produced in a part of the brain called the motor cortex, which is responsible for muscle movement. To move a cursor on a screen, you do not think 'move left' in natural language. Instead, you imagine a specific motion like hitting a ball with a tennis racket. Training the machine to realise which electrical signals correspond to your imagined movements, however, is time consuming and difficult. And while this method works well for directing objects on a screen, its drawbacks become apparent when you try using it to communicate. At best, you can use the cursor to select letters displayed on an on-screen keyboard. Even a practised mind would be lucky to write 15 words per minute with that approach. Speaking, we can manage 150.

Matching the speed at which we can think and talk would lead to devices that could instantly translate the electrical signals of someone's inner voice into sound produced by a speech synthesiser. To do this, it is necessary to focus only on the signals coming from the brain areas that govern speech. However, real mind reading requires some way to intercept those signals before they hit the motor cortex.

The translation of thoughts to language in the brain is an incredibly complex and largely mysterious process, but this much is known: before they end up in the motor cortex, thoughts destined to become spoken words pass through two 'staging areas' associated with the perception and expression of speech.

The first is called Wernicke's area, which deals with semantics – in this case, ideas based in meaning, which can include images, smells or emotional memories. Damage to Wernicke's area can result in the loss of semantic associations: words can't make sense when they are decoupled from their meaning. Suffer a stroke in that region, for example, and you will have trouble understanding not just what others are telling you, but what you yourself are thinking.

The second is called Broca's area, agreed to be the brain's speech-processing centre. Here, semantics are translated into phonetics and, ultimately, word components. From here, the assembled sentences take a quick trip to the motor cortex, which activates the muscles that will turn the desired words into speech.

Injure Broca's area, and though you might know what you want to say, you just can't send those impulses.

When you listen to your inner voice, two things are happening. You 'hear' yourself producing language in Wernicke's area as you construct it in Broca's area. The key to mind reading seems to lie in these two areas.

44 The work of Bradley Greger in 2010 broke new ground by marking the first-ever excursion beyond the motor cortex into the brain's language centres. His team used electrodes placed inside the skull to detect the electrical signatures of whole words, such as 'yes', 'no', 'hot', 'cold', 'thirsty', 'hungry', etc. Promising as it is, this approach requires a new signal to be learned for each new word. English contains a quarter of a million distinct words. And though this was the first instance of monitoring Wernicke's area, it still relied largely on the facial motor cortex.

Greger decided there might be another way. The building blocks of language are called phonemes, and the English language has about 40 of them – the 'kuh' sound in 'school', for example, the 'sh' in 'shy'. Every English word contains some subset of these components. Decode the brain signals that correspond to the phonemes, and you would have a system to unlock any word at the moment someone thinks it.

In 2011, Eric Leuthardt and his colleague Gerwin Schalk positioned electrodes over the language regions of four fully conscious people and were able to detect the phonemes 'oo', 'ah', 'eh' and 'ee'. What they also discovered was that spoken phonemes activated both the language areas and the motor cortex, while imagined speech – that inner voice – boosted the activity of neurons in Wernicke's area. Leuthardt had effectively read his subjects' minds. 'I would call it brain reading,' he says. To arrive at whole words, Leuthardt's next step is to expand his library of sounds and to find out how the production of phonemes translates across different languages.

For now, the research is primarily aimed at improving the lives of people with locked-in syndrome, but the ability to explore the brain's language centres could revolutionise other fields. The consequences of these findings could ripple out to more general audiences who might like to use extreme hands-free mobile communication technologies that can be manipulated by inner voice alone. For linguists, it could provide previously unobtainable insight into the neural origins and structures of language. Knowing what someone is thinking without needing words at all would be functionally indistinguishable from telepathy.

Questions 27–32

Do the following statements agree with the claims of the writer in the Reading Passage?

Write

YES	*if the statement agrees with the claims of the writer*
NO	*if the statement contradicts the claims of the writer*
NOT GIVEN	*if it is impossible to say what the writer thinks about this*

27 Our inner voice can sometimes distract us when we are reading or writing.

28 The possibility of reading minds has both positive and negative implications.

29 Little progress was made in understanding electrical activity in the brain between 1924 and the mid-1990s.

30 Machines can be readily trained to interpret electrical signals from the brain that correspond to movements on a keyboard.

31 Much has been written about the potential use of speech synthesisers with paralysed patients.

32 It has been proven that the perception and expression of speech occur in different parts of the brain.

Questions 33–36

Complete each sentence with the correct ending, A–G.

33 In Wernicke's area, our thoughts

34 It is only in Broca's area that ideas we wish to express

35 The muscles that articulate our sentences

36 The words and sentences that we speak

A	receive impulses from the motor cortex.
B	pass directly to the motor cortex.
C	are processed into language.
D	require a listener.
E	consist of decoded phonemes.
F	are largely non-verbal.
G	match the sounds that they make.

Questions 37–40

Choose the correct letter, A, B, C or D.

37 What does the underlined phrase 'broke new ground' in line 44 mean?

    A   built on the work of others

    B   produced unusual or unexpected results

    C   proved earlier theories on the subject to be false

    D   achieved something that had not been done before

38 What was most significant about Leuthardt and Schalk's work?

    A   They succeeded in grouping certain phonemes into words.

    B   They linked the production of certain phonemes to recognisable brain activity.

    C   Their methods worked for speakers of languages other than English.

    D   Their subjects were awake during the course of their experiments.

39 What does the writer conclude about mind reading?

    A   It could become a form of entertainment.

    B   It may contribute to studies on language acquisition.

    C   Most people are keenly awaiting the possibility of doing it.

    D   Mobile technologies may become unreliable because of it.

40 What is the main purpose of the writer of this passage?

    A   to give an account of the developments in mind-reading research

    B   to show how scientists' attitudes towards mind reading have changed

    C   to explain why mind-reading research should be given more funding

    D   to fully explore the arguments for and against mind reading

WRITING

WRITING TASK 1

You should spend about 20 minutes on this task.

The graph and chart below give information about 3D cinema screens and film releases.

Summarise the information by selecting and reporting the main features, and make comparisons where relevant.

Write at least 150 words.

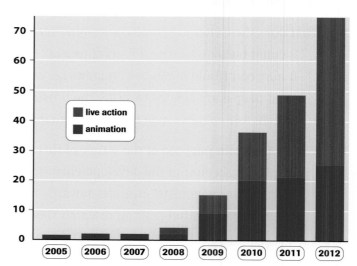

Global digital 3D screens   **Global 3D cinema releases**

WRITING TASK 2

You should spend about 40 minutes on this task.

Write about the following topic.

These days, too many people maintain their health by relying on doctors and medicine, rather than by following a healthy lifestyle.

To what extent do you agree with this statement?

Give reasons for your answer and include any relevant examples from your own knowledge or experience.

Write at least 250 words.

SPEAKING

PART 1

4–5 minutes

Examiner

Now, in this first part, I'd like to ask some questions about yourself. Do you work or are you a student?

- Why did you choose the subjects/course you are studying?
- What do you like about your university/ college building?
- How much time do you spend on campus a week?
- How much work do you do at home?
- What would you like to change about your studies/course?

- Why did you choose your present job?
- What do you like about your work environment?
- What are your working hours each week?
- How much work do you take home?
- What would you like to change about your job?

Let's talk about healthy lifestyles now.

- How often do you find time to relax?
- What's your ideal form of relaxation?
- What activities did you do as a child to stay healthy?
- How healthy do you think your diet is? Why?
- What's your favourite snack between meals?

I'd like to talk about outer space now.

- What aspects of space and space travel did you study at school?
- What do you think you can see through a space telescope?
- What news articles have there been in your country about space travel?
- Would you rather see a documentary about space or a science-fiction film? Why?
- Do you think you will ever take a holiday on the Moon? Why? / Why not?

PART 2

2–3 minutes

> **Examiner**
>
> *Now I'm going to give you a topic and I'd like you to talk about it for one to two minutes. Before you talk, you'll have one minute to think about what you're going to say – you can make some notes if you wish. Do you understand? Here is some paper and a pencil for making notes and here is your topic. I'd like you describe an area of your country that is well known for its natural beauty.*

> **Describe an area of your country that is well known for its natural beauty.**
>
> **You should say**
>
>   **where this area is**
>
>   **what people can see and do there**
>
>   **how you can get there**
>
> **and explain why this area is considered to be so beautiful.**

> *All right? Remember, you have one to two minutes for this, so don't worry if I stop you. I will tell you when the time is up. Can you start speaking now, please?*
> * How can children be encouraged to take an interest in areas of natural beauty?
> * Is it ever appropriate to charge visitors to enter areas of natural beauty? When?

PART 3

4–5 minutes

> **Examiner**
>
> *We've been talking about areas of natural beauty, and I'd like to ask you some more general questions about this.*
>
> *Let's consider the importance of areas of natural beauty.*
> * Why do countries value their beautiful landscapes and wildlife?
> * What disadvantages does tourism bring to these places?
> * How do adults and children differ in the way they experience places of natural beauty?
>
> *Let's move on to talk about protecting areas of natural beauty.*
> * What can individuals do to help protect areas of natural beauty?
> * Why is it sometimes difficult for governments to make decisions about protecting these places?
> * When are authorities justified in banning people from visiting areas of natural beauty?

Recording scripts

Interviewer Hi there – can I help you with anything?

Dominika Oh, hi … I'm interested in the possibility of a career with TGS when I graduate. So I thought I'd come here and see if there are any opportunities suitable for people like me.

I: OK. I'll take a few details from you, and then we can contact you when we start our recruitment programme.

D: Oh great.

I: So if you were to work with us, what area would you want to focus on?

D: I'm hoping to make a career in the field of marketing. I'm quite an outgoing person.

I: OK. I'll just feed that into the computer. And what's your name?

D: It's Dominika Alexandrovna.

I: OK … Can you just spell your surname for me?

D: Sure. It's A-L-E-X-A-N-D-R-O-V-N-A.

I: Thanks – it's important to spell names correctly in business!

D: Yeah!

I: And where are you from, Dominika?

D: Well, I was born in Poland actually, and my mum's Polish, but I'm Russian because we moved to Moscow when I was very small for my father's job.

I: Well I must say, your *English* is very good.

D: Thanks. I've been here a couple of years now.

I: OK, well, we usually get in touch with students a bit later on … and the easiest way for us to communicate with you is by email.

D: Oh yes – I can give you my email address.

I: Fine. Then we can send you any links that you need to read and attach the application forms.

D: Oh great … well, my email address is Dom, D-O-M 54 at qmail.com

I: Right – thanks. As you know, we like to encourage young people to start working for us as soon as they graduate.

D: Uh-huh.

I: Obviously our interest is related to the class of degree that you get.

D: Well, I'm hoping to get a 2:1. My tutors are all pretty confident that I will.

I: That's good … So, which university are you studying at?

D: I'm just finishing my course at London University.

I: And I assume you're in the school of business …

D: Yes, I've been doing a BA.

I: And is that part time?

D: No – I'm a full-time student. I haven't actually had any experience of business yet. I want to concentrate on getting my qualifications first.

I: OK. How have you found the course?

D: Oh – it's been really good. I've really improved my communication skills, and I've learned how to work in a team as well.

I: Well, that's good if you want to work in a global company. So when do you finish?

D: Um – well, it's a 22-month course and I finish in two weeks' time.

I: I see. So when would you be available for an interview?

D: Well, I think the 21st of July. I'm taking a holiday on the 12th of July for a week and I'd need a couple of days to sort myself out after that.

I: We're obviously interested in your business qualifications, but it also helps if you've done anything in your spare time that shows you have some business-related skills.

D: Um – well, I did run a competition last year for the charity 'Save the Children'.

I: That's just the sort of thing I mean … shows you have some management skills. Right … and, apart from work and study, what do you like to do in your free time?

D: I'm quite good at cooking. I make sure I eat well … you know, when you're a student, it's easy to forget to eat or to eat a lot of junk food. I do things like watch some of the cookery programmes on TV and then I copy them.

I: Great!

D: I'm not very sporty, but I do go swimming at least twice a week. I like to keep in shape.

I: Have you done any other work in the past that would be relevant to a marketing career?

D: Um, I did help my father with his business, but it wasn't really a job. I didn't get paid … But I have been a children's tutor. I got that job through the people at my homestay.

I: That's good. So if you worked for us, how would you see your career developing?

D: What do you mean?

I: Well, are you ambitious? Do you want to get to the top?

D: I guess I'd like to get into management … you know … I'd like to work my way up the ladder and end up as a project manager.

I: Well, that's about all I need to ask you for now. I'll let you walk around and look at some of our displays.

D: Thanks.

I: Can I just ask how you first heard about the fair?

D: Oh – from a friend. She told me about it last week, and then I looked it up on the Internet.

I: OK, thanks.

CD1 Track 2

Student 1

Well, a couple of years ago, I decided that I wanted to work in the hotel industry. I used to have a casual part-time job as a waiter when I was 16. So that's why I've been doing a hotel-management course for the past two years. I like dealing with the public – I think I'm quite an outgoing person. Yeah, I'm looking forward to graduating and getting into full-time employment.

CD1 Track 3

Student 2

Yes, when we were children, we used to have a very affectionate black and white cat. She would sit on our laps at night and … well, I know that cats don't talk, but this one did! She would make these high-pitched noises when we came home after school. I guess she wanted food or something, but as children, we used to think she was a real person.

CD1 Track 4

Student 3

I've never been very creative, but … but, er, I've got a nephew. He's two – he's a toddler now. And last month, while I was looking after him, er, we built a house together out of this old cardboard box. He absolutely loved it, and my sister and her husband were really impressed. They were used to seeing me as someone who couldn't play or make things, but I proved them wrong!

CD1 Track 5

Student 4

As a teenager, I didn't use to do very much exercise at all, I just got used to being lazy! But now I'm older, I'm more aware of my health. I joined a gym last year and I've been making use of its facilities – you know, the pool and the tennis courts. I think my fitness level's a bit better than it used to be!

CD1 Track 6

1. A couple of years ago, I decided that I wanted to work in the hotel industry.
2. So that's why I've been doing a hotel-management course for the past two years.
3. I know that cats don't talk, but this one did!

4. He's two – he's a toddler now.
5. I think my fitness level's a bit better than it used to be!

CD1 Track 7

1. I really don't like having animals in the home.
2. I go running in the afternoon because I feel more energetic at that time of day.
3. I think everyone's too busy these days to make anything by hand!
4. I tried sewing at school, but I just couldn't do it.
5. My brother did badly at school, yet he earns more than I do!

CD1 Track 8

Narrator: You will hear someone talking about a colour exhibition.

Announcer: Now, I'd like to welcome onto our show today Darren Whitlock, who's going to tell us about a very vibrant exhibition.

Darren: Thanks, Melanie. Yes, in fact, it's an exhibition called 'Eye for colour'. It's packed with hands-on exhibits and interactive displays and it explores the endless ways in which colour shapes our world.

Now, there are 40 exhibits altogether that come under six main sections. Sadly, I haven't got time to tell you about them all today, so let me just give you a taste of what's on offer.

So to start off, there's a section simply entitled 'Seeing colour', which is, well – as the title suggests – about how we do just that. And it's a good starting point, because basically, you look at the museum gallery through a giant eyeball that's standing on a circular foot. What you don't know is that this houses a 32" camera and screen, and the overall effect of these is quite amazing.

Another section that's very interesting is called 'Colour in culture'. Here, there are a number of activities designed to illustrate the powerful links that exist between colour and certain aspects of our lifestyle, and this is done through a range of images and objects. You can visit the colour café that contains meals that really make you question how conditioned you are … How hungry do you feel if you're faced with a plate of pink and green fried eggs and blue sausages, for example? This section also includes activities that give visitors some idea of what it's like to view the world with a visual disability, which is something that many people have to do.

Then there's a 'Colour in nature' section, designed to illustrate the many amazing colours that we see everywhere around us – from rainbows to autumn leaves – and to give us an idea of what it's like surviving in the external environment. So you can try camouflaging yourself. This really is one for the kids – dressing up in a suit and then selecting a background where, to all intents and purposes, you disappear. And you can look at the world through the eyes of a dog or fish … what do these creatures really see?

I'd recommend ending the trip with a visit to the 'mood room', which explores the influence of colour on the way we feel. Here, you can lie back and listen to music as a projector subtly alters the lighting in the room and with it, the atmosphere. How does each colour affect your emotions? You'll be surprised!

CD1 Track 9

Now, while the exhibition's been running, the organisers have carried out a study of the favourite colours of their younger visitors. Over 2,600 children have responded to this, and there were lots and lots of colours to choose from, so the scores weren't high for each individual colour, even if the colours were – like blue – of average popularity. Clearly, the bold colours were the winners. Though purple, which I would have expected to be a high scorer, had just 1.73% of the votes, unlike deep pink, which came next to top. In the middle ground along with purple – which was still pretty popular compared to others – was lime green – the first shade of green to be anywhere near the top. One two-year-old commented that red was the only colour she knew, which is perhaps why that was more popular with children than anything else. Needless to say, all the tans and beiges came near the bottom. In fact, the lighter the colours, the less popular they were – even the light pinks.

So why did the kids go for these striking colours? As adults, it's all about clothes … what we think suits us or is fashionable. But these youngsters are looking outward more and they go for colours that hit them … that they pick out over and above the rest. It's less to do with how they feel – whether it calms them down or whatever – and more about immediate impact. And, of course, there are associations with football that led a lot of both boys and girls to go for particular colours – in fact, more children seemed to comment on this than anything else, whereas adults would be more likely to go for something worn by someone they really like. So, all in all, it says a lot about …

CD1 Track 10

Well, one of the most colourful things that I've ever bought is a sort of doll that I got when I was on holiday in Java. Um, it's actually a puppet, and it has a special name in Indonesia, but I'm afraid I can't remember what it is. Um, let me see, I decided to buy this doll because we'd been to a puppet theatre and seen a performance, and it was just fantastic … I mean, I've seen some terrible puppet shows in the past, but these dolls were … expressive – they came alive. Um, the story included a certain amount of fighting, which was probably quite frightening for children, but it was also magical, and the good guy won, which I like. Actually, my doll looks pretty old, even though it was made – you know, er, made in this era … er, by that I mean it wasn't made that long ago! It's only wooden, but dressed in really bright, attractive materials, like batik – a long red and gold dress and a tall, coloured hat. Also, as I mentioned before, it's an Indonesian puppet, which means it's supported by these, um, long, thin pieces of wood attached to it that are used to make the limbs move. I've got mine in my room, and people always notice it. Some of my friends think she's very scary, and others, like me, are really drawn to her.

I mean, she's so eye-catching, I think partly because of the colours, but also because, as I said, she has this sort of magic about her. For me, well, ultimately, I feel that she protects me from bad things and brings me good luck. So I'll always keep her.

CD1 Track 11

I mean, I've seen some terrible puppet shows in the past, but these dolls were expressive – they came alive.

CD1 Track 12

1   I decided to buy this doll because we'd been to a puppet theatre and seen a performance, and it was just fantastic.

2   The story included a certain amount of fighting, which was probably quite frightening for children, but it was also magical – and the good guy won, which I like.

3   Actually, my doll looks pretty old, even though it was made – you know – made in this era.

4   It's only wooden, but dressed in really bright, attractive materials, like batik.

5   Some of my friends think she's very scary, and others, like me, are really drawn to her.

6   I feel that she protects me from bad things and brings me good luck.

CD1 Track 13

Steve: Good morning, guys, come on in.

Mike: Thanks, Steve – it's good of you to spare us some of your time.

Flo: Yeah – we really appreciate it.

S: That's OK. So you're studying sports science, are you?

M: Yeah – we've only just started our course, actually – but as I explained on the phone, um, we have this seminar to do on sports injuries and we thought, who better to talk to than someone like yourself?

S: Fine, OK. So what would you like to know?

F: Well, we thought we'd start by asking you about some of the treatments and services you offer here at the clinic.

S: OK – well, as you know, physiotherapists deal with a whole range of different 'problem areas' in the body.

M: Yeah – what sort of techniques do you use to help people? I mean, I know you use massage – and I understand that's a key form of treatment …

S: Yeah. Well, we call it 'manual therapy', you know, because it's a hands-on treatment and it just involves manipulating the soft tissue around a joint to relieve stiffness and pain.

F: Is that something that a lot of people come here for?

S: Um – well, *we* generally decide what's best for the individual. This treatment can hurt sometimes, but it gets results more quickly than anything else.

F: And is that true whatever the injury?

S: For sports injuries, generally, yes. But it doesn't stop there – you have to do other things as well.

M: I've heard of something called 'stability training'. Do you do that?

S: Definitely. This is something that's designed to improve overall posture and body shape.

M: So it's for the back and neck?

F: I think I've heard of this … it works on everything and gives you more power.

S: Yeah – this is important – we improve your overall form, and that's quite good if you're tired or a bit weak.

F: Do you use any aids to boost performance?

S: Occasionally we recommend a pad or block for a sports shoe, but not often.

M: What about electrical equipment?

S: We do sometimes use electrotherapy, which is supposed to stimulate the body to repair itself.

F: So that's actually using a small electrical charge?

S: Yes, but there's growing evidence that the effect is limited.

M: So I guess you don't use it much?

S: No – we tend to avoid it most of the time.

M: I see. What if people don't have an injury but just want to get better at their sport? I mean, sometimes people know they do *something* wrong when they … swing a golf club, for example.

S: Ah – then we film them and show them exactly what they do. It's called video analysis.

F: That must be really helpful.

S: It's what everyone asks for … it outstrips all our other services – because it's great for so many activities – not just sporting ones.

M: Can you help people with sedentary activities?

S: Absolutely – we offer workstation analysis because so many people have asked us for it.

F: Yeah, I spend hours on my laptop, and as the day goes on, my posture gets worse and worse!

S: That's why we tend to suggest that people come at the end of the day for this.

M: I guess the problem is that everyone's built differently … I think we both need some help there.

CD1 Track 14

F: That was really interesting. So what happens when someone comes to your clinic?

S: Well, let's imagine you're the patient.

F: OK.

S: A common situation will be that you sustained an injury, say, a year ago. So it's not new … so you turn up with what we call an 'existing injury'.

F: Right. Like I sprained my ankle.

S: Exactly – that's a typical one.

F: OK, and I've been to the doctor, and he's sent me to the hospital for an X-ray, and then I've been prescribed a cream or even painkillers.

S: You've been through that medical route.

F: OK. And I had to rest it for a while, of course, and that meant not doing any sport. So I've come to you because I'm fed up, basically.

S: Yes – you need to get the joint moving again. So what we would do first is to assess the damage to the joint area.

F: I guess there's a whole range of problems that it could be, and some are more serious than others.

S: And we can't afford to make mistakes. Now, once we know what the problem is, we select a treatment – perhaps one that we talked about earlier – *plus* we design an exercise plan for you.

F: That's great if you stick to it.

S: Yes, that's the hard part for patients because they don't have time or they get bored. So we ask them to come back regularly – we make appointments – and we monitor the movement in the joint each time.

F: And you expect that to work?

S: Yes, and it usually does – quite quickly, in fact, and then we can go on to rehabilitation.

F: You mean getting them back into the sporting activity they used to do?

S: That's right. We have a fully equipped gym and we devise a training plan – well, a personal trainer does that, and they oversee the programme for at least a couple of months and make sure the patient carries it out.

F: It sounds really thorough. That's great, Steve, thanks.

CD1 Track 15

Faris: Well, I'm *quite* fit because I do a range of sports like running and tennis, but, um, I've always dreamed of taking part in a triathlon. I really like the idea of that. Um, a triathlon's a multi-sport event, but rather a hard one. It basically consists of swimming, cycling and running events, but you have to do them one after the other … you know, there are no breaks, so it would be quite a challenge! You can do various distances for each sport – there's an Olympic distance, which I wish I could do, but it would be too much for me. However, I think I'm likely to finish if I choose a shorter course. There's one that's, um, I think it involves a 750-metre swim, followed by 20 kilometres on the bike and then a five-kilometre run. As for when I'd take part in it, I'm not sure. Looking ahead, I don't expect I'll be able to tackle it until my academic year's ended. That means I'd be thinking in terms of maybe doing it in a year's time. That would be realistic, because I'd need time to train and really get into shape. It's not something that I could do in a hurry! Um, obviously it would be a really healthy thing to do because it would force me to get even fitter than I am now. Plus I'd have to eat well during the training period and get plenty of sleep and that sort of thing. Yeah, I'm actually looking forward to doing a triathlon. I'd really like to do it some time soon and I just hope I'll be successful at it.

Examiner: Have you always tried to do things that are healthy?

F: Oh, yes – well, probably. I think I've enjoyed doing sport and exercise since I was a child. And, er, I also try to eat well and get plenty of sleep.

CD1 Track 16

1 Well, I'm quite fit …

2 … taking part in a triathlon.

CD1 Track 17

1 … a triathlon's a multi-sport event, but rather a hard one.

2 As for when I'd take part in it, I'm not sure.

3 I'm actually looking forward to the triathlon.

CD1 Track 18

That would be realistic because I'd need time to train and really get into shape. It's not something that I could do in a hurry! Um, obviously it would be a really healthy thing to do because it would force me to get even fitter than I am now. Plus I'd have to eat well during the training period and get plenty of sleep and that sort of thing.

CD1 Track 19

We're going to have a look today at Aboriginal art and painting, which actually dates back 60,000 years, making it one of the oldest art traditions in the world. Now, as long as indigenous people have been living in Australia, they've been creating different types of art. So let's start by having a look at some examples of ancient art. It includes things like, as you can see here, rock paintings, bark paintings … even some sand drawings like this have been found. Then there's the whole area of body art, which is so important for ceremonial practice, and lastly, here are some examples of decorative art on weapons and tools.

The oldest art examples today are the rock paintings because, obviously, rock is more durable than other materials and so the art has been preserved. In fact, most of this work is inside caves – largely because there, it's been sheltered, hasn't been destroyed by the weather, while the paintings on outside rock surfaces have often been washed away over the years. Now, there are enormous variations in the style of Aboriginal rock art, depending on its age and location. Dot paintings are one of the best-known visual art forms of Aboriginal culture in which a surface is covered in small dots to reveal symbols. Typical ones include arrows like this – here's a water hole, and these are animal tracks. You get to see both the abstract dot paintings and more naturalistic art … you get both in rock art of various ages. As the ancient Aborigines didn't have a written language, the key purpose of much of this rock art was storytelling, which has had a great significance for younger generations.

Let's move on to look at the materials. Er, whatever they were painting, traditionally Aboriginal people all over Australia used pigment, such as ochre, to make paint. Ochre's very finely textured natural rock and, um, well, they used this because ochre is plentiful across most of Australia. It's coloured by iron oxide, which is the mineral that makes a lot of Australian outback soil – in places such as Ayers Rock – what is known as 'Uluru red', Uluru being the Aboriginal name for Ayers Rock. However, depending on the exact conditions under which it formed, the shade can be anything from yellow to orange, red, purple or dark brown. Today, ochre occurs in many archaeological sites, and archaeologists at one site have discovered what appears to be an artist's palette of ochres, dating back 18,000 years.

Preparing the ochre paints was time-consuming work. First, the appropriate rocks had to be found and collected. Then the rock had to be broken up and ground into a powder, and that had to be mixed with some sort of fluid to bind it into paint. Nowadays, the binder most commonly used is professional artist's acrylic binder, but in the past, Aboriginal people used things like tree sap, or something similar like bush honey. Other fluids must also have been used but wouldn't have held paint on rock or a piece of bark for thousands of years, so sadly those paintings would have been lost.

So, how have things changed? Well, modern Aboriginal is a mixture of the old and the new. Things changed in the 1970s really when Aboriginal people from many different parts of Australia, particularly south Australia, central and northern Australia, took up acrylic painting and began to paint on canvas.

Taking a modern approach has had many advantages. It saves artists a great deal of time, and they can still choose to use the traditional yellowish-reddish-brownish colours if they wish to. But perhaps the most important fact is that, unlike bark and rock paintings, the modern paintings are easy to sell. In fact, painting on canvas has given Aboriginal people an opportunity to showcase their art to the world and keep their ancient culture alive. Modern Aboriginal art, particularly dot painting, has taken off and started selling on a big scale internationally. Aboriginal art can also be found on pottery and various musical instruments like didgeridoos and clapping sticks. Together, these have become some of the most popular souvenirs in Australia. Their artists, like other artists in the world, are now able to earn a living doing something they are passionate about.

CD1 Track 20

Examiner: What can young children learn from doing art at school?

Naresh: Well, I think broadly speaking, they can learn a great deal. The majority of pre-school children, for example, are incredibly creative and experiment with paints and all sorts of other art materials and they just love getting their hands dirty. Older students tend to be less enthusiastic, but many of them still enjoy art and, well, I guess if you don't try it, you won't know whether you're any good at it.

E: Why do you think secondary schools give arts subjects a low priority?

N: Well, generally, there are quite a few reasons. These days, a lot of head teachers seem to be more concerned about exam results than giving the students an all-round education. That's obviously going to have an influence on how significant art is in the school curriculum. Another possible reason is that many educational institutions don't tend to have the money to provide all the materials you need for art courses. They seem to be more worried about buying technological equipment these days.

CD1 Track 21

Speaker 1

I think attitudes to art have changed a lot since my parents were at school. Thirty years ago, schools taught a whole range of arts and crafts subjects, but nowadays there doesn't seem to be much choice.

CD1 Track 22

Speaker 2

I think attitudes to art have changed a lot since my parents were at school. Thirty years ago, schools taught a whole range of arts and crafts subjects, but nowadays there doesn't seem to be much choice.

CD1 Track 23

Speaker 3

I think attitudes to art have changed a lot since my parents were at school. Thirty years ago, schools taught a whole range of arts and crafts subjects, but nowadays there doesn't seem to be much choice.

CD1 Track 24

Examiner: What can young children learn from doing art at school?

Naresh: Well, I think broadly speaking they can learn a great deal. The majority of pre-school children, for example, are incredibly creative and experiment with paints and all sorts of other art materials, and they just love getting their hands dirty. Older students tend to be less enthusiastic, but many of them still enjoy art and, well, I guess if you don't try it, you won't know whether you're any good at it.

CD1 Track 25

Examiner: Why do you think secondary schools give arts subjects a low priority?

Naresh: Well, generally, there are quite a few reasons. These days, a lot of head teachers seem to be more concerned about exam results than giving the students an all-round education. That's obviously going to have an influence on how significant art is in the school curriculum. Another possible reason is that many educational institutions don't tend to have the money to provide all the materials you need for art courses. They seem to be more worried about buying technological equipment these days.

CD1 Track 26

Juni: Hi, Milton – I didn't see you this afternoon. You missed a really good talk.

Milton: Oh, did I? That's a pity – it was Mr Brand's talk about fossils, wasn't it?

J: Yeah. I hadn't really expected to enjoy it, but it was fascinating.

M: I thought it would be. I'd been planning to go to the talk, but then when I was in the lab this morning, I realised I hadn't done any reading for tomorrow's history seminar.

J: Well, I think he's going to repeat it some time, but it may be next year.

M: Perhaps you could tell me a bit about it, then?

J: Well, he talked about himself in the first part.

M: I saw on the notice that went round that he went to America to study and met a famous anthropologist.

J: Yeah, that's right, but he said he got interested in fossils well before then – when he was about six, in fact – and he found the most amazing fossil on a school visit to a national park. He showed it to us – he still has it – though he said he wasn't looking for it at the time!

M: Most kids wouldn't recognise a fossil if they saw one!

J: I know – they want to watch adventure films or play with model dinosaurs. But apparently *he* spent his school holidays hunting for fossils in the farm pits near his home.

M: So does he lecture on the subject now?

J: Yes – but he also runs a business organising fossil hunts for groups of adults and children.

M: Aw … Wouldn't it be great if we could do something like that?

J: He showed us a lot of pictures …

M: So they all go out in a group to the cliffs or somewhere with little hammers, do they?

J: Yeah – apparently, the kids tell everyone that's the best bit – tapping the stones to see if anything's there.

M: Do they know what they're looking for?

J: Yeah. They get shown some examples of what they might find first.

M: And do they actually get to find any fossils?

J: Yes – Mr Brand showed some photos of children proudly holding up their fossils for the camera at the end of the day.

M: If they take them home, I bet they become prized possessions in their rooms as well!

J: For sure. He said he never stops being amazed at how close you can be to a fossil.

M: I guess the children aren't aware of history that much.

J: No, but, for them, the key thing they learn is that if they keep looking, they *will* find something.

M: Mmm – you have to wait … it's not for people who want instant success. So why don't we go on one of these hunts?

J: Well, yes, I'm quite keen. The hunts are fully booked until the end of the year, unfortunately.

M: I could talk to some of the other students and see if we can form a group.

J: That's a good idea. I'll give him a call. Then, if we have enough people, we might be able to get him to do an extra one for us.

M: I'll look on his website when I get back to the dorm just to get a bit more information.

CD1 Track 27

Milton: So what did he talk about in the second part?

Juni: Well, that was more theoretical, but just as interesting, and there were lots of visuals. You know how fossils are formed?

M: Not exactly. We all know they're the remains of living organisms, sort of entombed in rock, but I don't know how they get to be there.

J: Well, he basically went through the stages that make that happen.

M: So did he talk about the conditions that bring about fossilisation?

J: Yes – and he used a fish as an example. Here, I'll show you my notes.

M: Wow, these are great diagrams, Juni!

J: Thanks.

M: OK … er, Stage 1 … Ah yes, that's right – a lot of fossils form underwater, don't they?

J: Yeah – like as soon as a fish dies, it sinks to the bottom of the ocean, and as long as a predator doesn't come along, it just lies there.

M: Undisturbed.

J: That's right.

M: And since the ocean bed's soft – well, much of it is, plus it's muddy as well – the fish gradually gets covered over and can't be seen any more.

J: Mmm. Apparently for a fossil to begin to form, you also need conditions where the light is minimal and there's very little oxygen.

M: … so the organic matter doesn't break down too quickly.

J: Yes, and you know there are fault lines, even on the sea bed, and the rocks can move.

M: Yeah, so once the fish gets buried – I guess that has to happen quite quickly?

J: Mm-hm, all the sand and sediment piles up into layers, and the huge pressure and weight of all the layers compacts it and you move on to Stage 2, where it gets heavier and heavier until it becomes hard rock.

M: There'd be no water left, so the fish skeleton would be entombed. It can stay like that for millions of years, can't it?

J: It can, but during that time, the bone in the skeleton is replaced by minerals.

M: I see, and these minerals sort of mimic the shape of the skeleton.

J: Yes – and that's how you get a fossil.

M: But how do we find them if they're buried so far down?

J: Again, it's all down to the movement of the Earth's plates. In the last stage, many millions of years after the fossil has formed, the rock may lift and eventually be above sea level.

M: Meanwhile, the surface of the rock wears away?

J: Yes, another natural process called erosion wears away the rock until one day, you can see the tip of the fossil.

M: And you break open the rock – and there it is.

J: It's incredible really.

CD1 Track 28

Actually, there are a number of objects that I could talk about in my home, so it's quite hard for me to decide what to choose. However, I'm going to talk about a very special necklace that I keep in my attic. First, I think I'll tell you where it came from. Basically, it was an inheritance from my grandmother, who was 95 years old when she died! As far as I know, *she'd* been given it by someone – possibly an aunt – who'd bought it in a market in India. It's a pity I didn't ask my grandmother. I'd know its origins for certain if I'd asked her. Anyway, undoubtedly it's pretty ancient now – probably an antique – although I've no idea what it's worth. But, as my mother says, you can't put a price on something that has sentimental value. If I were to lose it, I'd be really upset! Just looking at it, I don't think you get an idea of its age. You wouldn't realise how old it was unless you examined it closely. I wouldn't say that it's strikingly beautiful or something you'd choose to put on to go out for the evening. It's just a long line of blue beads that are quite chipped and faded now. They look pretty worthless – not as eye-catching as the gold necklace that I got for my 21st birthday! Actually, I don't *use* the beads for anything because, as I said earlier, I don't wear them. They're not at all fashionable. In fact, I don't really like beads, but, having said that, I'll always keep them. If I were to throw the beads out, I wouldn't be able to forgive myself. I'll pass them on to my children, so that they become an equally important family treasure for them. It's funny to think, but if it hadn't been for my granny's aunt, I wouldn't have inherited that necklace.

CD1 Track 29

Examiner: Why do you think some people like to keep old things, while others don't have any interest in doing this?'

Margarete: Actually, I'm sure there are all sorts of reasons, but perhaps the main one is space. You know, if I were to live in a small apartment, I wouldn't be able to store much. On the whole, people who are hoarders tend to have large attics or spare rooms or cupboards where they can put things.'

Johannes: I think it must be a question of personality … and by that I mean, well, some people are really sentimental, so they don't like to throw away things like cards or presents – even though they don't want them any more. I guess, you know, were they to throw them away, they'd feel a sense of loss. Whereas other people, maybe, don't care that much – they're just happy just to focus on the present.

CD1 Track 30

Well, old things are full of memories, and I think that's the main reason why people keep them. Perhaps the most obvious example is photographs. I mean, although people might get rid of the ones that they don't like themselves in, they often keep others because they remind them of a special person or event.

CD2 Track 1

Good morning, everyone. So – we're looking at animation technology today … something we're all very familiar with from seeing blockbuster films such as *Toy Story* and *Shrek*. But, um, I'd like to start by looking at how animation began, and how the technical side of things developed.

Not long after the invention of the first camera by Thomas Edison in 1889, a photographer by the name of J. Stuart Blackton developed the first technique for animated film. It consisted of a series of drawings and, er, he drew a number of 'funny faces' and then filmed one after the other. This gave the impression of motion and changing facial expression. But it was a very slow process and a long way from being anything like a film. Then a Frenchman, Émile Cohl, moved things on a bit by using scenes and figures cut out of paper instead. This meant things could be done more quickly. It was possible to build up a small scene, though a very large number of cut-outs were required to do this. And, of course, it was all still taking place during the era of silent film.

Eventually, Walt Disney came along. He wanted his film characters to look more 'real' and so he found ways to do this. Er, it took weeks to produce a single film sequence, but in 1928, the first talking animated film came out that had been made using hand-painted slides known as 'cels' – these were placed one on top of the other and then quickly removed. And that first film launched the career of Mickey Mouse – if you remember him. Disney then went on to produce the first full-length colour animated film in 1937 – *Snow White and the Seven Dwarfs* – which earned him the first of his 37 Oscars.

Animation changed very little over the next 50 years or so until the advent of computers and the work of a company called Pixar. Pixar Animation Studios was a graphics group until Steve Jobs invested 10 million dollars in the company. Now it has become a Hollywood icon, with earnings of over 6.3 billion dollars and numerous film awards. In fact, Pixar's films act rather like a timeline of technological developments in computer graphics. So, let's have a look at some of them. Pixar's debut feature film was *Toy Story*, and this was the first film to be completely animated by computers. When it was released in 1995, many features of the film were seen as outstanding. It is still considered to be one of the most significant achievements in the history of film animation. A later film, *Monsters, Inc.*, which came out in 2001, added a new animation feature, which was the on-screen representation of animal fur. This helped to enhance the appeal of one of the film's central characters. Two years after that, the award-winning film *Finding Nemo* – a tale of the lives of some very appealing and visually enchanting fish – pioneered new techniques in digital lighting, which were used to create realistic-looking water. This was an essential feature of the film. Many scenes took place underwater and relied on a certain level of brilliance and clarity throughout. Had they got it wrong, the entire effect would have been lost. And a film called *The Incredibles* in 2004 brought with it credible human characters and advances in the simulation of crowds.

So each of these films introduced new types of physical phenomena, and these days 3D animation can re-create most real-world scenarios. Yet cinema audiences have increasingly high expectations. So how do companies like Pixar plan to meet the challenges of the future?

Well, firstly, studios still struggle to create digital humans that audiences like. Up to now, they've been criticised for looking robotic. So the focus for producers now is on simulating more realistic human skin and more detailed facial movement. Both developments are bringing close the day when there will be convincing digital actors on screen.

A second aspect that Pixar hope to improve on is the speed at which they can actually produce each frame of animated film. Things have moved on, but the time it takes to do this is basically staying the same. Faster computers help, but work done by companies involved in the production of video games is also hoped to improve things.

A further challenge is colour. Pixar is looking ahead to how it can better use its colour palettes and produce more brilliant images. And lastly, the company is hoping to build on methods to stylise its images in films. It seems reality has been the goal for many years, but now they are also trying to break new ground and come up with other concepts. The result could be a new breed of animated films that don't look real or like anything that has gone before.

Now let's take a closer look at …

CD2 Track 2

Well, the website I'm going to talk about is called CD Baby. Um, it sounds like a music website for babies, but it isn't that at all. What it is is, it's basically a site where you can listen to ordinary people, I mean people who aren't famous, you know, not professionals. You can listen to their music, and they might be a solo artist or a band or whatever. You can buy their CDs on the site, or just play some selected tracks – there are all sorts of … many different types of music like jazz, blues, folk or rock. So … what people do is they make a CD in a recording studio somewhere. I don't know whether some people set up the recording equipment in their own home … you know, there's so much software around that you can use if you have the right kind of knowledge and skill, and, um, then they have to make some copies of their CD and send them to CD Baby. I meant to say earlier – it's an American site … I think it's based in Oregon, so the CDs have to be sent there. And there are a few online forms that you have to fill in because you're basically selling something over the Internet. Um, it's mainly young people who put their music on the site – though there's no age limit – and they're usually talented musicians and composers. Some of them might have their own bands or play regularly somewhere and they hope a talent scout will spot them on the website! As well as musicians, anyone can listen to the site and order the CDs online if they want to. I love this website because you get to hear original music, and whatever you choose, it's always really good.

CD2 Track 3

Speaker A

Oh, absolutely. I mean, a significant advantage for anyone is that you can stay in touch with so many people using sites like Facebook. Another is that it really doesn't matter how far away they are. Friends that you might otherwise lose can look at your photos and chat to you at night.

CD2 Track 4

Speaker B

They could be right – yeah, a lot of people would agree with that. To be fair, I think it depends on how much time they spend on it and what purpose they use it for. If they come straight home from school and spend three hours in their room chatting on social networking sites, then I'd say there aren't many benefits to doing that.

CD2 Track 5

Speaker C

I think so, yes. Although it provides a lot of useful information, I think one of the main drawbacks of using it in education is that children just copy what they read and don't bother trying to understand it. A real benefit to children of using books is that they're often better written or they're designed with a certain age group in mind.

CD2 Track 6

Examiner: Would you agree that most people find it easier to read the news on the Internet?'

Student 1: Not really. It's convenient sometimes, but I don't think it's as enjoyable.

Student 2: Yeah – a lot of young people do that these days.

CD2 Track 7

Examiner: Some people say it isn't good for children to use the Internet a lot in their free time – what do you think?

Student 2: That could be right, yeah. A lot of people would agree with that.

E: Would you agree that the Internet has a negative effect on children's social lives?

Student 1: Oh, well, actually, I think it has a positive one.

CD2 Track 8

Examiner: Some people say we've reached the point where technology is intruding on our private lives. Would you agree?

A: Oh, completely. There are CCTV cameras everywhere.

B: I don't think people notice really – they're just used to it.

C: I would, yes. Everywhere you go, there are screens of one kind or another.

D: Well, you can't stop it – new developments are happening all the time.

E: I'm not sure. In some ways it's a nuisance, but in others it isn't.

CD2 Track 9

Narrator: You will hear two students talking to their tutor about a photography assignment.

Tutor: So, you're off to Glen Affric next week in the Highlands of Scotland for your photography assignment.

Brett: Yes, that's right.

T: So have you got the map I gave you of Loch Affric and the surrounding area?

B: Yup – here's mine.

Mica: … and mine. *Loch* means 'lake', right?

T: Yes, that's right. Now, you've read up on it, so is there anything in particular that you want to look out for?

B: Well, as I said, I'd love to get some really good shots of the pine trees, particularly old ones.

M: You're going to see them all over … Look, there's a particularly big area of forest to the south-east here and several smaller ones.

T: Yes, they're OK, but if you look at where the two lochs meet …

B: Um, where it narrows in the centre of the map?

T: That's right. You'll find some of the oldest pines there – up to 200 years old.

B: Great – I'll mark that.

M: What about red deer? Can we hope to see any?

B: I guess they'd be more out in the open, in the non-wooded areas.

T: Well, they like an area near the edge of woodland.

M: So perhaps this largest area of forest – here, in the corner of the map?

T: Yes – they also need water, so between the woodland and the river – I'd try that spot. What you should also look for are red squirrels.

B: But they're so rare in Britain!

M: Not here, though. You might get a good picture of one among the pine trees near the loch.

B: Mm, close to the loch … um, perhaps this south side of Loch Affric.

T: Mmm. Not right on the edge, though – that's where you'd look for birds – but in this slightly bigger patch of woodland behind it.

B: Just away from the water a bit, then.

T: Yup. There's plenty of wildlife to tempt you. But remember to go for a good shot when you see it.

B: Yes, I remember what you said in your lecture – if you're in a good spot, the light is good; if an animal is about to move into a great position, then be ready and go for it. My problem's hesitation – I wait too long!

M: You lose the moment.

T: Well, a lot of inexperienced photographers have that particular problem.

M: What if you frighten your subject off?

T: If you do, it's like anything, you have to put it down to experience.

B: So you shouldn't wait too long, but don't take the shot too soon either – sometimes you've got to have patience.

T: That's one of the most important qualities if you're a wildlife photographer. You may have to sit for hours waiting for the perfect moment. But suddenly something will take your breath away and you'll realise it's all been worth it!

CD2 Track 10

Tutor: Right, so do you have any further questions about the trip?

Brett: Well, yeah – I was wondering about the weather – they're forecasting a lot of mist.

T: Well, yes, but I wouldn't worry – in the long run, you'll still get your pictures.

B: But …

T: You just have to be careful. You know, experts say there's no such thing as bad weather when it comes to photography.

Mica: What about driving rain?

T: Well, yes, that doesn't make things easy, but it does mean that you need to take the landscape into account. Perhaps to a greater degree than you would normally.

M: Is that because of shadow and things like that?

T: Well, you get shadow in good weather.

M: Yeah – I guess so.

B: Um, I'm really looking forward to photographing the Scots pine trees. I want to make the most of all the stunning reflections in the water.

T: Just take your time, and you might capture an amazing reflection – you really should profit from this with the water around you.

M: You were talking last week in your lecture about a piece of equipment called an angle finder, and I've been checking them out on the Internet …

T: Ah-hah, it's a clever little device – particularly useful if you're down on your knees trying to get really close to something in the grass, like an insect or bird.

B: I've got one actually – and what's great about it is that it prevents neck pain, because it's like a periscope on a submarine – you can lie down and look through it without hurting your neck.

M: Definitely worth buying, then!

T: Now, is there anything else?

B: Well, I've been looking at some wildlife paintings by Scottish artists. I thought they might help me get ideas.

M: That's a good suggestion.

T: Some designers can be helpful, too … they can help give you ideas about camera angles and how you use natural light .

M: Hmm, I'll look into that. One other thing … I know you said we should consider matters related to conservation when we choose a scene to photograph.

T: I made that point because, well, images like the ones you're going to take can sometimes reveal some of the conservation problems faced by species and habitats. It's just something to bear in mind.

CD2 Track 11

Daeng: Well, I'm going to talk about elephants, because they're an integral part of Thai culture and history. In the past, every Thai king had white elephants. Also, they used to be on our national flag and on our coins and banknotes. So Thai people are very fond of elephants. We even have an Elephant Day on March 13! Um, what else? Um, some Thai Buddhist temples have been built on the spot where an elephant died and, er, these temples contain things like an elephant shrine and elephant statues. As you can tell, elephants are everywhere! You can find them in the wild in Thailand, but also in cities and although the elephants were in captivity, they used to be an important part of the workforce in the forests – that was their primary occupation – but as a result of conservation programmes, there's less logging nowadays. Workers now bring them into the city, as this is the only way they can make a living.

Basically, elephant numbers are falling these days, and I think that's why there's been a lot of publicity about them recently. Cities aren't really the ideal environment for animals … they're full of pollution. On the other hand, elephants can damage roads and they can be dangerous for humans. So the government has cracked down on this, and some elephants have been moved out. In order to protect them, we now have an elephant conservation centre. Also, every year, there's a special event to help raise awareness and money to look after our elephants because they are such important creatures to us.

Examiner: Have you always liked elephants?

D: Oh yes, they're lovely creatures.

CD2 Track 12

Examiner: Is there any justification for continuing to keep animals in captivity?

Daeng: I'm not sure. Zoos became unpopular because animals were being kept in cages that were just much too small. But nowadays, many animals are kept in much larger enclosures and, well, children love seeing real animals – it helps with their education. Yeah, looking ahead, I can see a future for zoos. Also, certain species only survive if we protect them – like the giant panda. So,

I'd say there's a reasonable chance that zoos and similar places will carry on. Although it's highly likely that the word *zoo* will be completely replaced by *animal sanctuary* or something, but I think we need to have them.

CD2 Track 13

Examiner: Is wildlife preservation a global or national issue?

Per: Well, in the end, I think it's an issue that will be handled on an international level. I mean, woodland, animals, even insects – they belong to all of us – they don't recognise borders or cultural boundaries. If we don't protect forests and other animal habitats now, we may well see a very steep decline in animal numbers in the future and more extinctions. So we have to have a global plan; otherwise there's every possibility that there will be catastrophic consequences.

CD2 Track 14

Examiner: What future role do governments have to play in the preservation of their country's wildlife?

Lucrecia: As far as I can see, they must lead the way. I mean, ordinary people are interested to know whether they can do anything to help endangered species. You know, it seems like they want to play a role in that, so they give to charities and even do sponsored runs, and that raises awareness. But, in the end, it's only governments who can actually enforce laws and prevent people from participating in activities that damage the environment. Without new laws, there's very little chance of any real improvement in the foreseeable future.

CD2 Track 15

Also, certain species only survive if we protect them – like the giant panda.

CD2 Track 16

Although the elephants were in captivity, they used to be an important part of the workforce in the forests – that was their primary occupation – but as a result of conservation programmes, there's less logging nowadays.

CD2 Track 17

So we're talking about astronomy today – the scientific study of outer space – and I'm going to start by saying a bit about telescopes and then move on to look at some key features of amateur astronomy.

Now, one of the most powerful telescopes in the world today is the Hubble Space Telescope, named after Edwin Hubble. And, er, it's become rather symbolic in many ways … and that's quite appropriate really because, you know, in the early days, it was instruments – and particularly telescopes – that kicked off what was known as the 'scientific revolution'. We tend to think of science in terms of great minds conjuring up big ideas – we think of books – but in the field of science, instruments have always been more important.

And of course it was the Italian astronomer Galileo who started us star-gazing. He didn't come up with the world's first telescope, but he *was* the first scientist to add a lens to his telescope that magnified things in the sky enough to be able to study them. Until this time, scientists had been looking at objects on the Earth, but suddenly the skies held a much greater fascination for people. He said it best when he declared that his telescopes 'revealed the invisible'.

That was in the first part of the 17th century. Photography took longer to come about, so only artists were able to capture the celestial images seen in those days. We had to wait a further nearly 200 years, until 1839, for John William Draper, a chemistry professor, to produce the first recorded Moon photograph, which looks like this – black and white, of course.

Since that time, humans have built bigger, better, more powerful telescopes, and what can be seen through these in the present day is, well, truly amazing. Millions of pictures have appeared in magazines, books, on TV and on the Internet. Most professional astronomers don't care if the end result is beautiful, what they really want is research data – that's their main objective – but when the device capturing a distant star or galaxy is the Hubble Space Telescope or a large telescope housed in a mountaintop observatory, the result usually appears spectacular as well. Now, *amateur* astronomers often have a different objective. Many want nothing more than to capture a scene that will dazzle viewers. They aim to photograph things never seen before, um, like this beautiful solar eclipse that was captured in Greece … or this incredible image of the Moon with a plane crossing it. But needless to say, they've also made a great contribution to furthering astronomical research, and they do get their photographs and findings published in astronomy journals.

So let's have a look at what the amateurs can contribute. All astronomers are trying to find out, or understand, the origins of the solar system … how stars formed in the first place, and how the universe itself evolved in such a way. Amateur astronomers have a great deal of specialised knowledge that is highly valued in this regard. For example, they're very familiar with the sky and they know right away when something new appears or when the brightness of an object alters – increases or decreases. They know how to tell the difference between, say, planets and comets or stars, or even artificial satellites – many ordinary people wouldn't have any of these skills. And another vital skill is that they know how to make accurate measurements. Knowing the distance of one object from another or from Earth, for example, is essential information if you want to make a valuable contribution to astrophysics.

So that's what they know. When you look at what they can do to help the professionals … well, in general, there are two main types of observation that are important. Firstly, they are always watching space; they keep a constant eye on the skies for any new discovery, such as an exploding star that has reached the end of its life and lets off a tremendous amount of energy, or a comet – a very small object made of dust and ice orbiting the Sun.

Secondly, they constantly observe the evolution of stars, planets and other celestial features. And the information they gather is essential to our understanding of these objects. It tells us, for example, how stars live and die, and how they interact with neighbouring stars.

In both types of observation, professionals can see advantages in the enormous patience and passion that amateurs have for their hobby. This doesn't just mean spending a whole night looking at the stars. We're talking about observations that involve spending years of evenings on the roof or in the back garden. It's not possible for professional astronomers to undertake these long-term studies or to spend huge amounts of time observing a single object. But amateurs can – and they do – and that's why they are so important to the field of astronomy.

CD2 Track 18

Examiner: Let's talk about attitudes towards space travel. What do you think fascinates humans about outer space?

Pauline: Well, it's a 'new frontier' and it represents the 'unknown', and humans have a natural tendency to want to explore unknown places. It goes right back to the early explorers who travelled across the globe. You know, it's like the time when people were discovering that the Earth was round, not flat, and that there's a gravitational force. Over the centuries, one discovery has led to another so that we know a great deal more about Earth now, but we still know relatively little about outer space. We're still a bit obsessed with it.

E: Do you think that's why some stories about space travel have been so 'imaginative'?

P: Oh definitely, yes. Because, well, anything could be out there so – to make it exciting, particularly in films – you can just imagine what that might be. You know, so there are horror films that are designed to make you afraid of extra-terrestrial life, there are TV programmes like *Star Trek* that have a huge cult following, and then there are box-office hits like *Avatar* – that was even bigger in America than the Harry Potter films.

E: How do you think people's attitudes towards space exploration have changed since the first Moon landings?

P: Mm, I think there's possibly less interest now, since it's no longer new and exciting. Back in the 1960s, when the Moon landing took place, everybody was very impressed. It was an incredible moment, and it made the human race come together and see that we can achieve something that's 'out of this world'. But I think we've reached the point now where the next step is going to be too risky and too difficult. And – well – as far as I'm concerned, it's a waste of money.

E: To what extent do you think governments will continue to fund projects in search of life on other planets?

P: I think it's unlikely that they'll continue because it's too expensive. At a time when most countries are struggling to make ends meet, who wants to spend billions on space travel? As far as the solar system's concerned, we've a reasonably good understanding of what's on other planets and we're pretty certain that they wouldn't sustain life. So there's little point in sending people up there. I think governments may well continue to send space probes to see what they come up with, but why risk people's lives?

CD2 Track 19

As far as I'm concerned, it's a waste of money.

CD2 Track 20

1 I've no idea.
2 What's the point?
3 make both ends meet
4 it's like the time when
5 on the other hand
6 over the years

CD2 Track 21

1 Well, it's hard to say. I think that over the decades, people have lost interest.
2 You know, if you go back to the time of Galileo, no one even thought about travelling into space.
3 As far as space is concerned, I don't think we have any idea what's out there.
4 A lot of people say, 'What's the point in space exploration?', but as far as I can see, that's a bit short-sighted.
5 Actually, I can't wait to see what the Mars robot comes up with. I think the whole space thing is just out of this world.

CD2 Track 22

Narrator: You will hear a woman talking on the phone to a campsite manager.

Man: Hi, Lake Pane Campground. Can I help you?

Woman: Oh, hi, yes, um, I wonder if we could book a site on your campground?

M: Sure. My computer's down at the moment, so I just need to get a form. OK – how many nights would you like to stay for?

W: Um, well, ideally, we'd like to stay for five.

M: Five nights, OK.

(pause)

M: Hi, Lake Pane Campground. Can I help you?

W: Oh, hi, yes, um, I wonder if we could book a site on your campground?

M: Sure. My computer's down at the moment, so I just need to get a form. OK – how many nights would you like to stay for?

W: Um, well, ideally, we'd like to stay for five.

M: Five nights, OK. So when are you planning to arrive?

W: Well, we'll be travelling around the area from mid-<u>July</u> and we think we'll be at the lake by about the 24th.

M: Let's see. July's a busy time. We could probably fit you in, but to be honest, if you want five nights, it would be better to get here a day earlier. We've got a big group coming at the end of the month.

W: OK – the 23rd's fine. We weren't sure so …

M: Great. Do you just want somewhere to park and pitch a tent, or do you have an RV?

W: An RV?

M: Yeah – you know, a recreational vehicle … a campervan.

W: Oh, right – yes, we're driving a van, so …

M: OK – that's fine. So, um, what name is it, please?

W: It's Hepworth, that's H-E-P-W-O-R-T-H.

M: OK, thanks. I've heard that name before.

W: Well, it's quite common in England – particularly in Yorkshire. That's where we're from.

M: I was going to ask if you were in the UK. It's a really good line, isn't it?

W: Yes.

M: Would this be your contact number?

W: Yes – it's 07968 355630.

M: Great, thanks.

W: Do you want my home number as well?

M: No – that's fine.

W: OK.

M: We supply a number of facilities. I don't know if you're familiar with the way campgrounds work here.

W: It would be good if you could explain.

M: Well, you're coming in the RV, so would you like to hook up to our electricity?

W: Oh, yes, please.

M: You can also attach your vehicle to the water taps here.

W: I hope it's all easy to do!

M: Yeah – you just plug into the electricity and switch on the water. The people who hire out the RVs will explain it all.

W: OK – and what about waste water?

M: Sure – you can have a site with a sewer – or I think you guys call it a drain – that's a bit extra. Not all campgrounds have that facility, you see.

W: Fine, we'll have it. So what's the total and …

(pause)

M: OK – I've allocated you a site, so you need to note the code down.

W: Right, I'll just get a pen.

M: Most of our sites are coded using letters and numbers … EW or SEW.

W: Mm-hm

M: So yours is one of the SEW ones and it's number 47.

W: Got that.

M: That's the area that has all the requirements you need.

W: Is it easy to find when you get there?

M: What time will you be arriving?

W: I'm not sure, but it could be quite late.

M: OK, so the reception could be closed. We close at six.

W: Oh dear.

M: It's OK – I'll tell you where to go. As you come in the campground entrance, you'll see our office.

W: Uh-huh.

M: Drive past the front door … there's another office next to ours, that's the business office. Yeah, and there's a <u>pool</u> behind that.

W: OK – it would be good to have a swim!

M: It's open till eight, so feel free to use it. Keep going past all those … to the end of the track. At the top, you'll come to a … at the very end, there's a laundry.

W: OK.

M: Turn left at the laundry and you'll see your own site straight ahead of you. They're all clearly labelled.

W: That sounds easy enough.

M: Just before you hang up … um … we've had a few problems with campers … with, um, stuff left lying around.

W: Oh!

M: Well, it may be an oversight, but we do ask our visitors to take away all their litter.

W: Of course. Otherwise someone has to clear it up!

M: That's right. Also, in the morning … you know … we do have washrooms, and once the reception's open, you'll be able to get a key for the shower.

W: Right.

M: You can keep it while you're on the site, but could you return it when you leave?

W: I'll make sure we get it back to you.

M: Yeah – otherwise we don't have enough to go around.

W: OK – well, thank you very much. See you soon!

M: Yeah – bye.

CD2 Track 23

Narrator: You will hear someone talking on the radio about colours.

Presenter: Well it's a 'colourful' start to the day on DB Radio. Kathy, what have you got to tell us?

Kathy: Thanks, Briony. I thought I'd talk about two areas today where colour plays a huge role in our lives – and they are food and fashion. So, let's start with food and more specifically, food colouring.

In many parts of the world today, people like the food they purchase to be the 'right' colour. So if we buy tinned or canned vegetables, such as green peas, it's highly likely that the contents have been enhanced through the use of colouring agents. Peas are naturally green, you might say. But they may not be green all over or they may not be the most pleasing shade of green. So a natural additive or two can quickly sort that out, just as it can the perfectly minty green ice cream that we buy our children.

Children are a big market for food and are easily tempted by colour. Breakfast cereals, for instance, that come in various shades of brown are often altered using caramel, a natural brown food colouring derived from caramelised sugar. This also gives the cereals a shiny, mouth-watering appeal which is hugely tempting for consumers.

In fact, natural food colouring goes back a long way. One of the oldest – or perhaps the most well-known natural food colours – is red or 'cochineal', named after the insects used to make it. Aztec Indians created a crimson dye from the bodies of crushed beetles. Producing cochineal is very costly, so it was unpopular with consumers for some years. But health scares linking artificial red dyes to cancer have meant that more shoppers are buying cochineal again.

Now, there's one food colour that manufacturers use with a certain amount of caution and that's blue. Our ancestors believed that food this colour was dangerous. If you think about it, very few naturally occurring foods are blue, and there is little demand for the colouring. In fact, if you're trying to lose weight, experts suggest that you put your food on a blue plate. It's almost guaranteed to kill your appetite.

(pause)

OK, let's look at another area where colour is a key issue. If you say you've bought something new to wear, often the first question people will ask is 'What colour is it?' Yet the answer doesn't necessarily indicate that the colour was your preferred choice. As consumers, we have to balance how we feel in certain colours with what is fashionable at the time. You think you've suddenly developed a desire to wear orange, whereas, in fact, the shops are full of it, and you've ended up buying an orange shirt – that may or may not suit you – simply because it's 'this season's colour'.

Well, the interesting thing here is that 'colourists', as they're called in the business, have to look ahead and say what colour models will be wearing in fashion shows several years in advance. To get this right, they have to consider how long it will take to produce the cloth dyes, they have to set up deals with suppliers, and bear in mind the constant changes in consumer taste. So what may seem to be this season's colour has actually been agreed years before.

So what do we think about the colours we wear? Like everything, our tastes alter with age. In general, though, we think that black makes people look and feel thinner, while red does the opposite; white goes with everything, whereas yellow is harder to match, and nothing alters the fact that there are certain colours that we never feel comfortable wearing.

And finally – whether it's food or fashion, anyone in the business field knows that it isn't enough to get a product the right colour. Even the packaging has to be carefully designed in order to maximise sales. It's no good, for instance, wrapping an item in brown paper if you want it to stand out. Much better to go for eye-catching colours or, in fact, in today's world, green has become very popular because it promotes the view that the company cares about the environment. In addition to their products, businesses also have to think about the people who come up with the ideas. If you surround your workers with drab colours, they'll come up with equally dull ideas. This isn't rocket science. We used to associate red with creativity in business, but it turns out – according to a recent study – that blue is a much better stimulus for creative thought. So the colour's not all bad!

CD2 Track 24

Narrator: You will hear a tutor and two students discussing international mobility.

Tutor: Hi Nils, hi Eva. Come in and sit down. You wanted to talk about your research paper, is that right?

Nils: Yes, we've drawn up an outline for the introduction and done some preliminary interviews.

T: And how did that go?

Eva: We've come across some interesting findings.

T: OK – let's go through what you've done so far. What's the subject?

N: Right, so we're doing our paper on international student mobility.

E: We're looking at the overall picture – you know, where overseas students are going in the world to study and why … and we think that picture's changing.

T: Sounds interesting.

E: The first thing we've looked at is numbers, and as part of that, um, how many students there are in total who are studying outside their own country …

N: That *seems* easy. It looks like it's around three million.

E: Yeah, but the problem is that the definition of the term 'international student' varies across countries.

N: Yeah, and because of that, the figure *could* be much higher.

T: I see.

E: Our next question was... well, we wanted to know what the breakdown of numbers is around the world – you know, how many students go where. But we're not sure how accurate those figures are either.

N: Yeah, even though it's the fastest-growing sector of higher education, some ministries don't include the students at private institutions in their count.

E: Mm, it's quite frustrating. Anyway, um, next we wanted to know where the majority of students come from.

N: This is something that's changing quite rapidly.

T: Well, that would be an interesting point. What's changing?

E: Most people know that the largest group of international students comes from East Asia.

N: But what we hadn't realised is that figures for the US have quadrupled over the past 20 years, and a lot more students from Europe are also now studying abroad.

T: Ah-hah.

N: Yeah – we need to look at some more figures there.

E: Lastly, we looked at the countries that students go to – and the trends there.

N: Yeah, our question really was about the destinations of international students and whether they're changing.

E: And they are! Countries like China are providing more higher education opportunities for their own students and for students from places like Britain.

N: This means that higher education is becoming more … well, there are high levels of competition.

E: But with that there's also a spirit of exchange – it's not so one-sided any more.

(pause)

T: So you said you'd done some preliminary interviews?

E: Yes – we thought we'd start by talking to some of the international students in our city.

N: Just to help us design the web interviews we plan to do.

T: OK.

E: We wanted to find out if there are common factors that students consider to be important when they choose an overseas course.

N: Obviously, these will vary across the international student population, but we thought some, like cost, might be significant.

E: Surprisingly, a lot of students said they left finances to their parents, but they did want to know that their university was a good one.

N: They said they decided about this by talking to friends at home – not by looking at how many degrees or publications the staff had.

E: That's right. But they *were* interested in the *degrees* they were taking and whether when they finished their course they'd get a good job.

T: OK. What else did you ask them about?

N: What sort of incentives they think source countries should offer students – to encourage them to return home after they've graduated.

T: A very interesting question. What did you find?

E: Well, many said that if they chose to get another qualification, they'd stay or move to a third country to do this.

N: Yeah, so there doesn't seem to be much point in offering scholarships to get them to return home to study.

T: What about grants for research?

N: Post-graduation, that was much more popular, especially if the system let them compete individually for these.

E: And many students were keen to go home and get a job if they could be sure they'd have a good income and lifestyle.

N: For example, they felt that the government should perhaps offer tax exemptions so that they could afford to live in a nice area.

T: Some countries have created special work zones for incoming graduates, particularly in the science field.

N: Yeah, and some of these include apartment blocks as well.

E: Mmm. But as many of the students we talked to were Arts students, this didn't seem to appeal to them.

T: OK, well, I think that's a pretty good start, let's just …

CD2 Track 25

Narrator: You will hear a lecture on lions.

Lecturer: As part of this series of lectures on wildlife, I'm going to talk today about lions, about their history and about some of the work that's been done with lions in recent years.

When we think of lions, we tend to think of Africa, as this is the only area of the world where they still exist in the wild, apart from some small groups in the Indian forest of Gir. But you might be surprised to know that lions were once virtually everywhere on the planet. In fact, if you go back 500,000 years, there were more lions roaming the world than dogs or monkeys. You could bump into one in London, Moscow or LA, in every part of Africa, apart from the desert; in fact, the only continents that were and have always been lion-free were the frozen plains of Antarctica – which were obviously much too inhospitable for this jungle creature – and Australia, though there is plenty of bushland there.

So what happened? Well, we know for certain that as recently as the 1800s – that's just 200 years ago – lions were being hunted to extinction in some parts of the world, sometimes just for sport. But long before that, about 10,000 years ago, lions started to disappear from various corners of the globe. Scientists believe there was the usual battle with our human ancestors for food, in the form of other, smaller creatures, with many lions also being killed to make clothing.

So lions may have gone from Europe, but there are plenty of prehistoric paintings to witness their presence. And they reveal some interesting facts.

Let's take a look … These cave paintings were found in France – the outlines are slightly blurred because they were hand-drawn using materials like charcoal or ochre. But the images are still very clear and the interesting thing is that, as you can see, in the past, lions were actually a lot bigger than they are now – they come up to this man's waist! You may think the size has been exaggerated because of the man's fear, but there's plenty of fossil evidence that supports the larger proportions these animals once had, when you compare them with the African lions of the present day. The other curious thing here is that none of the male lions seen in cave paintings like this have the long, black or blond hair around their necks and faces that is called a mane. Now, the lion's mane is another interesting feature of these creatures. No one seems to know much about it – there are none in cave paintings like these – and, even today, the date when the lion's mane first appeared is unknown, and there is disagreement among scientists as to what its purpose is.

A lot of work has gone into researching this. If you think about it, no other cat has a mane. So why does a lion have one? And a lion's mane can be various lengths and colours, not unlike human hair: some are long, some are short; they can be black, brown or blond and they can be in good or bad condition. What scientists do know is that when lions fight, they tend to go for each other's necks and, at first, this led some researchers to believe that the mane acts as a form of protection during battles with neighbouring prides. That may be partly true. But not everyone agrees it's the whole explanation. One leading lion expert believes that manes are more to do with attracting females and scaring off males, and he's run an experiment to test this theory out.

What he did was to make five toy lions and put them in the lions' territory. He made sure they all looked different – some had long, light-coloured manes, some had short, dark ones and so on. He put these in places where they were sure to be seen, and for a while the lions ignored them. But eventually they went up to the models. And, well, the female lions were attracted to the ones that had long, dark manes. The male lions weren't, they just kept away from them – what interested them were the ones with short, blond manes. They approached these and bit or clawed them quite aggressively.

When the results of this study were compared with the real-world situation, it was found that lions with long, dark manes tend to be the healthiest, while ones with short, blond manes are more likely to be injured or sick. Thus, the team concluded that a lion's mane is effectively a status symbol; that it shows how strong and healthy the lion is and, as a result, makes the lion more attractive to females.

Acknowledgements

Text acknowledgements
The authors and publishers acknowledge the following sources of copyright material and are grateful for the permissions granted. While every effort has been made, it has not always been possible to identify the sources of all the material used, or to trace all copyright holders. If any omissions are brought to our notice, we will be happy to include the appropriate acknowledgements on reprinting.

Guardian News & Media Ltd for the text on p. 11 adapted from 'The MIT factor: celebrating 150 years of maverick genius' by Ed Pilkington, *The Guardian* 18/05/2011. Copyright © Guardian News & Media Ltd 2011;
For the Graphs on p. 15 and p. 17 adapted from 'Statistics Canada, Trends in University Graduation 1997–2007' and 'International graduates, Canadian Universities, 2001–2006'. Reproduced and distributed on an 'as is' basis with the permission of Statistics Canada;
Text on pp. 19–20 adapted from *The Surprise in the Learning of Colour Worlds* by Michael Ramscar, Kirsten Thorpe, Katie Denny, Department of Psychology, Stanford University;
National Museums Liverpool for the listening exercise on p. 23 adapted from Liverpool Museum World of Colour Exhibition. Courtesy of National Museums Liverpool;
Condé Nast for the text on pp. 32–33 from 'Placebos are getting more effective' by Steve Silberman. *Wired* 1/9/2009. Copyright © 2009 Condé Nast, for the text on pp. 63–64 from 'The New Way to be a Fifth Grader' by Clive Thompson. *Wired* 1/8/2011. Copyright © 2011 Condé Nast, for the text on pp. 138–139 from 'Hey Pencil Neck' by Ben Austen. *Wired* August 2011. Copyright © 2011 Condé Nast. All rights reserved. Reprinted with permission;
OECD for the chart on p. 39 adapted from OECD Health Data: Health Status, OECD Health Statistics (database) http://dx.doi.org/10.1787/data-00540-en;
World Health Organization for the table on p. 39 from World Health Organization data 2006. Reproduced with permission;
International Poster for the text on pp. 41–42 from 'A brief history of the poster'. www.internationalposter.com, Boston, MA. Reproduced with permission;
Gondwananet.com for the listening exercise on p. 44 adapted from 'Aboriginal Art History' www.gondwananet.com/aboriginal-art-history.html. Reproduced with permission;
Immediate Media Company Bristol Limited for the text on pp. 54–55 adapted from 'Last man standing' *BBC Focus Magazine* August 2011. Copyright © Immediate Media Company Bristol Limited 2012/© Kate Ravilious and Graham Southorn and for the text on pp. 135–136 adapted from 'Blast from the past' *BBC Knowledge Magazine* Nov/Dec 2011. Copyright © Immediate Media Company Bristol Limited 2012/© Cavan Scott;

Robert Chambers for the diagrams on pp. 60–61 adapted from http://geobytesgcse.blogspot.co.uk/2007/08/coastal-erosion-landforms-features-and.html. Reproduced with permission;
National Geographic for the text on pp. 77–78 adapted from 'Gold Dusters' by Jennifer Holland. Copyright © Jennifer Holland/National Geographic Stock. Reproduced with permission;
Royal Botanic Gardens, Kew for the charts on p. 82 adapted from www.kew.org/science/plants-at-risk.htm. With kind permission of the Board of Trustees of the Royal Botanic Gardens, Kew;
Futuretimeline.net for the graph on p. 83 adapted from 'Extinctions in tropical forests 2000-2100'. Copyright www.futuretimeline.net. Reproduced with permission;
Elsevier for the text on pp. 85–86 adapted from 'Fostering Links between environmental and space exploration: the Earth and Space Foundation' by Cockell, White, Messier, Stokes. *Space Policy* November 2002. Copyright © 2002, Elsevier. Reproduced with permission;
Tribune Media Services for the text on pp. 141–142 from 'Mind Readers: Eavesdropping on your inner voice' by Duncan Graham-Rowe, *New Scientist* 25/5/2011. Copyright © 2011 Reed Business Information – UK. All rights reserved. Distributed by Tribune Media Services;
IHS Screen Digest for the graph and chart on p. 144. Copyright © 2012 IHS Screen Digest. www.screendigest.com. Reproduced with permission.

Development of this publication has made use of the Cambridge English Corpus (CEC). The CEC is a computer database of contemporary spoken and written English, which currently stands at over one billion words. It includes British English, American English and other varieties of English. It also includes the Cambridge Learner Corpus, developed in collaboration with the University of Cambridge ESOL Examinations. Cambridge University Press has built up the CEC to provide evidence about language use that helps to produce better language teaching materials.

The *Cambridge Advanced Learner's Dictionary* is the world's most widely used dictionary for learners of English. Including all the words and phrases that learners are likely to come across, it also has easy-to-understand definitions and example sentences to show how the word is used in context. The *Cambridge Advanced Learner's Dictionary* is available online at dictionary.cambridge.org. © Cambridge University Press, third edition 2009, reproduced with permission.

Author acknowledgements

The authors would particularly like to thank Catriona Watson-Brown for editing the series so meticulously and Lynn Townsend and Dilys Silva at CUP for managing the project and providing invaluable support. Thanks also go to Louise Edgeworth, Julie Sontag, Diane Nicholls, Michelle Simpson and Diane Jones at CUP; to Tracey Cox and James Wyatt at Wild Apple; and to Leon Chambers for producing the audio.

Vanessa Jakeman would like to dedicate this book to her daughter Hannah, with love.

The publishers would like to thank the following for reviewing the material:
David Jay in the UK, Natalia Koliadina and Wayne Rimmer in Russia, and Sarah Fabel in Switzerland; thanks also to Kate Woodford for editing the Word lists.

Photo acknowledgements

The authors and publishers acknowledge the following sources of copyright material and are grateful for the permissions granted. While every effort has been made, it has not always been possible to identify the sources of all the material used, or to trace all copyright holders. If any omissions are brought to our notice, we will be happy to include the appropriate acknowledgements on reprinting.

The publishers are grateful to the following for permission to reproduce photographic material:

p.8(1): age footstock/Robert Harding; p.8(2): Echo/Cultura/ Getty Images; p.8(3): Dmitriy Shironosov/Alamy; p.8(4): Gamma-Rapho/Eric Vandeville/Getty Images; p.8(5): Jupiterimages/Pixland/Getty Images; p.8(6): West Coast Surfer/Mood Board/Rex Features; p.9: Getty Images News/ Peter Macdiarmid/Getty Images; p.11T: Time & Life Pictures/ Getty Images; p.11B: istock/Getty Images; p.13: Aerial Archives/Alamy; p.14T: Catchlight Visual Services/Alamy; p.14TC: Radius Images/Alamy; p.14BC: Terry Harris/Alamy; p.14B: commerceandculturestock /Flickr/Getty Images; p.16: i love images/teenagers/Alamy; p.18T: Karkas/Shutterstock; p.18TC: Jaak Nilson/Blend Images/Alamy; p.18C: Edmund Sumner/View Pictures/Rex Features; p.18BC: Elena Elisseeva/ Alamy; p.18B: Keith Lewis Archive/Alamy; p.19: Michael Hitoshi/Digital Vision/Getty Images; p.22R: VIEW Pictures Ltd/Alamy; p.22C: Valery Voennyy/Alamy; p.22L: David Mzareulyan/Shutterstock; p.23: Courtesy of National Museums Liverpool(Liverpool Museum, World of Colour Exhibition); p.24T: Stockbyte/Getty Images; p.24B: Sergey Sukhanov/ Alamy; p.25L: wxin/Shutterstock; p.25R: Fotosearch/ SuperStock; p.27: Anna Stowe/Alamy; p.30(1): ERproductions Ltd/Blend Images/Getty Images; p.30(2): Science Photo Library/Getty Images; p.30(3): Corbis Bridge/Alamy; p.30(4): Comstock/Getty Images; p.30(5): Karen Kasmauski/SF/ Superstock; p.30(6): Ace Stock Limited/Alamy; p.32: Selena/ Shutterstock; p.35: Art Directors & TRIP;
p.36T: Patrick Frilet/Rex Features; p.36BL: Inge Johnsson/ Alamy; p.36BR: Dieter Hawlan/Alamy; p.40(1): Bristol City Museum and Art Gallery, UK / The Bridgeman Art Library; p.40(2): Photo©Bonhams, London, UK/The Bridgeman Art Library; p.40(3): GFC Collection/Photoshot; p.40(4): age footstock/Robert Harding; p.40(5): Heritage Images/Hulton Archive/Getty Images; p.41T: INTERFOTO/Bildarchiv Hansmann/Mary Evans Picture Library; p.41B: Imagno/

Mary Evans Picture Library; p.43R: MPI/Getty Images; p.43C: Juha Eronen/Alamy; p.43L: Pictorial Press Ltd/Alamy; p.44L: Hemis/Alamy; p.44R: Hemis/Alamy; p.45L: Ted Mead/ Photolibrary/Getty Images; p.45R: UPPA/Photoshot; p.46T: Cathy Yeulet/Hemera/Getty Images; p.46C: Lane Oatey/ Getty Images; p.46B: F1 Online/Rex Features; p.47TL: Hill Street Studios/Sarah Golonka/Getty Images; p.47BL: Hill Street Studios/Blend Images/Getty images; p.47TR: Bob Daemmrich/Alamy; p.47BR: MBI/Alamy; p.49: Image Source/ DigitalVision/Getty Images; p.52(1): Yoshio Tomii/SuperStock; p.52(2): Jonathan Blair/Corbis Documentary/Getty Images; p.52(3): Werner Forman Archive/Dallas Museum of Art/ Heritage-Images; p.52(4): Helene Rogers/Art Directors & TRIP; p.52(5): Howard Grey/Stone/Getty Image; p.52(6): Nancy G Stock Photography, Nancy Greifenhagen/Alamy; p.54: De Agostini Picture Library/Getty Images; p.58B: age fotostock/ Robert Harding; p.58T: DEA/A. DAGLI ORTI/De Agostini Picture Library/Getty Images; p.58C: szefei wong/Alamy; p.59L: D.Hurst/Alamy; p.59R: Marcin Sadlowski/Alamy; p.62(1): ONOKY - Photononstop/Alamy; p.62(2): David J. Green - lifestyle themes/Alamy; p.62(3): Paul Rapson/Alamy; p.62(4): Montgomery Martin/Alamy; p.62(5): Lane Oatey/ Blue Jean Images/Getty Images; p.62(6): Jack Sullivan/Alamy; p.63: WireImage/Larry Busacca/Getty Images; p.64: Richard G. Bingham II/Alamy; p.66T: SNAP/Rex Features; p.66C: c.W. Disney/Everett/Rex Features; p.66B: Moviestore Collection/ Rex Features; p.68TL: Design Pics Inc./Alamy; p.68TC: Monkey Business Images/Rex Features; p.68TR: Quantum/ Glow Images; p.68B: ONOKY - Photononstop/Alamy; p.70T: Blend Images/Alamy; p.70B: imagebroker/Alamy; p.74(1): Christian Ziegler/Minden Pictures/FLPA; p.74(2): Anne Rodkin Photography/Getty Images; p.74(3): Michio Hoshino/ Minden Pictures/FLPA; p.74(4): Vittorio Ricci - Italy/Flickr/ Getty Images; p.74(5): Gilles Barbier/Imagebroker/FLPA; p.75T: F Pritz/Picture Press/Getty Images; p.75BL: Paul Harris/AWL Images/Getty Images; p.75BR: seawhisper/ Shutterstock; p.76: Peter Lewis/Corbis Documentary/Getty Images; p.78: Solvin Zankl /naturepl.com; p.79: Jose Fuste Raga/Corbis Documentary/Getty Images; p.80T: Monkey Business Images/Rex Features; p.80C: Samuelsson, Kristofer/ Johner Images /Getty Images; p.80B: WIN-Initiative/Getty Images; p.81: Dian Karlina/age fotostock/Getty Images; p.84(1): AFP/Stringer/Getty Images; p.84(2): NASA/Goddard Space Flight Center/Arizona State University; p.84(3): NASA/ Science Photo Library; p.84(4): Stocktrek/Getty Images; p.84(5): Dennis Hallinan/Alamy; p.84(6): RIA NOVOSTI/ Science Photo Library; p.85: 1971yes/Shutterstock; p.86: NASA, Steve Lee University of Colorado, Jim Bell Cornell University; p.88TR: iStockphoto/Thinkstock; p.88TL: sololos/ E+/Getty Images; p.88B: peresaz/Shutterstock; p.89T: Columbia/The Kobal Collection; p.89B: Universal/The Kobal Collection; p.90T: Radius Images/Alamy; p.90B: NASA/ Science Photo Library; p.92: Bloomberg/Getty Images; p.93: NASA Edgar D. Mitchell; p.136: luissantos84/iStock/Getty Images; p.139: luissantos84/iStock/Getty Images; p.142: Laguna Design/Science Photo Library.

Illustration acknowledgements

Andrew Painter: p61; Kate Rochester (Pickled Ink): pp60, 75; Kveta (Three in a Box): pp53, 105; Martin Sanders: p138; Peter Marriage: pp15, 17, 28, 37, 38, 39, 50, 82, 83, 102, 103, 104, 146